D1263134

WORD PROBLEMS

Research and Curriculum Reform

BALLOU LIBRARY
BUENA VISTA UNIVERSITY
610 WEST FOURTH STREET
STORM LAKE, IA 50588-1798

QA63 .R4 1999

Word problems : research an

The Studies in Mathematical Thinking and Learning Series
Alan Schoenfeld, Advisory Editor

WORD PROBLEMS

Research and Curriculum Reform

Stephen K. Reed
San Diego State University

LEA LAWRENCE ERLBAUM ASSOCIATES, PUBLISHERS
1999   Mahwah, New Jersey   London

Copyright © 1999 by Lawrence Erlbaum Associates, Inc.
  All rights reserved. No part of the book may be reproduced in
  any form, by photostat, microform, retrieval system, or any other
  means, without the prior written permission of the publisher.

Lawrence Erlbaum Associates, Inc., Publishers
10 Industrial Avenue
Mahwah, New Jersey 07430

Cover design by Kathryn Houghtaling Lacey

Library of Congress Cataloging-in-Publication Data

Reed, Stephen K.
  Word problems : research and curriculum reform / Stephen K. Reed.
    p.   cm. — (The studies in mathematical thinking and learning
  series)
  Includes bibliographical references (p.   ) and indexes.
  ISBN 0-8058-2660-2 (cloth : alk. paper). — ISBN 0-8058-2661-0
  (pbk. : alk. paper).
    1. Word problems (Mathematics)—Study and teaching. 2. Problem
  solving—Study and teaching. I. Title. II. Series : Studies in
  mathematical thinking and learning.
  QA63.R4 1999
  510'.76—dc21   98-43365
                                                     CIP

Books published by Lawrence Erlbaum Associates are printed on acid-free paper,
and their bindings are chosen for strength and durability.

Printed in the United States of America
10 9 8 7 6 5 4 3 2 1

This book is dedicated to the memory of Alba Thompson, whose contributions to the field of mathematics education were an inspiration to me and to countless colleagues and students.

Contents

Preface

The purpose of this book is to try to bring together ideas from the fields of cognitive psychology, mathematics education, and educational technology to achieve a better theoretical and practical understanding of how students attempt to solve word problems. I am a cognitive psychologist who has used algebra word problems in my research over the past 15 years. But like most other cognitive psychologists, my research interests have not focused as much on how students solve algebra word problems, as on more general theoretical issues such as how students transfer a solution from one problem to another problem. Algebra word problems just happened to be a convenient source of problems for my research, in large part because students have so much trouble solving them.

Nonetheless, when I began working with algebra word problems I naively thought that my work would be of some interest to professionals in the field of mathematics education. After all, I was working with word problems and transfer has always been a central issue for educators as well as for psychologists. But my work has had little influence on mathematics education, and work in mathematics education has had little influence on my work. Unfortunately, this is typical. Look at the reference section of any article published by a cognitive psychologist on mathematical problem solving and you will see mostly references to the work of other cognitive psychologists. Look at the reference section of any article published by a mathematics educator on mathematical problem solving and you will see mostly references to the work of other mathematics educators. The odds are not improved much by looking at the references of papers presented at the Psychology of Mathematics Education conventions. These are typically presented by faculty in mathematics education who reference other work in mathematics education.

There are a few exceptions, of course. A chapter by Putnam, Lampert, and Peterson (1990) in the *Review of Research in Education* on knowing mathematics in elementary schools has a wonderful section on how work in cognitive psychology has contributed to our understanding of understanding. I use this section in my cognition seminar in place of articles written by cognitive psychologists. But these kinds of articles are difficult to find. I therefore wanted to write a book in which I could bring together some ideas from both cognitive psychology and mathematics education.

Another reason for writing this book is that I have become interested in developing computer software that would help students solve word problems. I have been disappointed by the lag between the development of multimedia computers and the development of theory-driven software to run in the machines. We need software that is built on sound theory and experimentally tested to determine whether it is doing the job that it was designed to perform. But I needed to see a much bigger picture before I could begin this kind of work.

I once before had this urge to see a big picture. Late in my junior year as a psychology major at the University of Wisconsin I began to realize that obtaining a Ph.D. in psychology would likely make me a specialist in some small area of psychology. I thought that obtaining a Ph.D. in the History of Science would allow me to see the bigger picture by working in both the sciences and humanities. After consulting with the Chairman of the History of Science Department, I told a fellow student of my plans to obtain a doctorate in this area. His reply was "Why would anyone want to study the history of science when they could do science?" I didn't have an answer to that question and so went off to do science in a rather narrow area of psychology. Thirty years later my urge to see a bigger picture has returned.

A third reason for writing this book is to learn more about the mathematics reform movement that is occurring in our schools. Several months before I began writing this book there was a meeting of parents and educators at the middle school where our son was attending seventh grade. The purpose of the meeting was to discuss implementing a new mathematics curriculum in the San Diego Unified School District. I am embarrassed to admit that I was not among the approximately 200 parents who attended that meeting, many of whom were adamantly opposed to the new curriculum plans. However, I later talked to some of the parents who were at the meeting and obtained literature distributed by groups on both sides of the issue.

The debate made me realize that this book may have a wider audience than I initially believed. Although I initially thought that this book would be of interest only to people doing research on mathematical problem solving, I now believe that it also can be of benefit to people interested in instruction. I have therefore attempted to relate research findings to the larger issues of curriculum reform, beginning with a discussion in chapter 1 of the major issues in the debate between advocates of the old, basic-skills-driven curriculum and advocates of the new curriculum based on a set of standards published by the National Council of Teachers of Mathematics (NCTM, 1989).

In conclusion, readers should benefit by learning more about several different themes that are addressed in the book. First, I integrate research from both cognitive psychology and mathematics education to present a more coherent picture of how students attempt to solve word problems. Second, I discuss the transition that occurs as students progress from solving elementary problems in the lower grades to solving algebra word problems in the later grades. Third, I use word problems as a basis to describe current thinking about a number of general issues ranging from the organization of knowledge to the transfer of procedures to solve problems that differ from the instructional examples. Fourth, I draw connections between research topics and reform issues contained in the NCTM standards. And finally, I present some evaluative findings regarding the success of several different curriculum reform projects.

Writing this book would have been impossible without guidance from mathematics educators. I would like to thank my editor, Alan Schoenfeld, who already has the "big picture" for which I was searching. His insights often brought my search into sharper focus. Discussions with my colleagues at the Center for Research in Mathematics and Science Education were particularly beneficial. In addition, their books and journals saved me countless hours of library search.

I particularly want to acknowledge the influence of Alba Thompson on this book. Shortly after I immersed myself in reading literature in mathematics education, I sought her help in explaining Vergnaud's work on multiplicative structures. I realized this was an important contribution, but it was the most difficult article I read in preparing to write this book. She patiently and clearly explained the key points, as I am sure she must have done for hundreds of other topics and to hundreds of other students. Alba died suddenly several weeks later from a brain aneurysm. I never met anyone who showed a greater passion for her profession. I dedicate this book to her memory.

Stephen K. Reed

1

Introduction

I often elicit an emotional reaction when I tell people that I do research on solving algebra word problems. Some people are quite good at doing this and enjoy the challenge. More typically, people moan. They never did very well at solving word problems, and may feel helpless when their children need assistance with their homework. Gary Larson's cartoon (see Fig. 1.1) captures this typical reaction.

The purpose of this book is to try to bring together ideas from the fields of cognitive psychology, mathematics education, and educational technology to achieve a better theoretical and practical understanding of how students attempt to solve word problems. My perspective is that of a cognitive psychologist who does research on mathematical problem solving. Until recently, I had not paid much attention to curriculum reform in mathematics education, which is starting to find its way into classrooms across the country (Alper, Fendel, Fraser, & Resek, 1995; Heid & Zbiek, 1995; Kysh, 1995). But the current debate regarding the reform of mathematics education has brought these issues to the front pages of our newspapers. As newspaper articles continued to appear on this controversy between teaching basic skills and teaching concepts, I decided that research on mathematical problem solving would be of greater interest to me and my readers if I embedded it within the context of this ongoing debate. Therefore, I begin by giving a brief overview of the debate, which was stimulated by the publication of *Curriculum and Evaluation Standards for School Mathematics* (National Council of Teachers of Mathematics [NCTM], 1989).

THE FAR SIDE   By GARY LARSON

Hell's library

FIG. 1.1. THE FAR SIDE © 1987 FARWORKS, Inc. Printed by permission of Universal Press Syndicate. All rights reserved.

The NCTM Standards

Unlike countries in which a national curriculum exists in mathematics (e.g., Japan, United Kingdom, China), the United States has no national curriculum. The *Curriculum and Evaluation Standards for School Mathematics* (NCTM, 1989) represents an attempt to develop such a vision at a national level. There were numerous motivating factors for establishing a set of standards that could be used to change the way mathematics is taught in elementary and secondary schools (Putnam, Lampert, & Peterson, 1990). Critics of the current curriculum pointed to test scores that showed American students lagged behind students in other industrialized countries. Business leaders claimed that the labor force in our information-oriented society needed more sophisticated mathematical skills, particularly the ability to communicate with mathematical systems and solve a variety of complex problems.

Changes in the labor force had been brought about by advances in technology and information systems, but the learning and teaching of mathematics had not shifted correspondingly to meet these changes.

But the strongest push for a change came from mathematics educators who argued that current instruction focused too much on efficient computation and not enough on problem solving and mathematical understanding. Instruction should have a more conceptual orientation and less of a calculational orientation. Thompson, Philipp, Thompson, and Boyd (1994) expressed this view in the following way:

A teacher with a conceptual orientation is one whose actions are driven by:

- an image of a system of ideas and ways of thinking that she intends the students to develop;
- an image of how these ideas and ways of thinking can develop;
- ideas about features of materials, activities, and expositions and the students' engagement with them that can orient the students' attention in productive ways (a productive way of thinking generates a "method" that generalizes to other situations);
- an expectation and insistence that students be intellectually engaged in tasks and activities.

Conceptually oriented teachers often express the images described above in ways that focus students' attention away from the thoughtless application of procedures and toward a rich conception of situations, ideas, and relationships among ideas. (p. 86).

According to the NCTM, the curriculum should be broadened to place more emphasis on conceptual understanding and underrepresented topics in geometry, measurement, and statistics. In addition there should be greater emphasis on interacting with technology to facilitate calculations and graphing, as well as solving more difficult problems. These problems should include word problems with a variety of structures, everyday problems, and problems that take more than a few minutes to solve. Instruction should emphasize the acquisition of knowledge within the context of purposeful activity, rather than first learning computational skills for later application in solving problems. And finally, the nature of the classroom should shift away from students being passive recipients of mathematical knowledge to a classroom in which students are more actively engaged in acquiring knowledge.

According to the NCTM standards, the curriculum should therefore emphasize the following activities:

- The active involvement of students in constructing and applying mathematical ideas;

- Problem solving as a means as well as a goal of instruction;
- Effective questioning techniques that promote student interaction;
- The use of a variety of instructional formats (small groups, individual explorations, peer instruction, whole-class discussions, project work);
- The use of calculators and computers as tools for learning and doing mathematics;
- Student communication of mathematical ideas orally and in writing;
- The establishment and application of the interrelatedness of mathematical topics;
- The systematic maintenance of student learning, embedding review in the context of new topics and problem situations;
- The assessment of learning as an integral part of instruction.

The Backlash

My introduction to the controversial nature of these proposed changes in the curriculum occurred at the grass-roots level. Several months before I began writing this book there was a meeting of parents and educators at the middle school where our son was attending seventh grade. The purpose of the meeting was to discuss implementing a new mathematics curriculum in the San Diego Unified School District. The group opposing the curriculum change was led by a scientist at the Salk Institute in La Jolla. He was concerned that his children would not receive a firm foundation in mathematics if the new curriculum (called College Preparatory Mathematics, or CPM) was adopted. Many other parents had a similar concern. Their views are summarized in Box 1.1.

The group supporting curriculum change—the San Diego Unified School District—also came prepared with handouts. One titled *Myths and Realities about CPM* said that the course had been evaluated with over 10,000 students and revised three times before it was released for general use. It defended the NCTM standards and argued that students would spend time on the traditional content of algebra and geometry, but go beyond traditional content to develop higher order thinking skills. A San Diego teacher's view that we need to go beyond the basics is expressed in Box 1.2.

This debate has continued at a local, state, and national level. An article in the November 11, 1996, issue of the *Los Angeles Times* discussed the battle being fought in the state of California as both sides fought for positions on a board that would establish state guidelines for mathematics instuction. A month earlier, the cover story of an issue of *U.S. News & World Report* (Toch & Daniel, 1996) was on fixing schools. The story contrasted two different approaches to improving education; one building on the traditional approach as advocated in the book *The Schools We Need and Why*

Is "Reform" Math Right for Your Child?

Mathematically Correct is a San Diego Based group of parents and community members concerned about math education in our schools. Similar groups have recently formed throughout the state.

Broad changes in mathematics education are appearing in San Diego public schools. The new programs, often called *reform math, new-new math,* or *Whole math* are being introduced at all grade levels in response to controversial state guidelines. Our initial concerns about these programs arose from exposure to a curriculum called CPM *(College Preparatory Mathematics),* currently being taught at Muirlands and Standley Middle Schools. Similar programs will soon be introduced from Kindergarten to high school geometry.

Features of "Reform" Math that Concern Parents

- Constructivism ("Discovery Learning") — *This approach reduces the amount of material covered*
- Teachers are no longer information providers — *Instead, they are group facilitators. Questions of the teacher from individual students are discouraged*
- Emphasis on discussions and essays — *Takes time away from word problems and computational skills*
- Practice and drills are reduced — *Basic skills are less likely to become "automatic"*
- Group work, Group tests and Group Grades — *Individual contemplation, performance and time for consolidation of math knowledge is reduced*
- Extensive Use of Calculators — *Children become calculator-dependent, even for simple arithmetic*

What Do Parents Need to Know?

Although parents are told that the changes are based on new guidelines, parents need to know that all programs based on these guidelines are essentially **experimental** — they lack research support. Parents also need to know that these new guidelines are **controversial,** have been the subject of criticism by the members of the State School Board and many others, and are now the subject of public hearings as required by law.

Recommendations

- **Do not adopt radical changes,** such as Whole Math and Whole Language, without clear, well-documented, compelling, quantitative data to support them.
- **Require parental permission** before students are enrolled in experiments to test the value of such programs.
- Give parents of children at all levels in all schools **the right to choose a traditional math program.**

Box 1.1. Viewpoint of the mathematically correct organization.

We Don't Have Them (Hirsch, 1996), and one establishing progressive teaching methods as advocated in the book *Horace's Hope: What Works for the American High School* (Sizer, 1996). The article concluded that both sides can make a contribution: "Many progressives and traditionalists seem more eager to fight than to find common ground, routinely misrepresenting each other's views and needlessly polarizing debates at students' expense. It is left to the rest of us to break through the overheated rhetoric, finding in both sides important pieces of a national solution" (Toch & Daniel, 1996, p. 64).

Basic math was rote — and out of context

Re: "Back to basics" (Editorial, June 7):

I was taught mathematics the same way being advocated by the Mathematically Correct group (what a misnomer!). I was taught the basics, all right. I memorized formulas, followed recipes and was taught by rote. I was never asked to explain my own thinking, never given concrete materials to help me understand, never allowed to communicate my ideas or work with a partner and rarely encouraged to ask why.

Math problems were served up by the hundreds — always out of context, devoid of meaning and never having any connection to my life or the world around me.

Worse yet, we were never asked to figure anything out for ourselves. The teacher fed us the steps and we went through the motions. "Yours is not to reason why, just invert and multiply!" I hated math. And so did most everyone else.

This fall, I'll begin my 18th year as a classroom teacher and, long ago, I vowed never to allow my students to experience math the way I did.

RUSTY BRESSER
San Diego

Box 1.2. A teacher's response to the mathematically correct view (From *San Diego Union and Tribune*, June 22, 1997).

It is refreshing in this context to read the position taken by the Research Advisory Committee of the NCTM. Although the NCTM has been the moving force behind the progressive movment in mathematics education, the committee has stressed the importance of careful evaluation before accepting a new curriculum:

The process of designing innovative instructional materials or new approaches to teacher development frequently engenders a sense of conviction. This in turn can give rise to a tendency to advocate that others adopt a particular innovation. In such circumstances, the goal of research can easily become convincing others that an innovation is effective by searching for evidence that confirms untested conjectures. When this occurs, work conducted in classrooms is more akin to product promotion than it is to developmental research. The hallmark of developmental research as discussed in this article is that it views new approaches as unsubstantiated conjectures warranting a healthy skepticism. The overriding goal of research is not, then, to persuade others that an innovation works, but rather to examine the innovation critically, thereby investigating the conjectures and assumptions that it embodies. It is this openness to doubt and to the possibility of deconstructing an innovation that serves to distinguish developmental research from product promotion. (Cobb, 1996, p. 519)

The problem with evaluating entire courses is that there are many differences between the traditional courses and courses designed to fulfill the NCTM standards. Some of the recommended changes may work very well and others could be detrimental. Although I will include a fair amount of data in this book, including data on the success of various curriculum changes, I will be discussing research on specific topics more than research on the evaluation of entire courses. I believe that the study of specific issues in well-controlled experimental settings is providing the kind of data that will be useful for understanding mathematical reasoning, and for subsequently designing effective curriculum. But in the last chapter of the book I will look at the evaluation of curriculum changes that have already been implemented.

Research on Mathematics Learning

Most of the research discussed in this book is based on an approach called cognitive science that attempts to model the cognitive processes that students use to acquire and apply knowledge. Cognitive scientists have constructed information-processing models to represent how students perform a variety of tasks such as counting objects, doing multidigit subtraction, solving algebra and geometry problems, and making scientific discoveries. Greer and Verschaffel (1990) list four general characteristics of these theories. The first is the analysis of complex task performances in terms of knowledge structures and information-processing steps. The second is the assumption that mental processing is constrained by the characteristics of human memory. The third is the central role of schemas in organizing knowledge. The fourth is the formulation of models as computer programs.

The advantage of this approach is expressed by English and Halford (1995) in their book *Mathematics Education: Models and Processes*:

> Cognitive science has led to a greatly expanded knowledge of intelligence, both natural and artificial, and the field is progressing very rapidly. Its importance to mathematics education is that it provides the most detailed insights that are currently available into the way concepts are represented, and into the processes that are used in learning and reasoning. It provides the most scientific method yet devised for analyzing the real psychological processes that underlie mathematics. It offers great promise for increased efficiency in mathematics education, and it has been the single most important influence on the approach adopted in this book. (p. 14)

English and Halford (1995) then point out that the real benefit of cognitive science's discoveries for mathematics education will come from the application of the ideas in the classroom and home. The link between cognitive science and mathematics education is bidirectional because application of scientific principles in the classroom can help develop the science that generated those principles. But this view does not mean that the link is necessarily an easy one. As Davis (1996) explains:

The precision and elegance of this research comes at a price, however. And many teachers would argue that the price is too high. Experience in classrooms is both messy (in that there are many things that can be heard, seen, and done) and familiar (in that children quickly learn what sort of things to expect, the "rules of the game," as it were, and what sorts of things will be expected of them). There is no obvious way to bridge the gap between the messy, familiar world of a classroom and the novel, strange, impersonal, careful regulation of stimuli in a laboratory setting. It is partly due to this gap that those who work closely with teachers and children in classrooms tend to see matters very differently from those who work with subjects in laboratories. (pp. 101–102)

Although I agree with Professor Davis that the transition from laboratory to classroom will not always be an easy one, I believe that we need carefully controlled laboratory studies on specific topics that are taught in the classroom. But we also need researchers to collaborate with teachers to develop innovative classrooms as research sites to study students' and teachers' learning as it occurs in these instructional settings (Cobb, 1996). The outcome of both types of research should help us design curriculum based on cognitive models of how people learn.

Linking Research to Instruction

An example of how a cognitive model can guide instructional choices is illustrated by the work of Fuson and her colleagues at Northwestern University (Fuson, Hudson, & Pilar, 1997). The curriculum and teaching/learning framework is based on several years of research on how urban Latino children solve addition/subtraction word problems. The framework uses Fuson's conceptual phase model of solving word problems and specifies types of classroom activities for each phase in solving the problem. Figure 1.2 shows the link between various cognitive phases in solving word problems and classroom activities that can help students become better problem solvers. Although the phases represent stages in solving simple arithmetic problems, they are general enough to capture much of the more complex problem solving that is needed to solve algebra word problems. As students progress through school they move from using objects to using numerical notation to using algebraic notation to represent the problems.

The conceptual phase model describes three major kinds of activities that progress from building a *situation conception*, to forming a *mathematized conception*, to formulating a *solution method conception*. Building a situation conception during the initial phase requires understanding the meaning of the words that describe the problem, integrating the meanings to understand each sentence, and coordinating all these meanings into understanding the situation presented in the text. During this stage, objects, context, and space–time relations are in the foreground and mathematical

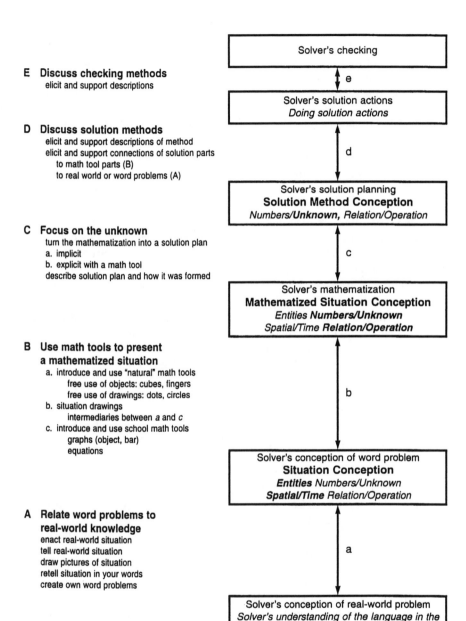

E Discuss checking methods
elicit and support descriptions

D Discuss solution methods
elicit and support descriptions of method
elicit and support connections of solution parts
to math tool parts (B)
to real world or word problems (A)

C Focus on the unknown
turn the mathematization into a solution plan
a. implicit
b. explicit with a math tool
describe solution plan and how it was formed

**B Use math tools to present
a mathematized situation**
a. introduce and use "natural" math tools
free use of objects: cubes, fingers
free use of drawings: dots, circles
b. situation drawings
intermediaries between a and c
c. introduce and use school math tools
graphs (object, bar)
equations

**A Relate word problems to
real-world knowledge**
enact real-world situation
tell real-world situation
draw pictures of situation
retell situation in your words
create own word problems

Solver's checking

e

Solver's solution actions
Doing solution actions

d

Solver's solution planning
Solution Method Conception
*Numbers/**Unknown**, Relation/Operation*

c

Solver's mathematization
Mathematized Situation Conception
*Entities **Numbers/Unknown***
*Spatial/Time **Relation/Operation***

b

Solver's conception of word problem
Situation Conception
***Entities** Numbers/Unknown*
***Spatial/Time** Relation/Operation*

a

Solver's conception of real-world problem
*Solver's understanding of the language in the
word problem and of the real-world situation*

Classroom Activities (PCMA)   Conceptual Phase Model

FIG. 1.2. Phases of classroom mathematical problem-solving activity. From
Fuson, Hudson, and Pilar (1997). Reproduced with permission.

9

aspects of the situation are in the background. Relevant classroom activities include encouraging students to retell the situation in their own words and to draw pictures of the situation.

During the second phase, the student needs to create a mathematized situation conception by focusing on the numbers and the unknown. In particular, students need to represent the space–time relations in the situation by mathematical operations. This requires the ability to model actions such as combining, adding to, taking from, and comparing. Using fingers, working with concrete objects, and drawing dots or circles to represent numbers are examples of classroom activities that help children form a mathematical representation of the problem.

The third phase is planning a solution method by focusing on the unknown in the problem and carrying out the steps needed to calculate the unknown. Classroom activities that discuss solution plans, describe connections among parts of the solution, and teach checking methods are particularly helpful at this stage. Of course, the phases shown in Fig. 1.2 are only a brief overview of the solution process. The challenge for researchers is to fill in the details of the cognitive processes that occur during each stage, and the challenge for instructional designers is to develop the implications of this research for creating an effective curriculum. I hope the material in this book will assist people in meeting both of these challenges.

Organization of the Book

Before reviewing research that directly examines the activities shown in Fig. 1.2, I will look at a broader context that should help frame these issues. The first section of the book, therefore, discusses general theoretical issues that should provide a helpful context for the material in the rest of the book. Chapter 2 is on rule learning. It focuses primarily on Anderson's 10-year effort to develop tutors based on his cognitive theory, Adoptive Control of Thought, or ACT (Anderson, Corbett, Koedinger, & Pelletier, 1995). It's the most successful example we have of a long-term development effort that has used a detailed cognitive theory to develop instruction. Yet, the project seems to be changing direction as Anderson has taken his computer tutors into the Pittsburgh schools to create a curriculum that is more closely aligned with the NCTM standards. The challenge is to try to more actively involve students in the instruction and to promote understanding of concepts. Chapter 3 shows how understanding often depends on how well we can link new ideas to previously acquired knowledge structures. The knowledge structures are called *schemas* and I will look at their characteristics in this chapter. Because these chapters are intended to provide background information, you may want to skim them if you are already familiar with the content. Or you may want to skim over some of the ACT model if you find the details too technical.

The second section of the book discusses word problems and examines the issue of how solving word problems evolves as children progress through elementary school and high school. Chapter 4 is on simple, one-step arithmetic story problems. A key issue is identifying a minimal set of relations (such as change, compare, group) that can be used to represent information in these problems. Chapter 5 discusses multistep problems in which these simple relations are combined to form more complex solutions. This requires planning to find the appropriate combination. Chapter 6 discusses algebra word problems. Here I look for similarities and differences between problems in an algebra course and the problems encountered in prealgebra courses.

The third section contains chapters on transferring what has been learned about solving a problem to solve related problems. How can students use the solution of an example problem to solve a test problem that doesn't quite match the example? Perhaps the same solution is used to solve both problems, but this fact isn't obvious because the two problems are about different situations—painters painting a fence versus pipes filling a swimming pool. Transfer between these isomorphic problems is the topic of chapter 7. Or perhaps the test problem is about the same situation as the example but the solution needs to be modified because one painter now works longer than the other. The topic of chapter 8 is adapting solutions. Chapter 9 discusses the transfer of general methods, such as using an appropriate diagram, rather than the transfer of specific solutions.

The fourth section contains three chapters on topics emphasized in the NCTM standards. Chapter 10 looks at research on the inclusion of problems that require students to model real-world situations. Recent research has shown that students often produce stereotypic solutions that make unreasonable assumptions, such as it takes four times as much time to run a distance that is four times as long. Chapter 11 looks at another recommendation of the NCTM standards: estimating answers to problems. Can students form a reasonable estimate of the answer without having to solve the problem? This chapter also reports research on estimation that measures students' understanding of functional relations. Chapter 12 reviews curriculum changes currently being implemented in the schools that are driven by the NCTM standards. When available, I will discuss program evaluations, but will also consider the implications of current research for making curriculum changes.

Summary

A set of standards proposed by the NCTM in 1989 is having a major influence on the design of mathematics curriculum. Low test scores and an increasingly information-oriented society are supplying the motivation for curriculum change. According to the NCTM standards, the curriculum should emphasize the active involvement of students in constructing and applying mathematical ideas, solving problems as a means as well as a goal of instruction, using effective questioning techniques that promote student interaction, using a variety of instructional formats, using calculators and computers as tools for learning, establishing and applying the interrelatedness of mathematical topics, systematically maintaining student learning, and assessing learning as an integral part of instruction. A concern of many parents, however, is that these changes will diminish the amount of time teachers can spend on teaching basic skills.

The major premise of this book is that curriculum changes should be guided by research in mathematics education. Research that has been influenced by advances in cognitive science is currently being conducted to understand how students perform standard calculations and attempt to solve a wide variety of problems. The cognitive science approach attempts to analyze performance on complex tasks in terms of the knowledge structures, information-processing steps, and memory demands required to solve problems. It provides a scientific method for analyzing the psychological processes that underlie classroom work in mathematics. A challenge, however, is to link the careful control of laboratory research with the messy world of the classroom.

The remainder of this book examines the research of cognitive scientists, and attempts to relate that research to issues raised by the NCTM standards. The next two chapters focus on two theoretical approaches: one that focuses on the smooth acquisition of rules that are modeled as production systems and one that focuses on using schematic structures to model understanding. The second section of the book reviews research on how students solve word problems. The three chapters trace the development of problem-solving skills from solving elementary word problems in the lower elementary grades to solving algebra problems in high school. The third section of the book discusses research on transfer that requires either abstracting solutions, modifying solutions, or representing solutions in a useful format. The last section of the book discusses topics that are recommended for emphasis by the NCTM standards such as real-world problems and estimation of answers, and concludes with an evaluation of several curriculum-reform programs.

KNOWLEDGE STRUCTURES

2

Learning Rules

At the center of the goals proposed by the NCTM standards is the desire to create a curriculum that will increase students' understanding of mathematical concepts and procedures. My objective in writing the two chapters in this section is to provide a theoretical context for thinking about learning with understanding. The chapters, therefore, contain examples of theories of learning, reasoning, and problem solving that have been formulated by cognitive psychologists. Chapter 2 looks at theories that emphasize rule learning, whereas chapter 3 focuses on the organization of conceptual knowledge.

In order to solve problems, we have to carry out a series of actions such as constructing and solving an equation. These actions can be theoretically represented as a set of rules. Our focus in this chapter is on a rule-based theory of learning called ACT* (J. R. Anderson, 1983). There are two reasons why this theory is important. First, it represents a tremendous theoretical accomplishment. It is the most detailed and extensively tested theory of learning that has been developed by cognitive psychologists. Second, the theory has been used to develop computer-based tutors for geometry, algebra, and a computer programming language called LISP, giving us the opportunity to see how theoretical ideas can be applied to the classroom (Anderson, Corbett, Koedinger, & Pelletier, 1995).

In spite of these successes, there is a concern among many mathematics educators that theories such as ACT* place too great an emphasis on the efficient learning of procedures, while neglecting conceptual understanding. For example, we have all learned when it is necessary to "borrow" when subtracting numbers, but do we have a good conceptual understanding of what borrowing signifies? It is a concern with these kinds of issues that motivated the NCTM standards.

Why should we care about rule-based theories of skill learning such as ACT* if our goal is to enhance conceptual understanding? I have two answers to this question. The first is that learning to perform complex cognitive tasks such as reading or solving mathematics problems usually requires the successful integration of many component skills. Let's take reading as an example. Comprehension depends on understanding the ideas in the text, but understanding depends on the successful execution of many skills. Children learn to read by learning to recognize letters, then to recognize words, pronounce words, interpret the meanings of individual words, combine these meanings to understand sentences, and combine sentences to connect ideas throughout the text.

According to a theory proposed by LaBerge and Samuels (1974), students would never learn to read unless they could automate some of these components. The reason is that we have a limited amount of cognitive capacity for performing tasks (Kahneman, 1973) and this capacity would become quickly overloaded if each component skill required substantial mental effort. For example, a child who is investing all his mental effort in recognizing individual words has little mental effort left over to integrate the meanings of the words. The proposed solution is to practice performing the component skills until they can be performed fairly automatically, requiring little cognitive effort. The basic skills for solving word problems—understanding the text, determining temporal and spatial relations, eliminating irrelevant information, identifying the unknown variable, selecting the correct arithmetic operations, determining what to equate in an equation—need to be practiced enough to prevent this mental overload.

A second answer for why rule-based theories such as ACT* are important is because they provide a framework for translating understanding into action. Although it is correct to say that ACT* in recent years has emphasized the efficient learning of procedures rather than the acquisition of conceptual knowledge, it would be incorrect to say that understanding can not be represented in a rule-based system. A good research example of acquiring understanding is the self-explanation effect (Chi, Bassok, Lewis, Reimann, & Glaser, 1989; Chi, De Leuw, Chiu, & LaVancher, 1994) that I will look at in the next chapter. A model of this process is that students' enhanced understanding of problem solutions by explaining those solutions occurs because they create rules that are not mentioned explicitly in the textbook (VanLehn, Jones, & Chi, 1992). But this is getting ahead of the story. Let's first look at how rule learning occurs according to ACT*.

The ACT* Theory

The Architecture of Cognition (J. R. Anderson, 1983) describes the ACT* theory of learning and problem solving. The theory proposes that acquiring a cognitive skill requires learning thousands of rules that relate task goals to actions and the consequences of those actions. The rules are expressed as productions that specify what action to take when a condition is satisfied. For example, a production rule for a geometry proof might be:

IF the goal is to prove two triangles are congruent
THEN set as a subgoal to prove that corresponding parts are congruent

Notice that the condition follows the IF part of the conditional rule and the action follows the THEN part of the rule.

Table 2.1 shows how production rules can be used to solve multicolumn subtraction problems (Anderson, 1995). The rules specify what to do during various stages in solving the problem and depend on the current goal (such as borrow from a column) and the numbers in the problem (such as whether the top digit is zero). Notice that the emphasis is on the corrrect execution of procedures, rather than on why the procedures work.

The production rules are part of what we call procedural knowledge. ACT*, like many other theories in cognitive science, makes a distinction between *declarative* knowledge and *procedural* knowledge. Declarative knowl-

TABLE 2.1
Production Rules for Multicolumn Subtraction

If the goal is to solve a subtraction problem,
Then make the subgoal to process the rightmost column.

If there is an answer in the current column
     and there is a column to the left,
Then make the subgoal to process the column to the left.

If the goal is to process a column
     and there is no bottom digit,
Then write the top digit as the answer.

If the goal is to process a column
     and the top digit is not smaller than the bottom digit,
Then write the difference between the digits as the answer.

If the goal is to process a column
     and the top digit is smaller than the bottom digit,
Then add 10 to the top digit
     and set as a subgoal to borrow from the column to the left.

If the goal is to borrow from a column
     and the top digit in that column is not zero,
Then decrement the digit by 1.

If the goal is to borrow from a column
     and the top digit in that column is zero,
Then replace the zero by 9
     and set as subgoal to borrow from the column to the left.

Note. From Cognitive Psychology and Its Implications (4th ed.), by Anderson (1995). Reprinted with permission from W. H. Freeman.

edge refers to our knowledge of facts such as a triangle has three sides, or 8 − 5 = 3. Procedural knowledge relates actions to goals and allows us to carry out tasks such as constructing a geometry proof or finding the sum of 863 + 598.

Figure 2.1 shows that, in addition to a declarative memory and a production memory, a working memory is a key component in the ACT* framework. Working memory contains the information that the system can currently access, consisting of information retrieved from long-term declarative memory as well as temporary information created by encoding processes and the action of productions. In the *match* process, information in working memory is matched to conditions specified in the productions. *Execution* of a production places the consequences of the action of the production into working memory. Thus, working memory plays a major role in coordinating information in the world with declarative and procedural knowledge.

A key assumption of ACT* is that all knowledge begins as declarative knowledge through observation or instruction. Acquiring a cognitive skill, therefore, requires converting this declarative knowledge into procedural knowledge through practice in solving problems. As we have all learned, it is difficult to become a good problem solver without practice in solving problems. Practice strengthens production rules in the sense that once created, further application of the rules produces more rapid and less errorful execution. It can also lead to composition of rules in which several

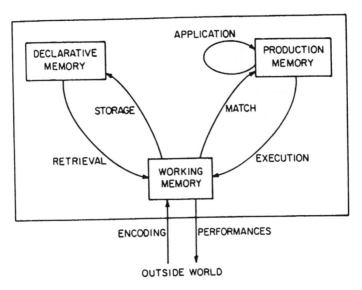

FIG. 2.1. A general framework for the ACT* production system. From Anderson (1983).

simple rules are combined into a more complex rule that specifies taking several actions rather than a single action.

ACT* provides a theoretical framework for representing an important component of learning mathematics—the efficient execution of procedural skills. In fact, the assumptions of ACT* have been used to develop computer tutors that can facilitate the acquisition of skills. This research has not only produced effective tutors, but has contributed to our theoretical knowledge of skill acquisition.

ACT* and Computer Tutors

Anderson's initial motivation in developing intelligent tutoring systems for geometry, LISP, and algebra was to learn more about skill acquisition than to produce practical results in the classroom. He considered tutoring to be a significant test of the ACT* theory to see if he could train students to act like a production-rule model of a task. In an effort to draw a tighter connection between ACT* and the design of tutors Anderson, Boyle, Farrell, and Reisser (1987) formulated eight principles that followed from the theory.

Principle 1: Represent student competence as a production set. This approach shares with a behaviorist approach the idea of decomposing a skill into components and organizing instruction around these components. The difference is the nature of the components. Production rules are organized around (more abstract) goal structures rather than stimulus–response associations.

Principle 2: Communicate the goal structure underlying problem solving. A major assumption of the ACT* theory is that solving a problem requires decomposing a problem into a set of goals and subgoals. Work with the tutors revealed that tasks such as generating geometry proofs or writing recursive programs were difficult because the goal structure was not adequately communicated to students.

Principle 3: Provide instruction in the problem-solving context. This principle was based on research showing the context specificity of learning, as is emphasized in the situated learning movement. This has been implemented by allowing students to refer back to appropriate instruction while solving problems.

Principle 4: Promote abstract understanding of the problem-solving knowledge. A limitation of situated learning is that students develop overly specific knowledge as they solve problems. In other words, the condition side of a production rule is not sufficiently general. The challenge is to try to teach correct abstractions through providing help and error messages.

Principle 5: Minimize working memory load. This principle was motivated by the ACT*'s assumption that learning a new production rule requires maintaining in short-term memory all the information relevant to the rule's condition and action. This requires minimizing both the presentation of irrelevant information and the amount of instruction during problem solving because processing the instructions contributes to working memory load. Minimizing working memory load leads to a curriculum design in which only a limited amount of new information is taught at a time.

Principle 6: Provide immediate feedback regarding errors. The ACT* theory claims that new productions are created from records of problem solving actions. The longer one waits until an error is corrected, the longer the span of problem solving over which the student would have wait to integrate the production. Providing immediate feedback turned out to be the most controversial of the tutoring principles and, as we will see later, was modified in the revision of the ACT* theory.

Principle 7: Adjust the grain size of instruction with learning. This principle was motivated by the composition learning assumption that single productions can be combined into a single production that did in one step what had been accomplished in several steps. Therefore, it seemed reasonable to design a tutor that could process the student's problem solving in ever larger units of analysis.

Principle 8: Facilitate successive approximations to the target skill. Students typically can not perform all the steps when beginning to learn a skill. The tutor needs to fill in the missing steps but should shift more of the work to the student as learning progresses.

Constructing tutors based on these principles turned out to be quite successful (see Anderson et al., 1995). The geometry tutor was evaluated during the 1986–1987 school year by comparing classes with the tutor to classes without the tutor, taught by the same teacher. In a paper-and-pencil test on proof skills students who had one-on-one experience with the tutor averaged more than a one letter grade higher on the test than students who did not have access to the tutor.

The LISP tutor was evaluated during a minicourse taught during the fall of 1984 in which students attended lectures and completed the same set of programming exercises either with or without the tutor. Students who completed the exercises on the tutor were 30% faster and performed 43% better on a posttest. A subsequent evaluation more closely approximated the self-paced design of a currently taught course. In this evaluation students using the tutor completed the exercises 64% faster and scored 30% higher on a posttest than did students using a standard LISP environment.

ACT-R

In spite of the initial early successes in applying the principles of ACT*, results of this research has produced occasional revisions of the theory. For example, the initial conception of the relationship between declarative knowledge and procedural knowledge has changed and is now most clearly formulated in the most recent version of the ACT theory described in the book *Rules of the Mind* (Anderson, 1993). This version, called Adaptive Control of Thought–Rational (ACT-R), made two major changes in how declarative knowledge leads to the formation of procedural knowledge.

The first was that the original theory emphasized that students learn to solve problems from their declarative memory for instructions. The emphasis now is on declarative memory for examples. The major reason for this shift of emphasis is that research has shown that students rely extensively on examples to help them solve problems in academic domains such as mathematics, science, and computer programming (Anderson & Fincham, 1994; Pirolli, 1991; Reed, Willis, & Guarino, 1994).

A second major change in the conception of how declarative knowledge is converted to procedural knowledge concerns the long-term storage of declarative knowledge. ACT-R does not assume that it is necessary to store in long-term memory the solution of an example; it is only necessary to keep part of the example solution active in working memory during the solution of an analogous problem. Often students look up example solutions in resources such as a textbook without committing the solutions to long-term memory.

Another change in ACT* that has been a consequence of designing and evaluating tutors is the role of feedback in directing students toward one of the correct solution paths generated by the model. Early tutors required students to always stay on a correct path by providing immediate, corrective feedback when they made a wrong choice. But does immediate feedback work best?

To answer this question, Corbett and Anderson (1991) compared four feedback conditions while students used the LISP tutor on programming exercises (discussed by Anderson et al., 1995). The *immediate feedback* condition corrected students as soon as they made an error. The *error-flagging* condition identified an error as soon as it occurred but the student had the option of requesting immediate feedback, trying to fix the error without feedback, or returning later to the error. The *no feedback* condition provided no feedback but indicated whether the solution was correct when queried by the student. The *demand* condition also required students to query the tutor but provided corrective feedback when requested.

The results showed that there were no significant differences among the three feedback groups on a paper-and-pencil posttest. Mean scores were 55% correct for the immediate-feedback tutor, 55% correct for the error-flag tutor, and 58% correct for the demand-feedback tutor. Only the no-feedback control group did significantly worse (43% correct). This group failed to solve 25% of the training problems, whereas students who received feedback necessarily had correct solutions to all the training problems. Posttest performance therefore was influenced by whether students had access to the correct solutions of example problems, rather than by the details of how this feedback was provided.

The current ACT-R theory claims that students build productions by evaluating problem solutions. It does not matter whether all the steps occur together in time, only that they be represented in the final solution. The principle theoretical justification for immediate feedback no longer exists in ACT-R. The current design of tutors therefore provides a variety of feedback options and allows the teacher to make the selection.

Advantages of Rule-Based Models

One of the advantages of rule-based models is a diagnostic one. If correct performance on a task can be represented by a set of rules, then errors can be diagnosed as the application of a faulty rule. The assumption that at least some errors may result from learning an incorrect rule motivated one of the early applications of cognitive science to mathematics learning. Using techniques developed in the field of artificial intelligence, Brown and Burton (1978) developed a computer model that assumed that mistakes occur not because students do not follow rules very well but because they learned the wrong rules. If students follow the wrong rules, there should be a systematic pattern in their errors. A good diagnostic model should be able to identify the misconception ("bug") that causes this systematic pattern.

Brown and Burton's (1978) analysis revealed that there is a large number of possible bugs even for relatively simple procedures like addition and subtraction. This creates a challenge for a teacher or a computer tutor to identify the incorrect rule that is producing the errors. I once interacted with a version of Brown and Burton's program in which I was shown the answers to five problems and had to identify the incorrect rule that was producing the answers. I was then shown five additional problems and had to provide answers that would be produced by using my hypothesized faulty rule. If I produced the correct faulty answers, the computer assumed that I had discovered the incorrect rule and gave me a new set of faulty answers to analyze.

You can test your own ability to diagnose faulty rules by examining the three addition problems and three subtraction problems in Fig. 2.2. Each set of three problems has a bug that produces the erroneous answers. See whether you can identify the bug before reading further.

You may have found that error diagnosis can be difficult. The addition bug is that the student is treating each digit as a separate number. Thus 17 + 5 becomes 1 + 7 + 5. The subtraction bug is that the student "saves" her borrows and subtracts them all from the left-most digit. Notice that bugs can occasionally produce correct answers, such as for the last subtraction problem, which does not require borrowing. This can make diagnosis more challenging, as can cases in which any one of several bugs can account for the errors, there is more than one bug producing the errors, or a student occasionally makes random errors when applying a faulty rule.

Ben-Zeev (1996) has argued that rule-based errors often result in "rational errors" that follow from initially inducing an incorrect rule and then following it in a logically consistent manner. Unfortunately, instruction may be the blame for some of these rational errors. For instance, children often initially learn to subtract two-digit numbers in which the number subtracted in each column is the smaller of the two numbers in that column. They may therefore learn the faulty rule that the smaller number in each column should always be subtracted from the larger number. Rational errors are particularly likely to occur when rules are learned by rote memorization, without conceptual understanding (Schoenfeld, 1988).

In addition to the instructional advantage of diagnosing errors as faulty learned rules, models based on rules and production systems such as ACT* and ACT-R have played an important theoretical role in human and machine learning. In their introduction to the book *Production System Models of Learning and Development*, the editors distinguish between two related, but distinct views of the role of production system models (Neches, Langley, & Klahr, 1987). The first view treats production systems as a formal notation for expressing models. The object of interest is the content of the models

Addition problems

17	43	18
+ 5	+79	+6
13	23	13

Subtraction problems

662	831	563
-357	-158	-241
215	583	322

FIG. 2.2. Examples of "buggy" rules. Based on Brown and Burton (1978).

rather than the form of their expression. The second view treats production systems as a specific theory about the architecture of the human information-processing system. The claim is that people employ the functional equivalent of productions in reasoning, problem solving, and other intelligent behavior. It is this second view that they contrast with alternative views of how knowledge is organized.

Neches et al. (1987) argued, based on the ideas of Newell and Simon (1972), that production systems have a number of advantages for modeling human behavior. These include:

1. *Homogeneity*. Production systems represent knowledge in a very homogeneous format, with each rule having the same basic If–Then structure.
2. *Independence*. Production rules are relatively independent of each other, making it easy to insert a new rule or remove old rules. This makes them very useful for modeling the incremental nature of human learning.
3. *Parallel/serial nature*. Production systems combine a parallel recognition process with a serial application process; both seem consistent with much of human cognition. Recognition is parallel because it is necessary to evaluate all rules that satisfy the condition part of the production. Conflict resolution is then used to determine which action to take.
4. *Goal-driven behavior*. Production systems can be used to model the goal-driven character of human behavior. This is because the condition part of the rule typically specifies achieving a particular goal.
5. *Modeling memory*. The production-system framework specifies the interaction of short-term and long-term memory because the matching and conflict resolution aspects of selecting productions embody principles of retrieval and focus of attention.

Disadvantages of Rule-based Models

But rule-based models also have their limitations. One of the big limitations has been that it is not clear how to integrate the learning of declarative knowledge into rule-based systems. It is not surprising that applications of production-system models to tutoring have focused on rule-based problem solving such as constructing a geometry proof or writing a short program in LISP. Anderson et al. (1995) have not attempted to model knowledge domains that are largely declarative. For instance, after considering a tutor for an undergraduate course in cognitive psychology, they concluded that this body of knowledge is largely factual.

This distinction between modeling procedural knowledge and modeling declarative knowledge is most clearly seen in using production-system models to predict the amount of transfer from one task to another task. The most straightforward prediction of a production-system model is that the amount of transfer depends on the number of shared production rules between the two tasks (Singley & Anderson, 1989), a prediction supported by Kieras and Bovair (1986).

However, sometimes the amount of transfer is greater than would be expected from simply counting overlapping productions. Pennington, Nicolich, and Rahm (1995) tested the prediction that practice in one subskill (such as writing a computer program) would not transfer to a related subskill (such as evaluating a computer program) when different productions represent the two tasks. The results revealed that there was considerably more transfer than predicted from a production-system analysis. Pennington and her colleagues interpreted their findings as demonstrating that transfer resulted from the shared declarative knowledge between the two programming tasks. In other words, the two tasks shared the same factual knowledge, which was helpful even when this knowledge was used in different ways.

Another critique of a rule-based approach is that it does not show how people develop a deep understanding of a subject. In a particularly articulate review, Ohlsson (1990) argued that cognitive science has not yet created a revolution in instruction because current theories (which he calls the standard theory) are theories of action rather than theories of knowledge. Consequently, the standard theory is a theory of skill training that does not tell us much about how to teach concepts and principles:

> To be knowledgeable is to know what the world is like. The Standard Theory replaces this concept with the concept of procedural knowledge, in which knowledge is a collection of rules for what to do, for acting efficiently, and in which to be knowledgeable is to be able to attain goals with a minimum of cost. Skills are substituted for beliefs, general applicability for abstraction, the act of inferring for the inference itself, efficiency for rationality, and decision making for belief formation. But knowledge and action, theory and practice, are not the same; they may be closely related, but one cannot be substituted for the other. (p. 576)

Ohlsson's thesis was not that our current theory of cognition is of no use in the design of instruction; a theory of action is a prerequisite for developing a theory about the growth of knowledge. But the task for educational research now is to identify how conceptual understanding contributes to the selected actions. This would lead to a theory of how a person's world view becomes more comprehensive, elaborated, differentiated, internally consistent, and accurate.

Anderson's group has been moving in this direction. In reflecting on their 10-year history of tutor development, Anderson et al. (1995) stated that their current emphasis is on building tutors that can provide helpful information and useful problems. Although they admit that this may result in less emphasis on cognitive modeling, they believe that the cognitive modeling approach is still important.

This move has taken them in directions that provide new challenges to implementing the theory. The group is now working on a tutor for exploration and discovery in geometry that involves skills different from the ones taught in previous versions of the theory. In addition, Anderson's group has taken their tutors to the Pittsburgh public schools where further development is influenced by the needs of their client. These needs include curriculum development in mathematics that is consistent with a set of standards proposed by the NCTM (1989). Similar to Ohlsson's (1990) argument, the NCTM standards propose that a good education requires going beyond learning basic skills to create a deep level of mathematical understanding. In the next chapter I will take a closer look at how the schematic organization of declarative knowledge contributes to understanding.

Summary

An important theory of learning and problem solving is the ACT* theory developed by Anderson and his students at Carnegie Mellon University. The theory assumes that we learn to solve problems by acquiring rules that are formally represented as production rules. A production rule has the form IF (condition) THEN (action). The condition specifies the prerequisite for carrying out a particular action. Production rules are created from attempts to solve problems, using example solutions as the primary source of instruction. Errors result from learning an incorrect production rule such as IF (the goal is to subtract one digit from another) THEN (always subtract the smaller digit from the larger digit).

The principles of ACT* have been applied to build theoretically based computer tutors for algebra, geometry, and LISP that have been quite successful when compared with standard instruction. The major objective of the tutor is to determine which productions the student has learned in order to correct missing or faulty productions. Other principles include specifying the goal structure of the problem, promoting abstract understanding, minimizing working memory load, adjusting the grain size of instruction, and providing immediate feedback for errors. Principles such as immediate feedback, which did not receive consistent support from research using the tutor, resulted in revision of the theory.

One advantage of rule-based models is that they aid error diagnosis. To the extent that errors result from incorrectly learned rules, the instructor can attempt to identify and correct these rules. A specification of the rules required to solve a problem may also help prevent rationale errors in which instructional examples do not provide enough information about the conditions required for applying a rule. Theoretical advantages of production-system models include the homogeneous format of productions, the relative independence of the rules, the combination of a parallel recognition of conditions with a serial application of an action, the emphasis on goals for organizing actions, and the explicit attempt to model the role of short-term and long-term memory in applying the rules.

A disadvantage of rule-based models is that they are better at specifying actions than at representing declarative knowledge that is largely factual. This can result in predicting too little transfer between two tasks (such as writing and evaluating programs) that share substantial declarative knowledge, but different productions. A possible instructional disadvantage is that tutors based on learning rules may not pay enough attention to teaching conceptual understanding. The emphasis on selecting an appropriate action may occur at the expense of learning about the organization of concepts. Conceptual organization is the topic of the next chapter.

3

Conceptual Understanding

We saw in the previous chapter that people follow rules when they carry out actions. A challenge that has likely confronted teachers from the very beginning of teaching is how to convey the meaning of the rules. Do students really understand what they are doing, or have they rotely memorized a set of procedures?

Although production rules model procedural knowledge, they were not designed for modeling declarative knowledge specifying how we organize concepts. It is not even clear how the production rules, themselves, are organized. Are there simply huge lists in long-term memory consisting of thousands and thousands of rules?

One view of understanding is that it consists of conceptual (declarative) knowledge that underlies the meaningful use of procedures. Hiebert and Lefevre (1986) argue that the distinction between conceptual and procedural knowledge is useful for thinking about mathematics learning in order to help us better understand students' failures and successes. Conceptual knowledge, in their formulation, is knowledge that is rich in relationships of many different kinds. In contrast, procedural knowledge consists of rules or procedures that are used to complete tasks. The primary relation in procedural knowledge is "after," which is used to order the procedures. For instance, we perform actions in a specified order when doing multicolumn subtraction. When a column requires subtracting a larger number from a smaller number, it is necessary to borrow from the column to the left as the next action.

The challenge, then, is to find a way to model declarative knowledge that could organize the rules and provide conceptual understanding of what the rules mean. The challenge is very real, as pointed out by Hiebert and Carpenter (1992):

> One of the most widely accepted ideas within the mathematics education community is the idea that students should understand mathematics. The goal of many research and implementation efforts in mathematics education has been to promote learning with understanding. But achieving this goal has been like searching for the Holy Grail. There is a persistent belief in the merits of the goal, but designing school learning environments that successfully promote understanding has been difficult. (p. 65)

Hiebert and Carpenter used insights from work in cognitive science to analyze understanding, building on two assumptions regarding mental representations. The first is that some relationship exists between external and internal representations; that is, the form of an external representation (physical materials, pictures, symbols) influences how the student internally represents a concept or relationship. The second is that the internal representations can be related or connected to one another in useful ways.

In this chapter I look at ways of organizing conceptual knowledge. I first look at what it means to use rules in a meaningful way. Then I look at the assumptions of a particular framework (schema) that provides a general structure for organizing knowledge. Finally, I look at specific examples of how schemas can be used to increase our ability to comprehend text, evaluate logical statements, and solve problems. The examples in this chapter come from many different knowledge domains; in subsequent chapters I will apply the schema framework to word problems.

Meaningful Use of Procedures

Procedures may or may not be learned with meaning. Rote learning of procedures produces knowledge that is closely tied to the context in which it is learned. In contrast, procedures that are learned with meaning are closely tied to conceptual knowledge and can be more readily transferred to novel situations.

Hatano (1988) makes a similar argument in discussing mathematical understanding, but further specifies that conceptual knowledge focuses on the object of the procedures. The object may be either a physical object or a cognitive entity characterized by the rich relationships mentioned by Hiebert and Lefevre (1986). Conceptual knowledge enables one to understand why a procedure works because each step can be related to the object's properties or to changes in those properties (Lesgold, 1991, 1994). Expertise does not necessarily imply the possession of conceptual knowledge because "routine" experts can be both fast and accurate, without being able to adapt to new problems.

Chi, Bassok, Lewis, Reimann, and Glaser (1989) have found that one way of measuring understanding is to record the number of self-explanations that students provide during problem solving. Their study examined the learning of procedural skill from examples provided in a physics text. The examples did not always provide good explanations of why one should take a particular action in solving a problem, so the investigators hypothesized that the amount of learning would be related to how well students could generate their own explanations for the actions. The four students who did the best at solving problems at the end of the chapter (averaging 82% correct) spontaneously generated an average of 15.3 explanations per example. The four less successful students (averaging 46% correct) spontaneously generated only 2.8 explanations per example. In addition, the good solvers were quite accurate at evaluating their own comprehension, whereas the poor problem solvers usually thought they understood. A third difference was that the good solvers used examples as a reference source, but poor problem solvers reread them in search of an exact solution procedure.

Chi and her colleagues contrasted their approach with Anderson's ACT* theory that was examined in the previous chapter. Whereas Anderson emphasized the conversion of already encoded knowledge into fast, skillful problem solving, Chi emphasized the encoding stage, believing that how well individuals learn to solve problems is due largely to the completeness of the encoding, rather than to the efficiency with which they can convert the encoded instructions into a skill. In a subsequent paper Chi and VanLehn (1991) analyzed the content of the self-explanations. Self-explanations either (a) combined a set of action steps into a goal or inferred a solution plan, (b) expanded or refined the preconditions of an action, (c) stated additional consequences of an action, or (d) interpreted mathematical statements. Table 3.1 shows how frequently each type of self-explanation was given by the good and the poor solvers. Particularly noteworthy is the high frequency of self-explanations that mentioned either the preconditions or consequences of an action. Preconditions and consequences of actions are the two components of the production rules that were considered in the pre-

TABLE 3.1
Frequency of Self-Explanations for Good and Poor Problem Solvers

	Good	Poor	Total
Strategic, plan like, or goal oriented	9	4	13
Expand or refine preconditions	46	24	70
Explicate consequences of actions	78	19	97
Give meaning to quantitative expressions	16	2	18
Uncodable	5	1	6

Note. From Chi et al. (1994).

vious chapter, illustrating that most of the explanations focused on the meaningful use of procedures.

Supporting the meaningful use of procedures is what Chi and VanLehn (1991) refer to as *constituent knowledge*. There are four kinds of constituent knowledge that helped students solve the physics problems. First, there is a knowledge of *systems* that provides a mental model of an entire configuration such as a block on an inclined plane, or two masses supported by a string. Second, there is knowledge of *technical procedures* such as choosing a reference frame and projecting force vectors onto the axes. Third, there is a knowledge of *principles* that consists mostly of qualitative versions of Newton's laws. Fourth, there is a knowledge of *concepts* such as body, tension, weight, acceleration, and force.

A challenge raised by these different kinds of knowledge structures is identifying how are they organized to support the meaningful use of procedures. Schemas are general frameworks for organizing knowledge that offer a promising approach. In the next section the major assumptions of schema theory are contrasted with the assumptions of a stimulus–response associationist theory.

Schema Theory

One way to organize existing knowledge is through relatively stable, internal networks called *schemas*. Schemas are constructed at a relatively high level of generality and provide a framework for interpreting specific events (Thorndyke, 1984). Schema theory refers to a collection of models that presume that we encode such knowledge clusters into memory and use them to comprehend and store our experiences.

During the time period that American psychologists were predominantly influenced by stimulus-response theories of behavior, psychologists such as Bartlett in England and Piaget in Switzerland were arguing that behavior is influenced by larger units of knowledge organized into schema (Brewer & Nakamura, 1984). The schema theory that Bartlett (1932) developed in his book *Remembering* has inspired many of the modern versions of schema theory. He defined a schema as an active organization of past experiences in which the mind abstracts a more general cognitive structure to represent many particular instances of those experiences. Bartlett's book consists of an elaboration of schema theory and shows its application to experimental results that he had collected on memory for figures, pictures, and stories.

A fundamental assumption of Bartlett's schema theory is that all new information interacts with old information represented in the schema. This interaction was noticed by Bartlett in the errors people made in recall. Many of the errors were more regular, more meaningful, and more conventional than the original material, suggesting that the material had been integrated with prior knowledge.

To clarify the concept of a schema, Brewer and Nakamura (1984) point out that there a number of fundamental differences between schema theory and the stimulus-response approach to psychology. These include:

1. Atomistic versus Molar. A stimulus-response theory is atomistic and is based on small units of knowledge (a single stimulus). A schema is a much larger unit, showing how knowledge combines into clusters.

2. Associationistic versus Nonassociationistic. A stimulus-response theory requires learning an association between a stimulus and a response. A schema provides a knowledge structure for interpreting and encoding aspects of a particular experience.

3. Particularistic versus Generic. A stimulus-response theory shows the association between a particular stimulus and a particular response. A schema is more general and represents a variety of particular instances, much like a prototype represents the particular instances of a category.

4. Passive versus Active. The association between a stimulus and a response can be learned in a passive manner. Invoking a schema is a more active process in which a particular experience is matched to the schema that best fits that experience.

Bartlett's ideas had little theoretical impact during his lifetime. In the United States behaviorism and stimulus-response psychology had a strong hold on theory construction. In England his theory was taken more seriously, but by the early 1970s even his own students thought the theory was a failure. A dramatic turn of events occurred in 1975 when a number of prominent American cognitive scientists argued that schema are needed to organize knowledge in artificial intelligence, cognitive psychology, linguistics, and motor performance. These theorists adopted the major assumptions of Bartlett's theory, but were more specific about what these knowledge structures looked like.

Two of the strongest advocates for the importance of schema were Minsky (1975) for representing knowledge in artificial intelligence programs and Rumelhart (1980) for representing knowledge in cognitive psychology. One of the main contributions from artificial intelligence has been that programming languages allow more detailed specification of schema organization than was possible in earlier formulations. Although Bartlett emphasized that schema were organized, he was not always very specific about what the organization was. Rumelhart indicated that a schema theory is basically a theory about how knowledge is represented and about how that representation facilitates the use of knowledge in various ways. Schemas are used to interpret sensory data, retrieve information from memory, organize action, and solve problems. The following section illustrates how schemas are used in comprehending text, reasoning about logical rules, and solving problems.

Text Comprehension

A central issue for psychologists interested in studying comprehension is specifying how people use their previously acquired knowledge to understand text (Kintsch, 1994). The influence of prior knowledge on the comprehension and recall of ideas was dramatically illustrated in a study by Bransford and Johnson (1973). They asked people to listen to a paragraph and try to comprehend and remember it. After listening to the paragraph, subjects rated how easy it was to comprehend and then tried to recall as many ideas as they could. You can get some feeling for the task by reading the following passage from Bransford and Johnson (1973) once and then trying to recall as much as you can.

> The procedure is actually quite simple. First you arrange things into different groups. Of course, one pile may be sufficient depending on how much there is to do. If you have to go somewhere else due to lack of facilities, that is the next step; otherwise you are pretty well set. It is important not to overdo things. That is, it is better to do too few things at once than too many. In the short run this may not seem important, but complications can easily arise. A mistake can be expensive as well. At first the whole procedure will seem complicated. Soon, however, it will become just another facet of life. It is difficult to foresee any end to the necessity for this task in the immediate future, but then one never can tell. After the procedure is completed, one arranges the materials into different groups again. Then they can be put into their appropriate places. Eventually they will be used once more, and the whole cycle will then have to be repeated. However, that is part of life. (p. 400)

The paragraph actually describes a very familiar procedure, but the ideas are presented so abstractly that the procedure is difficult to recognize. People who read the passage without a hint recalled only 2.8 ideas from a maximum of 18. A different group of subjects, who were informed after reading the passage that it referred to washing clothes, didn't do any better; they recalled only 2.7 ideas. But subjects who were told before they read the passage that it described washing clothes recalled 5.8 ideas. The results indicate that background knowledge isn't sufficient if people don't recognize the appropriate context. Although everyone is familiar with the procedure used to wash clothes, people didn't recognize the procedure because the passage was so abstract. Providing the appropriate context before the passage, therefore, increased both comprehension and recall.

The results suggest that relating abstract ideas to a familiar schema does more than provide useful retrieval cues. Since recall was improved only when people knew the topic before reading the passage, the experiment suggests that providing a familiar context improved comprehension, which in turn improved recall. When the abstract ideas were difficult to comprehend, they were quickly forgotten, and providing the hint after the passage had no effect on recall.

The integration of new information into existing knowledge structures can be encouraged by asking students to self-explain the material as they read a text. This is shown in a study by Chi, De Leuw, Chiu, and LaVancher (1994) in which they attempted to replicate the self-explanation effect with some major changes. The changes included:

- Self-explaining expository text rather than worked-out examples;
- Focusing on declarative understanding of concepts (as assessed by question answering) rather than learning a procedural skill (as assessed by problem solving);
- Using a different domain (biology instead of physics);
- Using a different age group (eighth-graders instead of college students); and most important,
- Prompting students for self-explanations rather than relying on spontaneous generation of self-explanations.

The reason the self-explanation effect might generalize to the declarative understanding of text is that, like in the explanation of problem solutions, textbooks often omit information that is useful for constructing a complete understanding.

Students in Chi's study took a pretest on the circulatory system, read a passage describing the system, and then took a posttest on the system. Those students in the prompted group were told to explain the meaning of each sentence in the passage after they finished reading it. In addition, the passage contained a set of specific function prompts that asked them explicitly about the function of a particular component. Students in the control group were not prompted for either self-explanations or functions, but read the passage twice. Although both prompted and unprompted students showed better performance on the posttest, the amount of gain was significantly higher for the prompted students. This is particularly impressive considering that the studied text was very well written, the unprompted students read the text twice, and the greater gain was obtained by merely eliciting self-explanations.

What is learned by self-explaining? Chi and her collaborators have three suggestions. The first characteristic of self-explaining is that it is a constructive activity. Constructed declarative knowledge was observed in Chi et al.'s (1994) study, and constructed procedural knowledge was observed in Chi et al.'s (1989) study on solving physics problems. The second characteristic is that self-explaining encourages the integration of new knowledge with existing knowledge. Making this connection is important, as was shown in the Bransford and Johnson (1973) experiments. The third characteristic is that because self-explaining is a continuous, ongoing process, it provides an opportunity to find conflicts in one's evolving mental structures.

The next section examines how making connections with schematic structures influences performance on a logical reasoning task called the four-card selection problem (Wason & Johnson-Laird, 1972).

Logical Reasoning

Imagine that you are shown four cards, each containing a *D*, a *K*, a 3, or a 7. The experimenter tells you that each card has a letter on one side and a number on the other side and then asks which cards you would have to turn over to determine the truth of the sentence *Every card that has a D on one side has a 3 on the other side*. Try to answer this question before reading further.

The correct answer is that you would have to turn over the cards containing a *D* and a 7. The selection of a *D* is fairly obvious; the rule would be false if the other side of the card did not contain a 3. The rule would also be false if you turned over the card containing the 7 and found a *D* on the other side. It is not necessary to turn over the card containing the 3, although this is a common mistake. The rule does not specify what should be on the opposite side of a 3; it only specifies what should be on the opposite side of a *D*. For example, finding a *K* on one side of the card and a 3 on the other side would not make the rule false.

Experiments using this task reveal that the implications of a conditional rule are not very clear to most people. The combined results of four experiments indicated that only 5 of 128 subjects correctly turned over only the two correct cards (Wason & Shapiro, 1971). The most popular choice was to turn over the two cards mentioned in the rule—the letter *D* and the number 3 for the above example.

Wason and Johnson-Laird (1972) argued that people make mistakes because they seek information that would verify the rule rather than information that would falsify it. Only the latter information is necessary. Turning over the card containing the 3 would verify the rule if a *D* were found on the other side, but it's not logically necessary to turn over this card because the rule does not specify what should be on the other side. It is necessary to turn over the 7, but people usually overlook this card because they are not seeking ways to disprove the rule.

Wason and Shapiro (1971) hypothesized that the poor performance in this task was due in part to the abstract material. They predicted that using more realistic materials related to everyday knowledge would make the task significantly easier. Data from a letter-sorting task designed by Johnson-Laird, Legrenzi, and Legrenzi (1972) supported this hypothesis. The subjects were British, and at that time in Britain it cost more to send a sealed letter than an unsealed letter. Subjects in the realistic condition were asked to imagine that they worked at a post office, and their job was to make sure that the letters conformed to each of the following rules: *if a letter is sealed, then it has a 50-lira stamp on it,* and *a letter is sealed only if it has a 50-lira stamp on it.* Two letters were face down, revealing either a sealed or an unsealed envelope, and two letters were face up, revealing either a 40-lira or a 50-lira stamp. Subjects in the symbolic condition were asked to test two abstract rules involving letters with an *A* or a *D* on one side and a 3 or a 5 on the other side. Seventeen of the 24 subjects in the realistic condition were correct on both rules, compared with none of the 24 subjects in the symbolic condition.

A question raised by these findings is why people improve when they are given realistic information. Do they become better reasoners, or do they recall specific experiences from memory that eliminate the need to reason? Research by Griggs and Cox (1982) initially suggested that the latter explanation is more appropriate. They tested undergraduates at the University of Florida on a variation of Johnson-Laird's letter task and found that students did as poorly on the realistic task as on the abstract task. Griggs and Cox proposed that the good performance reported by Johnson-Laird et al. (1972) could be explained by their British subjects' personal knowledge about the postal rule and its counterexamples. The American subjects, in contrast, lacked personal experience that they could retrieve from memory, because U.S. rates were the same for sealed and unsealed letters.

A more recent view, however, is more encouraging about our reasoning abilities than the memory retrieval explanation proposed by Griggs and Cox. According to this view, we possess *pragmatic reasoning schemas* that are general knowledge structures that enable us to reason about a variety of situations that can be interpreted by the schema (Cheng, Holyoak, Nisbett, & Oliver, 1986). Two examples of pragmatic reasoning schemas are the *permission schema* and *obligation schema.* Permission requires that a condition be satisfied (being old enough) before some action (drinking beer) may be taken. According to this hypothesis, people should do well in evaluating permission statements even for situations that are unfamiliar to them. Imagine that you are hired to enforce the rule *If a passenger wishes to enter the country, then he or she must have had had an inoculation against cholera.* You are shown the four cards PASSENGER *A* WISHES TO ENTER THE COUNTRY, PASSENGER *B* DOES NOT WISH TO ENTER THE COUNTRY, PASSENGER *C*

HAS BEEN INOCULATED, PASSENGER *D* HAS NOT BEEN INOCULATED. Which cards would you have to turn over to obtain more information in order to enforce the rule?

People should also do well in reasoning about situations that involve obligation, such as *If any urithium miner gets lung cancer then the company will pay the miner a sickness pension.* An obligation requires that some action (paying a sickness pension) must be taken if some condition (having lung cancer) is satisfied. Research supports the hypothesis that people do much better in evaluating conditional statements about permission and obligation than in evaluating conditional statements about arbitrary relations (Cheng et al., 1986). By the way, the answer to the question in the previous paragraph is that it is necessary to find out more information about passengers *A* and *D* by turning over the cards.

Problem Solving

Early information-processing models of problem solving (Newell & Simon, 1972) were formulated for how people solve puzzles such as the Tower of Hanoi and the missionaries–cannibals problem. Solving puzzles typically requires general strategies for searching for a solution, rather than extensive declarative knowledge about the puzzle (VanLehn, 1989). Theories, therefore, emphasized search procedures that would guide the problem solver from the initial state of the problem (all the missionaries and cannibals on one side of the river) to the goal state (all the missionaries and cannibals across the river). An example of a search procedure is means–end analysis, in which the problem solver attempts to reduce differences between the current problem state and the goal state.

However, some problems are familiar ones so we can use our prior knowledge about possible solutions to reduce the need for searching for a solution. This distinction between using prior knowledge and searching for the solution is illustrated in Fig. 3.1, which shows three major stages in solving a problem (Gick, 1986). The problem solver first attempts to construct a representation of the problem by connecting it to prior knowledge.

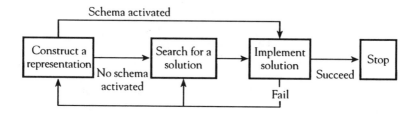

FIG. 3.1. Schematic diagram of the problem-solving process. From Gick (1986).

Certain features of the problem may activate a schema for solving the problem if the problem solver does find a connection with prior knowledge. The schema contains information about the typical problem goals, constraints, and solution procedures for that kind of problem. If schema activation occurs during the construction of a problem representation, the solver can proceed directly to the third stage and implement the solution. There is very little need to search for a solution because the appropriate solution procedures are activated by recognizing the particular problem type.

One of the challenges in using schematic knowledge is recognizing that a problem has the same (isomorphic) solution structure as a previously learned solution. A classic study on the difficulty of spontaneously noticing isomorphic solutions was conducted by Gick and Holyoak (1983). They investigated whether providing an isomorphic solution would help students solve Duncker's radiation problem. The problem requires using high-intensity rays to destroy a tumor. The rays can not be applied along a single path because they would destroy healthy tissue before reaching the tumor. The convergence solution involves dividing the rays so that they will have a high intensity only when they converge on the tumor. Although this is a clever solution, Duncker (1945) found that very few people solved the problem in this way.

Gick and Holyoak (1983) tested whether more people would discover the convergence solution if they were first exposed to an analogous story that used this solution. Their subjects initially read a military story that described a solution to a problem in which an army had to be divided in order to converge on a fortress. The instructions indicated that the story might provide hints for solving the radiation problem. The results showed that most people made use of the analogy. Over one half of those who read the story included the convergence solution among their proposed solutions, compared with only 8% of those who did not read the story. But when Gick and Holyoak omitted the hint to use the story, the number of convergence solutions greatly decreased. Their findings demonstrated that people could generate an analogous solution when prompted, but did not spontaneously recognize the similarity between the two problems.

People's inability to spontaneously notice the relation between isomorphic problems poses a challenge to make analogies more obvious. One reason that isomorphic solutions are often not obvious is that, although the analogy preserves relations among the concepts in a problem, the concepts themselves differ (Gentner, 1983). This point is illustrated in Table 3.2 for the military and radiation problems. Although the concepts (army and fortress; rays and tumor) differ in the two problems, the solutions preserve the relations of breaking up and converging. The similarity of the two solutions is represented at the bottom of the table by the convergence schema, in which the concepts are described more generally. The solutions

TABLE 3.2
Abstraction of a Convergence Schema

Military Problem

Initial state
   Goal: Use army to capture fortress.
   Resources: Sufficiently large army.
   Constraint: Unable to send entire army along one road.
Solution plan: Send small groups along multiple roads simultaneously
Outcome: Fortress captured by army.

Radiation Problem

Initial state
   Goal: Use rays to destroy tumor.
   Resources: Sufficiently powerful rays.
   Constraint: Unable to administer high-intensity rays from one direction.
Solution plan: Administer low-intensity rays from multiple directions simultaneously.
Outcome: Tumor destroyed by rays.

Convergence Schema

Initial state
   Goal: Use force to overcome a central target.
   Resources: Sufficiently great force.
   Constraint: Unable to apply full force along one path.
Solution plan: Apply weak forces along multiple paths simultaneously.
Outcome: Central target overcome by force.

Note. From Gick and Holyoak (1983).

to both problems require breaking up a large force so that weak forces can be simultaneously applied along multiple paths.

   Gick and Holyoak (1983) discovered that people were likely to form this more general schema if they read and compared two analogous stories before trying to solve the radiation problem. For example, some students read the military story and a story about forming a circle around an oil fire in order to use many small hoses to spray foam on the fire. Students who described the relation between these two stories were much more likely to think of the convergence solution to the radiation problem than were students who read only a single analogous story. Creating the convergence schema requires that people compare two analogous stories, which makes them think about the solution in general terms. Reading the two analogous stories without comparing them is not very helpful, but requiring people to replace specific concepts by general ones helps them formulate the more general solution (Catrambone & Holyoak, 1989).

The advantage of creating a general schema, such as the convergence schema, is that it should be easier for subjects to recognize that the radiation problem is an example of a general schema than to recognize how it relates to a particular problem. But psychologists are still investigating the extent to which people create general schema, as opposed to recalling a particular problem (Ross, 1984) as a basis for analogy. After an extensive review of the literature on analogy, Reeves and Weisberg (1994) concluded that there is sufficient evidence to show that we use both specific problems and more abstract schemas in analogical reasoning. One promising theory is that we begin by using the solution of specific problems, but as we apply the isomorphic solution to other problems, we make comparison between problems and begin to form more abstract schemas (Ross & Kennedy, 1990). I will return to this issue in chapter 7 on abstracting solutions when we apply these ideas to word problems.

Summary

A challenge for instructors is to create learning conditions to help students learn rules in a meaningful way. This requires that students learn conceptual knowledge to support their use of procedural knowledge. Conceptual knowledge enables them to understand why a procedure works because each step can be related to properties of objects that support the procedures. Analyzing students' self-explanations as they study problem solutions provides a good measure of how well they understand the solution. Good problem solvers provide many more self-explanations than poor problem solvers, and can monitor their degree of understanding. The most frequent self-explanations evaluate the prerequisites and consequences of rule applications, illustrating an understanding of the problem-solving procedures.

A schema provides a framework for organizing both objects and procedures by providing general structures that can be filled in with the detailed properties of a particular instance. A fundamental assumption of schema theory is that all new information interacts with old information contained in an activated schema. In contrast to stimulus-response theory, which is based on small units of knowledge, a schema combines knowledge into larger clusters of related information. A stimulus-response theory requires learning an association between a stimulus and a response, but a schema provides a knowledge structure for interpreting experiences. A schema is also more generic and represents a variety of particular instances. And finally, although a stimulus-response association can be learned in a passive manner, invoking a schema is a more active process in which a particular experience is matched to the schema that best fits that experience.

Schematic knowledge can help us understand abstract ideas, organize our recall, interpret the implications of logical statements, and replace general search strategies for solving problems with more specific solutions. An example of how schemas aid text comprehension is illustrated by research in which people read a very abstract passage about a familiar situation. When the familiar situation is identified (such as washing clothes), comprehension and recall of ideas is much better than when the abstract situation cannot be matched to schematic knowledge. Comprehension of technical passages (such as an explanation of the circulatory system) is improved by asking students to explain the meaning of each sentence in the passage. Self-explanations help students connect new ideas to existing knowledge and identify inconsistencies as they attempt to construct a model of the situation.

Schematic knowledge also aids reasoning and problem solving. The four-card selection problem, which requires evaluation of a conditional rule, is very difficult when the content cannot be matched to schematic knowledge. However, when the content can be matched to a permission or an obligation schema, people vastly improve in their ability to evaluate the rule. Abstract schematic knowledge also helps us identify the similarity between isomorphic problems that have identical solution procedures but different story content. An example is the abstraction of a convergence schema by comparing two different stories that can be solved by convergence on a central target (fortress or oil fire).

In the next part of the book specific examples of how such schematic structures can help us solve word problems are presented.

PROBLEMS

4

Elementary Problems

It is now time to begin applying some of the general ideas about procedural and conceptual knowledge to word problems. We begin with arithmetic problems that children encounter in the lower elementary grades. These problems are interesting for two reasons. The first is that they provide a valuable source of information regarding the kinds of difficulties young children encounter when they begin working on mathematical problems. For instance, is successful performance at this age constrained by a lack of ability to do addition and subtraction or is successful performance constrained by an inability to understand the problems? The second reason these problems are useful is that it can later be seen whether the analysis of more complex problems builds on the same theoretical ideas used to analyze simple problems. Can the kinds of relations identified in simple problems be combined to form more complex problems, or do we need different kinds of knowledge structures to represent complex problems? This issue is explored in chapter 5 on multistep arithmetic problems and again in chapter 6 on algebra word problems.

Children's Strategies for Solving Problems

Children use a variety of strategies for solving elementary story problems. Here's an example of an exchange between a sixth-grade student named Ann (a pseudonym) and an interviewer (I) based on the problem:

> A bag of snack food has 4 vitamins and weighs 228 grams. How many grams of snack food are in 6 bags?

Ann: . . . you probably divide that.

I: Why division?

Ann: 'Cause there's a big number and a little number.

[After dividing 228 by 6 and obtaining 38, Ann continues]

Ann: Umm, no . . . times. You times.

I: Now what's changing your mind here, Ann?

Ann: Because the 38 is much less than that one [228], and that's only in one bag. That makes a lot of sense. That makes better sense, because that's more than that one [the 228].

I: What can you tell students [to help them]?

Ann: If you see a big number and a little number, go for the division. If that doesn't work, then you try the other ones.

This exchange between Ann and the interviewer is included in an article by Sowder (1988) on children's solution of story problems. Interviews of approximately 70 children in the middle grades revealed that children use a variety of strategies that differ in sophistication. These include:

- Use the arithmetic operation that the student feels most competent with, and/or has been recently discussed in the classroom;
- Use the size of the numbers to determine whether to add, subtract, multiply, or divide. Ann begins by selecting division because there is a big number and a small number in the problem;
- Try all the operations and choose the most reasonable answer.
- Look for key words to tell which operation to use, such as "all together" means add;
- Decide whether the answer should be larger (by adding or multiplying) or smaller (by subtracting or dividing) than the provided numbers. Ann concludes that her choice of division was the incorrect choice based on the reasonableness of the answer;
- Choose the operation the fits the meaning of the story.

Greer (1987, 1994) emphasized the numbers used in the problems has a tremendous influence on which arithmetic operation is selected in solving elementary story problems. For instance, in one of his studies he found three levels of difficulty depending on the type of number used as the multiplier. When it was an integer, 92% of the answers were correct; when it was a decimal greater than one, 71%; and when it was a decimal less than one, 53%. In contrast, the number used as the multiplicand had very little effect. One of the biggest misconceptions in children is that multiplication always makes bigger and division always makes smaller.

Diagnosing misconceptions is made more challenging by the fact that immature strategies can often produce correct answers. A key finding in Sowder's study was that correct answers are not a safe indicator of good thinking. Ann still does not have a mature strategy even though she eventually discovered the correct operation. A recent study of second graders reached the same conclusion (Mekhmandarov, Meron, & Peled, 1996). Many children who obtained a correct answer gave incorrect explanations, whereas other children who gave an incorrect answer revealed a partial understanding of the solution during an interview. The difficulty with assessing students' understanding from their numerical answers is that there are so few operations to choose among in one-step problems. Sowder, therefore, recommended a greater use of two-step problems in which it is more difficult to select the correct operations by chance.

The more mature strategies for solving word problems are based on the meaning of the text. The key-word strategy is a step in this direction but is limited. In the key-word strategy students are taught to look for an important word in the text that tells them what arithmetic operation to use. For example, teachers might tell students that they should add whenever they see the word *altogether*. According to Sowder (1988), the key-word strategy is taught by some well-meaning teachers who are not aware of how students can abuse it:

> The *spirit* of teaching key words—getting students to think about the situation—is all right, but students sometimes look only for the key words and ignore the whole context. It is, of course, also easy to write story problems with key words that alone, suggest *incorrect* operations for the problems. (pp. 230–231)

Nesher and Teubal (1975) gave examples of how key words can be misleading. The key word *more* usually suggests addition, but not in the problem:

> The milkman brought 11 bottles of milk on Sunday. That was 4 more than he brought on Monday. How many bottles did he bring on Monday?

Similarly, the key word *less* often suggests subtraction, but not in the problem:

> The milkman brought on Monday 7 bottles of milk. That was 4 bottles less than he brought on Sunday. How many bottles did he bring on Sunday?

Nesher and Teubal (1975) found that students provided correct answers much more frequently when the key words were consistent with the correct arithmetic operation.

Mayer and Hegarty (1996) distinguished between two general approaches to solving word problems, which they labeled the direct translation strategy and the problem model strategy. In the direct translation strategy, students focus only on numbers and key words, ignoring most other information that they consider to be nonessential. In the problem model strategy, students construct a mental model of the situation that focuses on how objects in the situation are related. Mayer and Hegarty cited a study by Lewis (1989) that was successful in greatly reducing errors when the key word was inconsistent with the correct arithmetic operation. Students first constructed the qualitative relation between numbers by indicating the relative placement of quantities on a number line. For instance, they indicated whether James or Megan had saved more money when informed that Megan had saved one fifth as much as James. The use of the number line was intended to help students learn how to build a problem model.

At a more general level, we can agree that we want our students to select arithmetic operations based on the meaning of the story. But how do students get beyond problems in which specific words are mapped onto specific numerical operations? The answer provided by psychologists and mathematics educators is that students need to analyze meaning at a higher level of generality that refers to changing, combining, and comparing quantities. The next section describes and evaluates a taxonomy that uses these more abstract categories to classify addition and subtraction problems.

A Taxonomy for Addition and Subtraction Problems

A major step forward in the analysis of addition and subtraction problems was the formulation of a taxonomy for describing the problems (Riley, Greeno, & Heller, 1983). Table 4.1 shows the taxonomy that consists of Change problems, Combine problems, and Compare problems. In Change problems some quantity is increased or decreased and the unknown is either the starting amount, the amount of the change, or the resulting amount. In Combine problems at least two quantities are combined and students are asked to find either the total amount or the amount in one of the subsets. In Compare problems a comparison is made between two quantities using the relation *more* or *less*. The unknown is either the referent, the compared quantity, or the difference between the two quantities.

Table 4.2 shows how well children in kindergarten through third grade did in using blocks to solve these problems (Riley et al., 1983). The experimenter read the problems slowly to the children, repeating when necessary. The problems were also made accessible to young children by keeping the numbers small enough so that the sum was less than 10.

The results of the Riley study revealed that the semantic structure of the problem, as defined by the taxonomy, had a major influence on the difficulty of the problem. For instance, Compare problems 3 and 6 in Table 4.1 are more difficult than Change 1 or Combine 1, even though all four problems require simple addition. The identity of the unknown also influenced the difficulty of the problem. A striking example is the rapid decline in the younger children's ability to solve Change problems as the unknown quantity varied from the result of the change to the amount of the change to the starting amount.

As an example, let's compare a problem in which the unknown is the amount of the change with a problem in which the unknown is the starting amount. An example of the first (Change 3) type is:

John had 5 marbles. He got some more. Now he has 8. How many did he get?

This problem was solved by 61% of the children in kindergarten. Contrast it with an example of the second (Change 5) type:

John had some marbles. He got 5 more. Now he has 8. How many did he have in the beginning?

This problem was solved by only 9% of the kindergarten children. Note that the Change 3 problem can be solved by starting with 5 fingers (or 5 blocks, when available) and counting additional fingers (blocks) until reaching 8 fingers (blocks). This strategy doesn't work for the Change 5 problem because the beginning amount is unknown.

Riley et al. (1983) proposed three models to simulate different levels in children's performance on these problems. The models differ in the ways information is represented and the ways in which quantitative information is manipulated. The least sophisticated model limits its representation of Change problems to the external display of blocks. This model can solve Change problems 1, 2, and 4 in which the solution uses blocks that can be directly inspected when the question is asked. For instance, in Change 4 the answer (5 blocks) can be directly observed after removing 3 blocks from the initial 8 blocks. The second model can maintain an internal representation of increases and decreases in blocks, allowing it to solve the Change 3 problem, but it still depends on an external display of objects. The third model has a more abstract understanding of part–whole relations that enables it to build a representation of the entire problem before actually solving it. This allows it to solve all of the Change problems, including problems 5 and 6, which require operating on the unknown start value. Riley's simulation models for the Combine and Compare problems have the same general characteristics as her models for the Change problems.

TABLE 4.1
Types of Elementary Problems

Action	*Static*

CHANGE
Result unknown
1. Joe had 3 marbles.
    Then Tom gave him 5 more marbles.
    How many marbles does Joe have now?
2. Joe had 8 marbles.
    Then he have 5 marbles to Tom.
    How many marbles does Joe have now?
Change unknown
3. Joe had 3 marbles.
    Then Tom gave him some more marbles.
    Now Joe has 8 marbles.
    How many marbles did Tom give him?
4. Joe had 8 marbles.
    Then he gave some marbles to Tom.
    Now Joe has 3 marbles.
    How many marbles did he give to
    tom?
Start unknown
5. Joe had some marbles.
    Then Tom gave him 5 more marbles.
    Now Joe has 8 marbles.
    How many marbles did Joe have in the
    beginning?
6. Joe had some marbles.
    Then he gave 5 marbles to Tom.
    Now Joe has 3 marbles.
    How many marbles did Joe have in the
    beginning?
EQUALIZING
1. Joe has 3 marbles.
    Tom has 8 marbles.
    What could Joe do to have as many
    marbles as Tom?
    (How many marbles does Joe need to
    have as many as Tom?)
2. Joe has 8 marbles.
    Tom has 3 marbles.
    What could Joe do to have as many
    marbles as Tom?
	COMBINE
	Combine value unknown
	1. Joe has 3 marbles.
	    Tom has 5 marbles.
	    How many marbles do they have altogether?
	Subset unknown
	2. Joe and Tom have 8 marbles altogether.
	    Joe has 3 marbles.
	    How many marbles does Tom have?
	COMPARE
	Difference unknown
	1. Joe has 8 marbles.
	    Tom has 5 marbles.
	    How many marbles does Joe have more than
	    Tom?
	2. Joe has 8 marbles.
	    Tom has 5 marbles.
	    How many marbles does Tom have less than
	    Joe?
	Compared quality unknown
	3. Joe has 3 marbles.
	    Tom has 5 more marbles than Joe.
	    How many marbles does Tom have?
	4. Joe has 8 marbles.
	    Tom has 5 marbles less than Joe.
	    How many marbles does Tom have?
	Referent unknown
	5. Joe has 8 marbles.
	    He has 5 more marbles than Tom.
	    How many marbles does Tom have?
	6. Joe has 3 marbles.
	    He has 5 marbles less than Tom.
	    How many marbles does Tom have?

Note. From Riley, Greeno, and Heller (1983).

Activating Schemas

Kintsch and Greeno (1985) further developed Riley's third model to present a more specific picture of the knowledge structures needed to solve Change, Combine, and Compare problems. Part of their model builds directly on Kintsch's previous work in constructing a general model of text comprehension. This part proposes that the problem text is transformed into a conceptual representation by grouping words into meaningful units called

TABLE 4.2
Effect of Problem Type on Proportion Correct

Problem Type	Grade			
	K	1	2	3
Change (1)	.87	1.00	1.00	1.00
Change (2)	1.00	1.00	1.00	1.00
Change (3)	.61	.56	1.00	1.00
Change (4)	.91	.78	1.00	1.00
Change (5)	.09	.28	.80	.95
Change (6)	.22	.39	.70	.80
Combine (1)	1.00	1.00	1.00	1.00
Combine (2)	.22	.39	.70	1.00
Compare (1)	.17	.28	.85	1.00
Compare (2)	.04	.22	.75	1.00
Compare (3)	.13	.17	.80	1.00
Compare (4)	.17	.28	.90	.95
Compare (5)	.17	.11	.65	.75
Compare (6)	.00	.06	.35	.75

Note. From Riley, Greeno, and Heller (1983).

propositions. But unlike general comprehension of text, understanding word problems also requires constructing a problem model that focuses on the part of the text that is required to solve the problem. In constructing the problem model, a student must infer information that is needed for solving the problem but is not stated in the text, and must exclude information in the text that is not needed in the solution. This requires activating schemas that represent the properties and relations of relevant information in the problem.

Table 4.3 shows the general form of a schema, which has the general properties that were discussed in the previous chapter. The schema is called a *set schema* and contains slots that can be filled in with the relevant information of a particular problem. The *object* slot refers to the kind of

TABLE 4.3
A Set Schema

Slot	Value
Object	<cnoun>
Quantity	<number>, SOME, HOW MANY
Specification	<owner>, <location>, <time>
Role	start, transfer, result; superset, subset; largeset, smallset, difference

Note. From Kintsch and Greeno (1985). Copyright © 1985 by the American Psychological Association. Reprinted with permission.

objects that the set contains. The *quantity* slot specifies how many objects are in the set, or specifies a term such as SOME or HOW MANY when the number of objects is the unknown variable. The *specification* slot contains information that distinguishes the set from others such as the owner, its location, or the time when it is specified. The *role* slot identifies how the set is related to other sets in the problem.

Notice that identifying the role is essential for determining how the various quantities specified in the problem should be combined to calculate the solution. Solving the problem requires activating more specialized schemas that apply to either a Change, Combine, or Compare problem. Change problems are solved by using a *transfer schema* in which there is a start amount that is modified by transferring some amount into or out of the start amount, producing a result amount. Combine problems are solved by using a *part–whole schema* consisting of subsets that combine to form a superset. Compare problems are solved by using a *more–less schema* that consists of a large set, a small set, and a difference set.

Let's try to make this more concrete by looking at the following example:

> Joe has 3 marbles. Tom has 5 marbles. How many marbles do they have altogether?

The first sentence activates a set in which the object is marbles, the quantity is 3, and Joe is the owner. The important role information cannot be identified at this point because there is not enough information. The second sentence activates a similar set, but has a different quantity and a different owner. The phrase "have altogether" in the last sentence results in forming a superset with the goal of finding its quantity as the answer to the problem. When a superset is created, the model assigns subset roles to the other sets such as the number of marbles possessed by Joe and by Tom. Once the complete superset schema has been filled in, with the goal of computing the quantity of the superset, a calculational strategy is triggered that provides the answer to the problem.

The calculational strategy is represented as procedures that are attached to the schema, using a technique called *procedural attachment* that was invented during work on artificial intelligence (Bobrow & Winograd, 1979). The information in a procedural attachment indicates the prerequisite conditions for invoking the procedures, stated in terms of the schema's components. The information also includes the consequences of performing the procedure, such as adding the quantities of the subsets to calculate the quantity of the superset. Note that this representation combines the procedural and schema approaches that were examined in the previous two chapters. Procedures specify the solution, but are organized around schematic information that identifies the formal structure of the problem from text information.

Comprehension Difficulties

The theory formulated by Kintsch and Greeno (1985) attempted to model good problem solvers—those who can solve the problems. An advantage of having the kinds of schematic structures postulated in the theory is that they enable good problem solvers to comprehend the problems in a more top-down manner by fitting problems into one of the schematic structures. This identification allows good problem solvers to compensate for omissions and ambiguities in the text by making the appropriate inferences.

But a theory about good problem solvers does not tell us why so many children have trouble with elementary story problems. One hypothesis is that children lack the part–whole, transfer, and more–less schemas that are needed to solve these problems. Another hypothesis is that children possess these schemas but have linguistic deficiencies that impair their ability to relate text information to their existing schemas (Cummins, Kintsch, Reusser, & Weimer, 1988).

A study by Hudson (1983) is often cited as evidence that difficulties in comprehension contribute to the poor performance of young children. In one of the problems she showed children 5 birds and 3 worms, and asked them "How many more birds are there than worms?" Only 17% of the nursery school children and 64% of the first graders could answer the question. But when asked "How many birds won't get a worm?" 83% of the nursery school children and 100% of the first graders answered correctly. Children indicated a fairly sophisticated understanding of part–whole set relations by counting the three worms, counting the same number of birds, and then counting the number of remaining birds. The results, therefore, suggested that children may understand part–whole set relations but lack the knowledge of how to map them onto linguistic statements such as *How many more X's are there than Y's?*

Cummins and her colleagues tested the hypothesis that linguistic deficiencies limit young children's understanding of word problems by asking them to both solve and recall the problems. They were not told whether a problem was to be solved first or recalled first until after the problem had been read. As predicted, recall accuracy (as measured by correct memory for the logical relations among sets) closely resembled solution accuracy. On 77% of the misrecall occasions, the problem was transformed into a simpler problem of the same type; difficult Compare problems were transformed into easier Compare problems and difficult Change problems were transformed into easier Change problems. Moreover, arithmetic errors were often correct answers to miscomprehended stories. Subtraction tended to be used to solve addition problems that were miscomprehended as subtraction problems, and vice versa.

Although these results are interesting, they do not provide direct support for the hypothesis that linguistic deficiencies produced the strong correlation between correct recall and correct solutions. Perhaps young children simply lack the schematic structures for the more difficult problems and this prevented both the recall and solution of these problems. As was seen in the previous chapter, appropriate schematic structures help us both to recall text and to solve problems.

More convincing evidence for the linguistic deficiency hypothesis came from a detailed simulation model based on observed comprehension difficulties (Cummins et al., 1988). Deficient linguistic knowledge was modeled by giving the simulation program correct schematic knowledge but deficient knowledge in interpreting key words and phrases. The simulation interpreted the word *some* as an adjective, the word *altogether* as *each*, and the phrase *have more than* as simply *have*. The model matched the children's responses on 15 of the 18 problems. Furthermore, the model more accurately simulated the response patterns than an alternative model that had correct linguistic knowledge but impaired schematic knowledge.

A more recent computer simulation model was created by LeBlanc and Weber-Russell (1996) to investigate the complex interaction between text comprehension and mathematical operations. The simulation is implemented as a bottom-up problem solver in which a novice attempts to solve the problem by integrating in a word-by-word manner the concepts in the text. This bottom-up approach is contrasted with a top-down strategy that activates a schema in memory (such as a Compare schema) for each particular type of problem. A significant finding from the simulation was that demands on working memory, as measured by the number of concepts to remember and the number of inferences to make while remembering those concepts, was a good predictor of students' success rate in solving problems. These results contribute to our understanding of how solving word problems relates to more general theories of text comprehension (Kintsch, 1988).

A practical consequence of the linguistic deficiency view is that changing the wording of problems should make them easier to solve. In fact, De Corte, Verschaffel, and De Win (1985) had earlier hypothesized that rewording the problems to make the semantic relations more explicit would help the children find a correct solution. They selected one case each of a Change, Combine, and Compare problem to see if the reworded problems would be easier to solve. Table 4.4 shows how the reworded problems differed from the traditional problems. In the usual statement of Change 5 problems, there is no explicit reference to the unknown start set. In a traditional Combine 2 problem, it is not stated explicitly that the given subset is at the same

TABLE 4.4
Examples of Standard (Series A) and Reworded Problems (Series B)

Type of problem	Series A	Series B
Change/start set unknown (Change 5)	Joe won 3 marbles. Now he has 5 marbles. How many marbles did Joe have in the beginning?	Joe had some marbles. He won 3 more marbles. Now he has 5 marbles. How many marbles did Joe have in the beginning?
	Bob got 2 cookies. Now he has 5 cookies. How many cookies did Bob have in the beginning?	Bob had some cookies. He got 2 more cookies. Now he has 5 cookies. How many cookies did Bob have in the beginning?
Combine/subset unknown (Combine 2)	Tom and Ann have 9 nuts altogether. Tom has 3 nuts. How many nuts does Ann have?	Tom and Ann have 9 nuts altogether. Three of these nuts belong to Tom. The rest belong to Ann. How many nuts does Ann have?
	Ann and Tom have 8 books altogether. Ann has 5 books. How many books does Tom have?	Ann and Tom have 8 books altogether. Five of these books belong to Ann. How many books does Tom have?
Compare/difference unknown (Compare 1)	Pete has 8 apples. Ann has 3 apples. How many apples does Pete have more than Ann?	There are 8 riders, but there are only 3 horses. How many riders won't get a horse?
	Ann has 6 puppies. Sue has 3 puppies. How many puppies does Ann have more than Sue?	There are 6 children, but there are only 3 chairs. How many children won't get a chair?

Note. From De Corte, Verschaffel, and De Win (1985). Copyright © 1985 by the American Psychological Association. Reprinted with permission.

time part of the superset. The traditional use of an abstract comparison term such as *more than* was eliminated by rewording the Compare 1 problem. The rewording was based on Hudson's (1983) findings but omitted the diagrams used in her study. Each of these changes made the problem significantly easier to solve by a group of first- and second-grade children.

Development of Conceptual Structures

Although understanding linguistic terms can contribute to the difficulty of young children's comprehension of word problems, it would be misleading to blame all errors on language. In contrast to theorists who focus on linguistic variables, Okamoto (1996) has recently proposed a model in which the development of mathematical knowledge determines the relative difficulty of elementary word problems. In her view, the two questions "How many more birds are there than worms?" and "How many birds won't get a worm?" differ in more than minor changes in wording. Success that kindergartners had in Hudson's (1983) study on "won't get" problems, but not on Compare problems, is because they had a conceptual understanding of one-to-one correspondences to solve "won't get" problems, but did not possess the higher levels of mathematical knowledge required to solve Compare problems.

Okamoto built her theory on the development of central conceptual structures, as proposed by Case (1992). Six-year-old children are assumed to represent real-world objects as mental objects on a single dimension, allowing them to add or subtract mental objects along this dimension. At this stage, they should be able to solve the Combine 1, Change 1, and Change 2 problems in Table 4.1. For instance, in the Change 1 problem, Joe starts with three marbles and receives five more marbles. By 8 years old, children can tentatively relate two number lines and the numbers themselves are treated as objects of manipulation. This enables them to solve all of the Change, Combine, and Compare problems except Compare 5 and 6. For instance, determining how many more marbles Joe has than Tom in Compare 1 requires comparing number lines for both Joe and Tom. By 10 years, children develop two, well-coordinated number lines that enable them to use numerical operations to reverse a direction of more or less. Compare 5 requires determining how many marbles Tom has if Joe has 8 marbles, which is 5 more marbles than Tom has. Support for the proposed theory comes from results that show the difficulty of solving the problems clusters into the three groups of problems specified by the three stages of her theory.

Okamoto concluded that new models need to specify the relation between linguistic and mathematical knowledge. An example is a model proposed by Fuson, Carroll, and Landis (1996) for addition and subtraction Compare problems. In the first (relational) level children can answer "Who had more/less?" but not "How much more/less?" In the second (language cue) level children are more likely to solve problems with equalizing language and problems in which finding the unknown quantity is directed by key words. In the third (matching situations) level children predominantly solve problems by using a matching conception in which the small quantity is taken from the big quantity. In the fourth (solve inconsistent) level children are able to solve inconsistent problems by using equalizing conceptions in which the relation given in the relational statement is reversed.

Dimensional Analysis in Multiplication
and Division Problems

This section addresses a more challenging set of problems than the addition and subtraction problems that have been discussed previously. One of the reasons why multiplication and division problems are more difficult than addition and subtraction problems is that they refer to several kinds of objects. Addition and subtraction problems typically refer to only one kind of object, such as apples or marbles or books (see Table 4.4). In contrast, multiplication and division problems often refer to more than one kind of object, and the object specified in the answer may differ from the objects specified in the problem.

Schwartz (1988) referred to the distinction between preserving and changing objects as referent-preserving and referent-transforming composition. The distinction is based on the premise that the purpose of mathematics is a modeling activity; a view that is similar to the object-oriented view of procedures that were discussed at the beginning of the previous chapter. Addition and subtraction are referent-preserving operations because they do not change the objects. Subtracting 5 marbles from 8 marbles gives 3 marbles. Multiplication and division are referent-transforming operations. Multiplying 9 feet × 12 feet to calculate the area of a room changes the dimensions from feet to square feet.

But Schwartz argued that there is an even more fundamental reason why multiplication and division change referents (dimensions) and it is based on the concept of an *intensive quantity*. An intensive quantity typically can not be directly measured but is a ratio of two (extensive) quantities that can be measured. For instance, when you pay $10 for 7 gallons of gas, the $10 and 7 gallons of gas are objects in the world. The price of the gas, in dollars per gallon, is an intensive quantity that refers to a quality of the gas rather than to objects such as money or gasoline.

Intensive quantities are important because they are referent-transforming operations. Imagine that you need 10 gallons of gas and want to calculate what it will cost. Solving the problem creates a change in dimensions from gallons to dollars. The change occurs by multiplying gallons by an intensive quantity, price per gallon.

Schwartz concluded that it is incorrect to assume that children's early number knowledge leads in a continuous way to understanding of the use of multiplication and division in modeling situations. An instructional strategy for teaching referent-transforming operations must, therefore, make explicit exactly how they differ from the previously learned referent-preserving operations in addition and subtraction problems.

Multiplicative Structures

Closely related to Schwartz's emphasis on dimensional analysis is the concept of a multiplicative conceptual field, proposed by Vergnaud (1984, 1988, 1994). A conceptual field is a set of situations that requires mastering several concepts of different natures that are nonetheless highly interrelated. The conceptual field of multiplicative structures includes concepts such as dimensional analysis, fraction, ratio, rate, multiplication, and division.

A major concern in our trying to understand students' understanding of multiplicative structures is to identify the mathematical relationships that they use when they choose an operation or a sequence of operations to solve a problem. Consider the following problem:

> Connie wants to buy 4 plastic cars. They cost $5 each. How much does she have to pay?

Even such a simple problem can be represented in alternative ways that have different implications for dimensional analysis. Figure 4.1 shows two different representations. Figure 4.1a represents a thought process in which 4 cars cost 4 times as much as 1 car. It shows a scalar representation of the problem in which both the number of cars and the number of dollars is multiplied by four. The ratios are scalar in the sense that they have no dimension. Notice that the arrows representing the multiplication do not cross dimensions—both cars and costs are increased by a factor of four. In contrast, the arrows in Fig. 4.1b cross dimensions by mapping from cars to costs. This represents a functional perspective that can be expressed symbolically as $f(x) = ax$, where cost is a linear function of the number of cars.

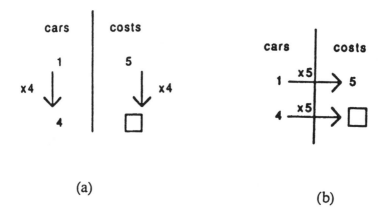

(a)

(b)

FIG. 4.1. Example of scalar (a) and functional (b) relations between numbers. From Vergnaud (1988).

Vergnaud (1994) claimed that the table-and-arrow diagrams in Fig. 4.1 offer many advantages as instructional aids including the use of vertical arrows to indicate ratios, horizontal arrows to represent functions, and parallelism to represent similar kinds of quantities. The table-and-arrow diagram is a prealgebraic representation that is less abstract than algebra but still retains the essential relationships between numbers. Students can, therefore, learn to use the diagrams before they learn how to use algebraic notation.

Nesher (1992) cited a study by Mechmandarov (1987) that supports these claims. The major findings of the study were that:

- Children weak in mathematics tended to voluntarily use the diagrams more often than children who were strong in mathematics (on 23% vs. 9% of the problems);
- When students voluntarily used the diagram, it was usually for more difficult problems, and they were more successful than students who did not use the diagram;
- Students who were required to use the diagrams for dimensional analysis significantly improved their performance on the same problems. For instance, performance improved from 20% to 55%, from 29% to 71%, and from 14% to 86% respectively, on three of the more difficult problems.

Nesher described two reasons why table-and-arrow diagrams (or mapping tables in her terminology) are helpful. First, the graphical schemes assist in the search for relevant dimensions. And second, the child does not have to work with intensive quantities but only with the more easily understood extensive quantities. Notice that in Fig. 4.1, the intensive quantity *cost per car* is separated into its two extensive components, *cars* and *cost*.

In general, researchers in this area have made many recommendations regarding how their findings could be used to improve instruction (Verschaffel & De Corte, 1996). The classification scheme shown in Table 4.1 can be used to insure that students receive a sufficiently rich variety of problem situations. Information about the relative difficulty of the different situations, different wordings, and different numbers can be used to select appropriate problems at various stages in the learning process. Knowledge about children's informal strategies can enable teachers to build on these strategies to teach more abstract concepts and skills. And finally, findings that have identified typical misconceptions can help teachers diagnose and correct students' errors.

In attempting to achieve some breadth in the coverage of major issues, depth has been sacrificed. This statement applies to this chapter more than to any other chapter in the book. Much of the work in mathematics education has focused on the issues raised in this chapter and the discussion has uncovered only the tip of the iceberg. For a more thorough overview of these issues, read Verschaffel and De Corte's (1993) review of addition/subtraction problems and Nesher's (1992) chapter on solving multiplication/division problems. More recently, Verschaffel and De Corte (1996) raised many unanswered questions about the issues discussed in this chapter, including how to better integrate the different variables investigated in addition/subtraction and in multiplication/division problems.

Summary

There are a wide variety of strategies that young children use to solve elementary word problems. Strategies include guessing, selecting a preferred or recently discussed arithmetic operation, looking for key words or at the magnitude of the numbers, deciding whether the answer should be larger or smaller than the given numbers, and choosing an operation that fits the meaning of the story. Direct translation strategies that focus on key words result in errors whenever a descriptive term (such as *more*) is inconsistent with the correct arithmetic operation (such as subtract).

A major step toward analyzing addition and subtraction problems was the development of a taxonomy that has been influential in guiding research. Results show that there is wide variation in problem difficulty depending on whether the problem is a Change, Combine, or Compare problem, and depending on which quantity in the problem is the unknown. Models developed by Riley, Greeno, and Heller (1983) simulate children's performance at three different levels of competence. The least sophisticated model relies on an external display of objects and the most sophisticated uses an abstract understanding of part–whole relations. Kintsch and Greeno (1985) further developed the most sophisticated model by showing how text information can be formally represented as set relations. Change problems can be represented by a transfer schema, Combine problems by a part–whole schema, and Compare problems by a more–less schema.

There have been two major approaches to explaining young children's errors on elementary problems. The linguistic approach assumes that a major source of difficulty is comprehending the meaning of the text. This approach claims that children possess the mathematical knowledge to solve the problems but have difficulty understanding the meaning of descriptive terms such as *some* and *altogether*. Simulations based on incorrect interpretation of these terms have accurately modeled errors, and rewording problems to clarify terms has resulted in reduced errors. But models based on conceptual development have been successful in predicting the relative difficulty of the different problem types in the Change–Combine–Compare taxonomy. For example, as children grow older, their growth in mathematical knowledge changes from being able to mentally represent objects on a single dimension to being able to represent objects mentally as numbers on two number lines that can incorporate reverse operations.

The solution of multiplication and division problems often requires combining information that refers to more than one kind of object. Multiplication and division change referents such as when we multiply 8 feet by 7 feet to obtain an answer in square feet. Referent changes also occur when using intensive quantities that represent a ratio of two (extensive) quantities, such as $1.45 per gallon. Vergnaud's analysis of multiplicative structures showed how even a simple problem, such as figuring out the total cost of buying 4 toy cars at $5 each, can be solved differently depending on whether it is solved as a scalar representation in which both cars and cost are multiplied by four, or as a functional representation in which cost is a linear function of the number of cars. Table-and-arrow diagrams, showing the relation among these numbers, have been helpful in improving children's understanding of these problems.

5

Multistep Problems

The previous chapter focused on elementary story problems that could be solved with a single arithmetic operation. Students had to decide whether to add, subtract, multiply, or divide. More complex arithmetic problems can be solved by formulating a plan for combining these elementary operations. Consider the following problem:

> Julie had a budget of $1,200 to furnish her new apartment. She found a five-piece living room set on sale for $625. She also found a queen-sized bed for $350 and a dresser for $195. How much money, if any, will Julie have left to buy various odds and ends for her apartment?

Note that this is basically a Change problem. Julie started with $1,200 and the student needs to find how much she had left after her purchases. But the amount of change has to be calculated by finding the total cost of her purchases. This is a Combine problem.

This chapter examines how multistep problems are solved by combining the elementary operations that were discussed in the previous chapter. Research on multistep problems has usually been conducted on computer systems that can coach students in constructing plans for solving these problems. This has both practical and theoretical advantages. The practical advantage is that there now exists computer coaches that can assist students in solving multistep problems. The theoretical advantage is that constructing solutions on the computer makes it easy to study the planning process that students use to solve these kinds of problems.

Three different systems that have been used to support and analyze solutions for multistep problems are compared and contrasted below. The first system called HERON (after the Greek mathematician who created some of the first mathematical word problems) was constructed by Reusser (1993) and his colleagues. In contrast to the solution trees of specific quantities constructed in HERON, Marshall's (1995) Story Problem Solver builds solutions from the abstract Change, Combine, and Compare schemas that were encountered in the previous chapter. A third system called Training Arithmetic Problem-solving Skills (TAPS) was constructed by Derry (1989) and her colleagues to instruct students on planning solutions for multistep problems.

Constructing Solution Trees

A computer-based planning environment designed by Reusser focuses on planning with specific information. Although the early work on schematic structures (Kintsch & Greeno, 1985; Marshall, Pribe, & Smith, 1987) influenced Reusser's design of HERON, his system does not require students to identify situations at these more abstract schematic levels. Students work only with domain-specific information (such as gallons of water) when entering information into the computer and don't have to identify whether a particular situation is an example of a more abstract schema, such as a Change or a Vary problem.

Reusser (1993) described his system as a graphics-based instructional tool for solving mathematical story problems. HERON gives the student a high degree of control both in conceptualizing the problem and in planning the mathematical solution. It does this by allowing students to construct the solution by creating solution trees that show how domain-specific relational schemata are combined to calculate the answer. Each relational schema consists of a pair of qualitatively and numerically specified situation units that allow the computation of a third unknown unit. A situational unit is specified by its situational role, a numerical value, and a unit of measurement.

The three examples of relational schemata presented in Fig. 5.1 should make this description more concrete. Each rectangle is a situation unit consisting of a particular role, numerical value, and unit of measurement. The unknown unit in the bottom rectangle (such as wages per month) is calculated from information entered into the top two units. The solution tree shows how single step problems, such as the three examples in Fig. 5.1, can be combined to solve multistep problems. An example of a multistep problem is the following:

> Little Simon and his father are watering their vegetable garden. The father has a 15-liter watering can. Simon's can holds one fifth of that. Both fill their cans 12 times. After that, there are still 24 liters in the rain barrel. How much water can the rain barrel hold? (presumably it was full when they started)

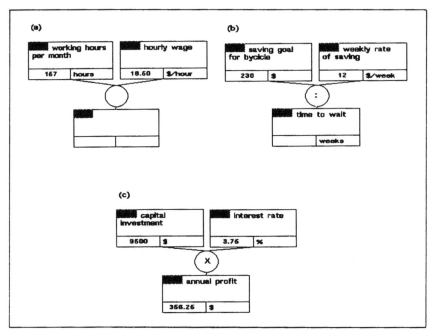

FIG. 5.1. Three examples of relational schemata in HERON. From *Computers as Cognitive Tools* (p. 162), by S. P. Lajoie and S. J. Derry (Eds.), 1993, Hillsdale, NJ: Lawrence Erlbaum Associates. Copyright 1993 by Lawrence Erlbaum Associates. Reprinted with permission.

Figure 5.2 shows the solution tree for this example. We know the final amount (24 liters) but need to calculate the amount of the change. The initial step finds the capacity of Little Simon's watering can by dividing the capacity of the father's can (15 liters) by 5. The combined capacity of both cans is then multiplied by the number of fillings to determine how much water is removed from the rain barrel. Finally, this amount is added to the amount of remaining water to determine the capacity of the barrel.

Although this problem contains a variety of abstract situational schema, students do not work at this level but instead work with the more concrete objects described in the problem. Identifying each situational unit as a particular situation (content of father's can) and supplying units (liters) emphasizes the object-oriented view of problem solving (Hatano, 1988; Lesgold, 1991) that was discussed in chapter 3 and the dimensional analysis of problems (Schwartz, 1988) that was discussed in chapter 4.

Reusser reported that it takes third graders about 20 minutes to become familiar with the entirely mouse-driven interface of his program. Information is entered into the solution tree by highlighting information in the problem

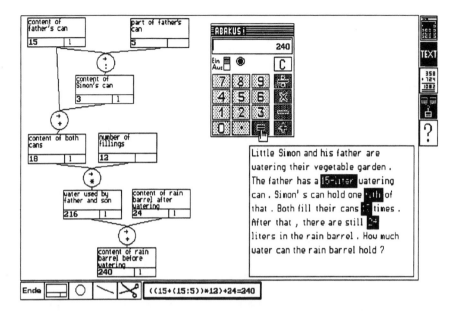

FIG. 5.2. A solution tree constructed in HERON. From *Computers as Cognitive Tools* (p. 168), by S. P. Lajoie and S. J. Derry (Eds.), 1993, Hillsdale, NJ: Lawrence Erlbaum Associates. Copyright 1993 by Lawrence Erlbaum Associates. Reprinted with permission.

text or in a menu. Depending on how the system is initialized, the student may get an error message when selecting irrelevant information. HERON is able to monitor the student's construction of a solution tree and provide feedback on four types of errors: mathematical operations, labels, units of measurement, and the inclusion or omission of (ir)relevant mathematical information.

Reusser argued that there are many reasons to consider solution trees as useful representational and conceptual tools:

- They provide a transparent means of representing the processes for understanding and solving a large class of word problems;
- They provide a flexible means for constraining knowledge construction;
- They illuminate the hidden construction processes by which the student determines the structure of the problem;
- They encourage generative understanding in that the student can begin constructing a solution tree without understanding the complete problem.

Identifying Basic Schematic Relations

In contrast to Reusser's approach, Marshall's tutor builds multistep solutions from the more abstract schematic structures that were identified in the previous chapter. The use of elementary schemas to construct solutions to single and multistep problems is the theme of Marshall's (1995) book *Schemas in Problem Solving*. Based on interviews with students and the theoretical work described in the previous chapter, she felt that the patterns of relations in story problems were critical to making correct choices about arithmetic operations. Her challenge was to develop a minimal set of schematic structures that would describe all possible relationships in story problems. The simple problems that were discussed in chapter 4 could then be represented by a single schema and more complex, multistep problems could be represented by a combination of elementary schemas.

Marshall's (1995) approach was based on the assumption that there is only a small number of basic situations that can be combined to form more complex situations. She argued that five situations are sufficient for describing relations within common arithmetic story problems: Change, Group, Compare, Restate, and Vary. The five categories are an expansion of the three categories (Change, Combine, Compare) described by Riley et al. (1983) for how children learn addition and subtraction. Marshall developed the Restate and Vary categories to represent multiplicative situations, and changed the label Combine to Group because it did not suggest as strongly addition as an operation. Table 5.1 shows an example problem for each of these five categories.

- A Change situation describes a permanent alteration over time in the quantity of some thing. There are three important numbers: the amount prior to a change (35 stamps), the extent of the change (8 more stamps), and the resulting amount after the change (43 stamps).
- A Group situation occurs when a number of small groups are combined into a large group. Three or more numbers are required: the number of members in each subgroup (18 boys, 17 girls) and the overall number in the combination (35 children).
- A Compare situation occurs whenever two things (15 minutes, 18 minutes) are contrasted to determine which of them is larger or smaller. The problem solver must determine whether the smaller or larger value is required if the relation is stated as a comparative adjective or adverb (quicker, longer, better buy).
- A Restate situation occurs when two things are described by a relational statement (twice as many kittens) such as *twice as great as* or *one half of*. The relationship holds only for the particular time frame of the story and cannot be generalized to a broader context.

TABLE 5.1
Examples of Five Schematic Situations

Change: Stan had 35 stamps in his stamp collection. His uncle sent him 8 more for a birthday present. How many stamps are now in his collection?

Group: In Mr. Harrison's third-grade class, there were 18 boys and 17 girls. How many children were in Mr. Harrison's class?

Compare: Bill walks a mile in 15 minutes. His brother Tom walks the same distance in 18 minutes. Which one is the faster walker?

Restate: At the pet store there are twice as many kittens as puppies in the store window. There are 8 kittens in the window. How many puppies are also in the window?

Vary: Mary bought a package of gum that had 5 sticks of gum in it. How many sticks would she have if she bought 3 packages of gum?

Note. From Marshall (1995). Reproduced with permission from Cambridge University Press.

- A Vary situation occurs when a relation between two things can be generalized over other time frames. Often these problems describe a hypothetical situation—how one amount (number of sticks of gum) changes as a function of a change in the other amount (number of packages).

Consider again the problem about Little Simon as viewed from an analysis into the more abstract relational schemas. The entire problem can be considered a Change situation in which the initial amount of water is the unknown variable. We know the final amount (24 liters) but need to calculate the amount of the change. We can do this by first dividing 15 liters by 5 (a Restate situation) to find the capacity of Little Simon's watering can. The combined capacity (a Group situation) is then multiplied by the number of fillings (a Vary situation) to determine how much water is removed from the rain barrel. Finally, this amount is added to the amount of remaining water to determine the capacity of the barrel.

In order to help students classify elementary problems into the five categories and to develop plans for multistep problems, Marshall designed a computer-implemented learning environment called the Story Problem Solver. The Story Problem Solver has been evaluated in several different studies including a thesis by Brewer (1988) that focused on the use of icons to represent the five semantic categories. Figure 5.3 shows the icons, each consisting of several geometric components for entering quantity information. For instance, the icon for a Change problem consists of an arrow linking two ovals; the first oval represents the initial amount of some object and the second oval represents the final amount of the object. In the middle is a rectangle that represents the amount of change.

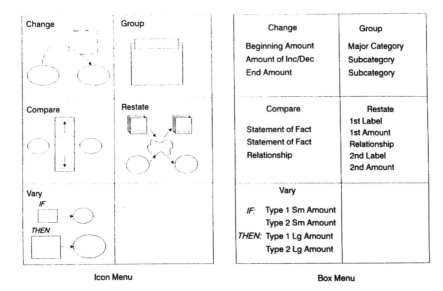

FIG. 5.3. Alternative menus for diagram and no-diagram groups. From *Schemas in Problem Solving*, by S. P. Marshall, 1995, Cambridge, England: Cambridge University Press. Copyright 1995 by Cambridge University Press. Reprinted with permission.

Brewer tested whether the use of icons would facilitate classifying problems and mapping quantities by comparing a Diagram group with a No-Diagram group that received only the labels shown on the right side of Fig. 5.3. The classification task required that students sort 20 simple story problems according to the 5 situations. The mapping task required placing numbers from the problems into the appropriate geometric components in the icon, or label, to show how the numbers were linked to parts of the schema. The two groups did not differ significantly in their ability to map numbers from the problem to the schematic slots, but the Diagram group was significantly better at classifying the problems. Marshall (1995) discussed several different ways in which icons can facilitate cognitive processing, including their role in showing the connection among the various parts of a schema.

Marshall (1995) subsequently developed a computer tutor to train students to solve multistep problems by combining the icons that represent the abstract schematic structures in the Story Problem Solver. After students acquired a familiarity with the five schematic situations described in the Story Problem Solver, they then worked with a more challenging computer environment called the Problem Solving Environment. This is particularly suitable for evaluating students' planning knowledge when the plans are based on Change, Group, Compare, Restate, and Vary relations.

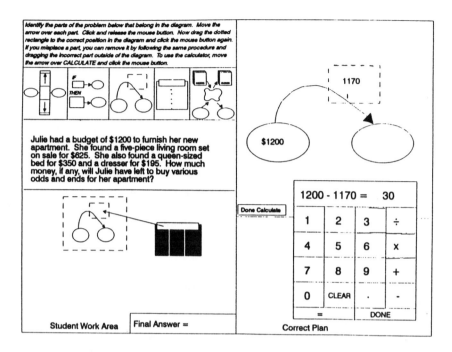

FIG. 5.4. A screen design for the problem solving environment. From *Schemas in Problem Solving*, by S. P. Marshall, 1995, Cambridge, England: Cambridge University Press. Copyright 1995 by Cambridge University Press. Reprinted with permission.

Let's return to the problem about Julie's purchases that was introduced at the beginning of the chapter to see how students would solve it in Marshall's tutor. Figure 5.4 shows the screen design for determining how much money Julie has left after making her purchases. Students solve these kinds of multistep problems by linking the icons representing the different schematic situations. In this (correct) example the student first selects the Change icon, moves it into Work Area, and enters $1,200 as the initial amount. The amount of change is found by moving the Group icon into the Work Area and linking it to the appropriate component in the Change icon. As a reminder to the student, the link is displayed as an arrow. Each of the three purchases is then entered as subgroups in the Group icon to calculate the amount spent ($1,170). Finally the amount spent is subtracted from the initial amount to find how much money Julie has left.

The advantage of using computer-based environments to make the construction process more transparent is that it can help teachers locate deficiencies in students' work and can help cognitive scientists construct theories of planning. Theories of planning play an important role in Derry's (1989) work, which also uses a computer learning environment to support planning.

Planning Theories

Derry used prior theoretical work and students' performance on her TAPS system to evaluate how students plan their solutions to multistep problems. Her group collected verbal protocols from students working with TAPS, and was influenced by two theoretical approaches in coding the protocols. The first was the theory of set relationships identified in Marshall's schema theory, which had been recently published in a technical report (Marshall et al., 1987). The second was J. R. Anderson's (1983) ACT* theory, which provided a general framework for thinking about how elementary schema could be combined to form the plans needed to solve multistep problems.

The protocol analyses assumed that a prerequisite skill for expert performance on word problems is the ability to recognize and manipulate relational schema that represent the set relations (such as Change, Combine or Group, Vary) that frequently occur in story problems. Solving single-relation problems involves not only identifying the correct relational schema but also attaching the correct arithmetic operation. When a problem is more complex, involving two or more schema, the solver must also be able to link multiple schema together to form a pathway to the goal. Here is where ACT* is useful. Derry used J. R. Anderson's (1983) theory to develop a problem-solving system that could monitor working memory for the activation of conceptual patterns, select and execute learned responses to the conceptual patterns, and set goals and plans to guide the solution.

Derry then developed a production system for multistep word problems based on the principles of ACT*. Some of the proposed (paraphrased) productions include:

- IF a schema has one unknown THEN compute the unknown;
- IF a schema has more than one unknown THEN either set subgoals for finding the unknowns or set the schema aside, eligible for later recall;
- IF there is a memory overload THEN either record or discard the information.

For example, returning to the problem at the beginning of this chapter, Julie's purchase of furniture could be represented as a Change schema with two unknowns—the amount of change and the amount of money she has left. Because the latter unknown is the goal, the subgoal of finding the amount of change could be set by using the Group schema to find the total cost of her purchases. Derry reported that many students avoid constructing complex subgoal structures, because holding several schemata in mind at once places a burden on working memory.

The TAPS tutor was designed to coach students in solving multistep problems based on a model of how experts solve these problems. Assessment procedures attempt to determine which of the expert components are either missing or inconsistently used by the student. As the student gains in expertise, tutorial prompts occur less frequently and are gradually phased out. This is done to encourage students to engage in self-monitoring, such as finding and repairing errors.

Solution Strategies

The ideas formulated for designing TAPS have been further developed by Derry (1994) in a computer-based instructional environment called Tutoring in Problem Solving (TiPS). Although the architecture was designed to generalize to problem-solving training in various subject domains, the current implementation uses the multistep story problems found in TAPS. TiPS was designed to support many learning objectives but the one most relevant to the current discussion is strategic planning.

Derry (1994) distinguished between two kinds of planning strategies— working backward and working forward—and argued that both should be explicitly taught. The distinction can be illustrated with the following problem from a damage control drill.

> Assume a situation in which a ship is taking on water at the rate of 400 gallons per minute and will sink after taking on 80 tons. There is one P-250 pump operational, which directs discharge of water overboard at a low pressure rate of approximately 300 gallons per minute. There is also a small hand-operated pump capable of pumping 65 gallons per minute. (Note: 1 gal weighs 8⅓ lb and 1 ton is 2,000 lb.) With both pumps working, how many hours does the ship have before sinking?

The working backward strategy starts with the problem goal and works backward to the information provided in the problem. The goal of finding how long it will take the ship to sink can be found from determining how many hours are needed to take on 80 tons of water. A reasonable subgoal would be to find the net inflow per minute by subtracting what is pumped out from the 400 gallons per minute coming in. One could then calculate the weight of the 35 gallons gained per minute and multiply by 60 to determine the amount of weight gain per hour. The total weight for sinking (80 tons × 2,000 lbs per ton) could then be divided by the amount of weight gain per hour to determine how many hours the ship has before sinking.

In contrast, the working forward strategy calculates quantities without developing a full plan for solving the problem. The problem solver works with computable chunks of the problem as they are read and understood. For example, the student might see the words *gallons* and *tons* in the first sentence and determine how many gallons of water weigh 80 tons before understanding how this fits into the overall solution of the problem. This approach can simplify the data but may result in unnecessary and potentially misleading calculations if they are not needed in the solution.

There are two cases in which working forward is particularly helpful. One case occurs when all the calculations that one could make are needed for the solution, so none would be unnecessary or misleading. Many problems taught in school satisfy this criterion. The other situation is when one essentially knows the correct procedure for solving the problem so does not need to do planning (VanLehn, 1989).

The transition from following a general planning strategy to applying a specific solution is particularly evident from the study of how people solve physics problems that use several equations to calculate the value of an unknown variable. Table 5.2 shows an example. Before reading further, you might want to determine how you would use the equations shown below the problem to calculate the distance the pile driver fell.

Research on how problem solvers solve these problems reveals that novices are more likely to use a general search strategy based on means/end analysis, whereas experts are more likely to work forward by referring to the equations in the order that they are actually needed (Larkin, McDermott, Simon, & Simon, 1980). Because the goal is to find the value of the unknown variable, the means/end strategy searches for an equation that contains the unknown variable. The unknown is distance in the example problem, so the novice would attempt to use Equation 1 in Table 5.2 to calculate distance by multiplying rate by time. The value for time (3.7 sec) is stated in the problem, but the value for rate is not stated (30.4 m/sec is the Final rate). The novice would then search for an equation that allows for the calculation of rate. This value is calculated from Equation 2 and then substituted into Equation 1 to solve the problem.

TABLE 5.2
Equations for Solving Motion Problems

Problem
A pile driver takes 3.7 sec to fall onto a pile. It hits the pile at 30.4 m/sec. How high was the pile driver raised?

Equations
1. Distance = rate x time
2. Rate = .5 x final rate
3. Final rate = acceleration x time

Note. From Sweller, Mawer, and Ward (1983).

Notice that the novice referred to the equations in the reverse order of how they were actually used. He first referred to Equation 1 because it contained the unknown variable, but he had to calculate a value in Equation 2 before solving Equation 1. In contrast, an expert refers to the equations in the order in which they are needed. An expert would go immediately to Equation 2, calculate rate, and then substitute the value into Equation 1. The expert has learned the correct sequence of steps and doesn't have to search for the solution. Searching for a solution should become more time consuming as the number of equations increases. For instance, if the example problem gave the rate of acceleration rather than the final velocity, it would be necessary to use all three equations.

Research has shown that students switch from a means/end to a working forward strategy as they become more experienced in solving problems. Sweller, Mawer, and Ward (1983) gave students a series of 25 motion problems like the one in Table 5.2. The average number of solutions based on a means/end strategy significantly declined from 3.9 for the first five problems to 2.2 for the last five problems.

Sweller (1988) argued that, although the means/end strategy is an efficient one for obtaining the goal, it is an inefficient strategy for learning the sequence of steps required to solve the problem. By eliminating differences between the current state and the goal state, the problem solver may rapidly obtain the goal but fail to remember the sequence of steps used. Remembering the steps is difficult because the learner's attention is focused on reducing differences, not on learning steps. Furthermore, reducing differences requires a relatively large amount of cognitive capacity, which is consequently unavailable for learning the solution.

A technique for encouraging students to learn the correct sequence of steps is to omit the goal by asking them to solve for as many variables as they can, rather than solving for a particular variable. If students were asked to use Equations 1 and 2 in Table 5.2 to solve for as many variables as they could, they would first solve for rate in Equation 2 and then substitute this value into Equation 1 to solve for distance. This approach encourages students to use a working forward strategy and eliminates the capacity demands of the means/end strategy that make it difficult to learn the correct sequence of steps.

A study of 20 high school students demonstrated the success of this approach (Sweller et al., 1983). Ten of the students were assigned to a goal condition (find the distance), and 10 students were assigned to a nongoal condition (calculate as many variables as you can). After practicing solving problems, students solved two test problems that had a specific goal. Nine of the 10 students in the nongoal group solved the test problems by working forward, but only 1 of the 10 students in the goal group solved the problems by working forward. The working forward strategy helped the nongoal students reduce search because they took significantly fewer steps in solving the test problems.

Although Larkin et al. (1980) found that experts typically use a working forward strategy on familiar problems, they suggested that experts might use a working backward strategy on complex, nonroutine problems. For these reasons, Derry (1994) recommended that both strategies be taught so students can use them as needed for thinking about complex problems.

Summary

Multistep arithmetic problems are solved by combining the elementary schematic operations that were considered in chapter 4. Reusser, Marshall, and Derry have each designed computer learning environments to assist students in solving multistep problems. Reusser's system allows students to construct solution trees by combining pairs of situation units (working hours per month, hourly wage) to form a third unit (wages per month). Although the arithmetic operations that combine pairs can be classified according to the more abstract schemas considered in the previous chapter, the focus is on identifying particular situations (content of father's can) and their corresponding units (liters). Solution trees provide a transparent means of representing the solution, constrain the selected operations, illuminate hidden cognitive processes, and allow students to "assemble" the solution without initially developing a complete plan.

Marshall's learning system, in contrast, builds directly on the abstract schematic structures. Her students received practice in identifying the parts of the problem as either a Change, Group, Compare, Restate, or Vary situation. The use of descriptive icons to represent these different categories helped students classify elementary problems into one of the categories. Marshall subsequently developed a computer tutor to train students to solve multistep problems by combining the icons. After students acquired a familiarity with the five schematic situations, they worked with a more challenging computer environment that is particularly suitable for evaluating students' planning knowledge when the plans are based on Change, Group, Compare, Restate, and Vary relations.

Derry's work was influenced by both the schematic structures developed by Marshall and the goal-oriented planning component of ACT*. Planning requires computing the unknown when there is only one unknown, setting subgoals when there is more than one unknown, and discarding information when working memory is overloaded. She recommended teaching students both a working forward strategy, which calculates quantities without developing a full plan, and a working backward strategy that starts with the problem goal and works backward by finding relevant information for producing the goal. Sweller, however, argued that students should be encouraged to develop the expert-like working forward strategy because the cognitive demands of working backward may prevent them from learning the correct sequence of steps for producing the solution. He encouraged the formulation of working forward strategies by asking students to solve for as many variables as they can, rather than asking them to solve for a particular variable.

There are a number of similarities that exist among the three planning systems discussed in this chapter. All three enable students to construct solutions by combining the more elementary relations in a multistep problem. The computer environments externalize the planning process by requiring students to make a series of decisions as they assemble the components. These decisions can be monitored and corrected through feedback. There are also differences among the systems that raise instructional questions. Is it useful to require students to categorize the elementary components according to the Change, Compare, Group, Restate, and Vary relations proposed by Marshall? Or is it better to emphasize a dimensional analysis as proposed by Reusser? The former approach is more abstract and may encourage transfer across different situations, whereas the latter approach is more concrete and consistent with an object-oriented approach to problem solving. When should teachers stress a working forward strategy and when should they stress a working backward strategy? Not enough research has been done yet to answer these questions, but the computer environments constructed by Reusser, Marshall, and Derry have not only raised these kinds of questions, but provided an instructional environment in which to search for the answers.

6

Algebra Problems

The transition from the elementary word problems discussed in chapter 4 to the multistep problems discussed in chapter 5 was relatively straightforward. Multistep problems can be solved by formulating a plan for combining the elementary schemas found in chapter 4. But the transition from arithmetic word problems to algebra word problems is more complicated. Although I have used algebra word problems in most of my research on problem solving, I have never been very confident that I could distinguish between algebra word problems and other kinds of problems. One reason is that this distinction seems to depend more on the approach used to solve the problem (whether or not the student uses algebra) than on the problem itself. A better distinction therefore is to distinguish among the different methods that students use to solve problems that we might typically classify as algebra word problems.

According to the NCTM standards, the ability to represent situations with algebraic quantities is a central skill that is a prerequisite to understanding many areas of mathematics. The first section of this chapter looks at what is involved in making this transition from arithmetic to algebra. The transition requires thinking differently about mathematical operations and about the meaning of symbols such as the equals sign. It also requires understanding how letters are used in equations to represent variables. The difficulty of representing relations between variables is illustrated in the extensive research that has been done on variations of the student–professor problem. One consequence of students' difficulty with algebra is that they often attempt to solve word problems by using nonalgebraic approaches. When this is possible, students typically do better by having access to a variety of strategies.

The success of both algebraic and nonalgebraic strategies depends on constructing a correct model of the situation described in the problem. Students are typically able to understand the situation—the challenge is to quantitatively model the situation to find the value of an unknown variable. This is particularly difficult when algebraic solutions are necessary. This chapter, therefore, looks at how an animation-based tutor that uses students' constructed equations to provide visual feedback can help students establish a correspondence between their situation model and an algebraic description of that situation.

The discussion then shifts to another issue that I feel is as important as the use of algebra to distinguish algebra word problems from the problems in the previous two chapters. Elementary and multistep arithmetic problems are usually not categorized according to the objects in the problem because the situation varies so greatly. For instance, knowing that the objects in the problem are apples tells us nothing about which arithmetic operations are needed to solve the problem. However, students typically use the described situations in algebra word problems to classify problems into categories such as work problems, distance problems, mixture problems, et cetera. This classification greatly influences how they attempt to solve the problems and use the solutions to solve transfer problems. As discussed in chapter 3, cognitive psychologists have generally argued that classification results in the activation of schema that aid in constructing solutions. However, many people in the mathematics education community argue that classification can be detrimental to problem solving. This issue is examined at the end of the chapter, and encountered again in several subsequent chapters. But let's begin by looking at the transition from arithmetic to algebra.

The Transition to Algebra

A straightforward application of the ideas that have been discussed in the previous two chapters would simply consider algebra word problems to be another example of multistep problems. To a certain extent this is true. Equations representing algebra word problems can be constructed from the elementary schemas that were described in chapter 4, and this approach formed the basis for constructing an animation-driven learning environment that is presented later in the chapter (Nathan, Kintsch, & Young, 1992). Yet, if this were all that were involved, algebra word problems should not be any more difficult than the multistep problems in chapter 5. Part of the difficulty in solving these problems, therefore, is related to learning algebra.

There has been an extensive amount of research by mathematics educators on the learning of algebra. Several of the major points were made by Kieran (1992) in her chapter for the *Handbook for Research on Mathematics Teaching and Learning*. Kieran pointed out that a study of the historical development of algebra suggests that algebra is currently conceived as the branch of mathematics that deals with symbolizing general numerical relationships and mathematical structures, and with operating on those structures. One of the major adjustments of novice algebra students concerning the symbolic representation of numbers is the translation of problem situations into equations. This change from an arithmetic to an algebraic perspective requires a new way of thinking about both the equals sign and the arithmetic operations in the equation.

Initially, elementary school students use the equals sign to announce a result, rather than as a way of expressing a symmetric relation of equality between the two "sides" of the equation. Kieran included the following problem as an example:

> Daniel went to visit his grandmother, who gave him $1.50. Then he bought a book costing $3.20. If he has $2.30 left, how much money did he have before visiting his grandmother?

Sixth graders will often write the solution as $2.30 + $3.20 = $5.50 − $1.50 = $4.00. Notice that the equals sign is used here as a left-to-right signal expressing a result, and thus requires an interpretational shift to use it appropriately in algebra (Vergnaud, 1984).

I must admit that when I first read the sixth graders' solution I had no idea what they were doing, or whether their answer was correct. Their solution was very different from how I would solve the problem using algebra. I would use some abstract symbol, such as M, to represent the initial amount of money and then add money gained and subtract money spent to equal the total amount of money left: $M + \$1.50 - \$3.20 = \$2.30$. Solving for M yields $4.00 so the sixth graders were correct. Part of my confusion in evaluating their solution resulted from their using operations that were the inverse of mine; they would subtract where I would add, and add where I would subtract.

Trying to understand their arithmetic solution required my making a perspective shift that was almost as great as would be required by them to understand my algebraic solution. In arithmetic the goal of finding the answer is usually accomplished by carrying out some sequence of operations on either the numbers in the problem or on intermediate values derived from these numbers. This can be accomplished by using a linear, sequential approach involving a string of inverse operations, without any formalizing of either the problem situation or method of solution. Although this will work for some problems, it creates a major challenge for learning algebra, as pointed out by Kieran (1992):

> Thus, the cognitive demands placed on algebra students include, on the one hand, treating symbolic representations which have little or no semantic con-

tent, as mathematical objects and operating upon these objects with processes that usually do not yield numerical solutions, and on the other hand, modifying their former interpretations of certain symbols and beginning to represent the relationships of word-problem situations with operations that are often the inverses of those that they used almost automatically for solving similar problems in arithmetic. (p. 394)

The Student–Professor Problem

The difficulty of working with symbols, rather than numbers, is illustrated by the notorious student–professor problem. Clement (1982) included the following problem among 6 questions given to 150 freshman engineering students:

> Write an equation using the variables S and P to represent the following statement: "There are six times as many students as professors at this university." Use S for the number of students and P for the number of professors.

Although Clement thought this should be a trivial problem for engineering majors, only 63% of the students wrote a correct equation. In a sample of 47 nonscience majors taking college algebra, only 43% of the equations were correct. The most common error was a reversal error ($6S = P$).

In order to try to understand the source of this error, Clement videotaped interviews with 15 freshman who were asked to think aloud as they worked on the student–professor and similar problems. Two sources of the reversal error were identified from the protocols: the word-order matching process and the static comparison process shown in Fig. 6.1. In word-order matching, the student simply assumes that the order of key words in the problem corresponds to the order of the symbols appearing in the equation. Clement referred to this approach as a syntactic strategy because it does not depend on the meaning of the expression. The static comparison process, in contrast, does consider the meaning of the expression. Students who use this strategy realize that there are more students than professors but do not know how express this relation. Therefore, they place the multiplier (6) next to the symbol associated with the larger group.

The correct approach requires an operative strategy in which a comparison of two unequal groups must be forced into the notation of an equation that shows two equal groups. This requires a hypothetical operation that makes the group of professors six times larger than it really is. The operative approach is encouraged when students are required to express comparative relations in a computer program. An earlier study by Clement and his colleagues found that significantly more students were able to solve these problems in this context because programming languages emphasize the role of operations on numbers in assignment statements.

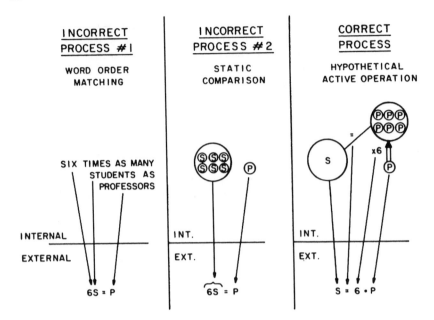

FIG. 6.1. Types of solution strategies for the student–professor problem. From Clement (1982). Reprinted with permission from the *Journal for Research in Mathematics Education*. Copyright 1982 by the National Council of Teachers of Mathematics.

Contributing to the notoriety of the student–professor problem is that supplying what we would typically consider helpful aids result in worse performance. Fisher (1988) thought she could reduce the use of a word-order matching strategy by changing the notation of the variables. If there is a tendency for S to be read as *students* and P as *professors*, then the variable notation N_s should encourage interpretation of the variable as the number of students and N_p as the number of professors. But the new notation resulted in fewer correct answers.

Sims-Knight and Kaput (1983) tried to help out by providing a concrete picture, which reduced the proportion of correct responses from 60% to 37%. Providing more familiar problems (5 pennies for every nickel) also reduced the number of correct answers. Philipp (1992) tried familiar problems in which the relation between the two variables was not stated explicitly in the problem:

> You have a pile of pennies and another pile of dimes. The value of the pile of pennies is the same as the value of the pile of dimes. Write this as an equation, using P for the number of pennies and D for the number of dimes.

You may have guessed by now that even this familiar problem was significantly more difficult than the student–professor problem. Philipp suggested that a possible explanation for this finding is that variables in the penny–dime problem contain more possible referents than variables in the student–professor problem. Interviewed students referred to the variable D as either the number of dimes, one dime, the value of one dime, or the value of all the dimes.

However, representing relations among variables is a challenge for students in grades 8, 9, and 10 even when the problem of multiple referents is avoided by using abstract symbols (MacGregor & Stacey, 1993). Only 37% of the students could use mathematical symbols to represent the statement "the number y is eight times the number z" and only 27% of the students could correctly express the relation "s is eight more than t." Approximately one half of the responses were reversal errors, such as $z = 8y$ and $t = s + 8$. MacGregor and Stacy stated that the reversals appear to be direct representations of cognitive models in which the numeral is associated with the larger variable. Their interpretation is consistent with Clement's (1982) static comparison explanation, but shows that concrete referents are not required to obtain reversal errors.

Alternative Solution Strategies

It is perhaps not surprising, given the difficulty of representing relations among variables, that students may try to avoid using algebra to solve problems. Although students are typically taught to solve algebra word problems by constructing and solving an algebraic equation, they may continue to rely to some extent on nonalgebraic solutions, even after acquiring considerable expertise in mathematical problem solving. This is revealed in a study of 85 upper-division computer science majors who had completed 3 university courses in calculus before enrolling in a course on artificial intelligence (Hall, Kibler, Wenger, & Truxaw, 1989). The students in the course were asked to solve the two distance-rate-time problems and the two work problems shown in Table 6.1. They were given 8 minutes for each problem and asked to write down all their work.

The investigators classified the solution attempts into several different categories based on the chosen strategy. The most widely used strategies were:

- Algebra: A solution is algebraic if it makes use of at least one equation to place constraints on the value of one or more variables (simple assignments such as $d = 880$ are not considered equations). Figure 6.2 shows one of the solutions in which the constructed equations were used to solve for the unknown variable.
- Model-based Reasoning: A solution was classified as model-based reasoning when a student "executes" a model of the problem situation along

TABLE 6.1
Problems Used by Hall et al. (1989)

Motion: opposite direction (MOD)

George rode out of town on the bus at an average speed of 24 miles per hour and

Two trains leave the same station at the same time. They travel in opposite directions. One train travels 60 km/h and the other 100 km/h. In how many hours will they be 880 km apart?

Motion: round trip (MRT)

George rode out of town on the bus at an average speed of 24 miles per hour and walked back at an average speed of 3 miles per hour. How far did he go if he was gone for 6 hours?

Work: together absolute (WT)

Mary can do a job in 5 hours and Jane can do the job in 4 hours. If they work together, how long will it take to do the job?

Work: competitive (WC)

Randy can fill a box with stamped envelopes in 5 minutes. His boss, Jo, can check a box of stamped envelopes in 2 minutes. Randy works filling boxes. When he is done, Jo starts checking his work. How many boxes were filled and checked if the entire project took 56 minutes?

---

the dimension defined by the unknown variable such as time, distance, or work. One subcategory is *simulation* and is illustrated by the student solving the train problem who systematically increments the time variable to determine how far apart the two trains are after each successive hour (see Fig. 6.3). The other subcategory is *generate-and-test* in which promising values are tested to see which one solves the problem. Figure 6.4 shows an example of this strategy for the train problem. Notice that the time values are not systematically incremented as in the simulation strategy.

• Ratio: These solutions use relations of proportionality between quantities and sometimes provide clever shortcuts to a solution. Figure 6.5 shows the use of ratios to solve a standard work problem. A key insight is that Jane will complete 5/9 of the job and Mary will complete 4/9 of the job when they work together. Because it takes Jane 4 hours to complete the entire job it will take her 5/9 × 4 hours (or 2 and 2/9 hours) to complete 5/9 of the job. Similarly, it will take Mary 4/9 × 5 hours (or 2 and 2/9 hours) to complete her 4/9 of the job.

• Diagram: These solutions include a picture to represent the situation.

Table 6.2 shows the percentage of students who used these strategies across the four problems. The strategies are not mutually exclusive and the fact the sum of these percentages is greater than 100 for each problem shows that students used more than one strategy in attempting to solve the problem. The finding that students used a diagram more often on the distance problems than on the less-spatial work problems is not surprising. But I was surprised by the uniformly high use of algebraic strategies across

George rode out of town on the bus at an average speed of 24 miles per hour and walked back at an average speed of 3 miles per hour. How far did he go if he was gone for six hours?

$$\text{bus distance} = (24 \text{ miles/hr})(x \text{ hours})$$

$$\text{walking distance} = (3 \text{ miles/hr})(6-x \text{ hours})$$

$$\text{bus distance} = \text{walking distance}$$

$$(24 \text{ miles/hr})(x \text{ hours}) = (3 \text{ miles/hr})(6-x \text{ hours})$$

$$24x = 18 - 3x$$

(1) $$27x = 18$$

$$x = \frac{18}{27} = \frac{2}{3} \text{ hours}$$

$$\text{bus distance} = (24 \text{ miles/hr})\left(\frac{2}{3} \text{ hours}\right)$$

$$\text{bus distance} = 16 \text{ miles} = \text{walking distance}$$

| One way = 16 miles |
| Round Trip = 32 miles |

FIG. 6.2. Example of an algebra strategy. From "Exploring the Episodic Structure of Algebra Story Problem Solving," by R. Hall, D. Kibler, E. Wenger, & C. Truxaw, 1989, *Cognition and Instruction*, 6, p. 249. Copyright 1989 by Lawrence Erlbaum Associates. Reprinted with permission.

all four problems because two of the problems—the opposite distance problem and the competitive work problem—seem to be more amenable to nonalgebraic solutions. As we saw in Figs. 6.4 and 6.5 model-based reasoning can be used to solve the opposite distance problem and the extensive use of diagrams for this problem may have been used to support a nonalgebraic solution. The frequent use of model-based reasoning and ratio strategies on the competitive work problem represent nonalgebraic alternatives for solving this problem.

Students were more successful in solving the two problems that depend less on an algebraic solution. The percentage of correct solutions was 91% for these two problems, compared to a 52% solution rate on the round-trip problem and a 61% solution rate on the work-together problem. The lower solution rates were primarily the result of conceptual errors rather than manipulation errors. Conceptual errors included errors of commission in which a student introduces an incorrect constraint and errors of omission

Two trains leave the same station at the same time. They travel in opposite directions. One train travels 60 km/h and the other 100 km/h. In how many hours will they be 880 km apart?

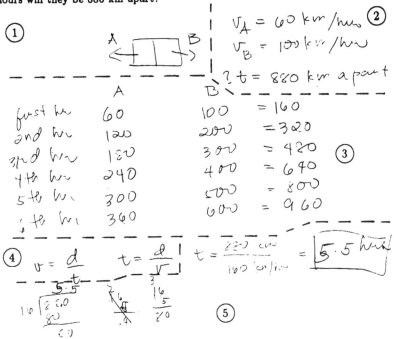

FIG. 6.3. Example of a simulation strategy. From "Exploring the Episodic Structure of Algebra Story Problem Solving," by R. Hall, D. Kibler, E. Wenger, & C. Truxaw, 1989, *Cognition and Instruction, 6,* p. 248. Copyright 1989 by Lawrence Erlbaum Associates. Reprinted with permission.

in which a student overlooks a critical constraint. Manipulation errors included arithmetic, algebraic, and variable errors. Table 6.2 shows the percentage of times these errors occurred during solution attempts across the four problems (multiple errors may occur during a solution attempt).

More recent work has shown the advantage of having multiple strategies for solving word problems. Koedinger and Tabachneck (1994) analyzed verbal protocols from 12 undergraduates at Carnegie Mellon University as they worked on two relatively simple algebra word problems containing a total of three questions. Students encountered an impasse on 23 of the 36 solution attempts. They retried the same strategy on four of these occasions and all four attempts resulted in failure to solve the problem. In contrast, 15 of the 19 cases in which students switched strategies resulted in successful solutions. The switches usually occurred from an algebraic strategy to one of the nonalgebraic strategies described previously. The emerging model of how students solve problems is that the flexible use of strategies can often

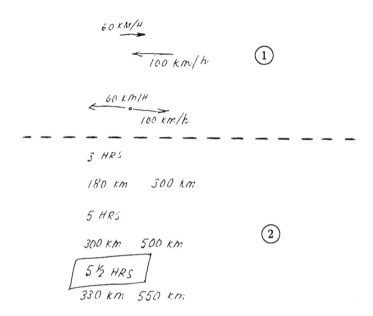

FIG. 6.4. Example of a generate-and-test strategy. From "Exploring the Episodic Structure of Algebra Story Problem Solving," by R. Hall, D. Kibler, E. Wenger, & C. Truxaw, 1989, *Cognition and Instruction, 6,* p. 250. Copyright 1989 by Lawrence Erlbaum Associates. Reprinted with permission.

Mary can do a job in 5 hours and Jane can do the job in 4 hours. If they work together, how long will it take to do the job?

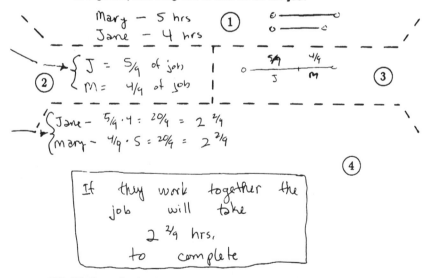

FIG. 6.5. Example of a ratio strategy. From "Exploring the Episodic Structure of Algebra Story Problem Solving," by R. Hall, D. Kibler, E. Wenger, & C. Truxaw, 1989, *Cognition and Instruction, 6,* p. 251. Copyright 1989 by Lawrence Erlbaum Associates. Reprinted with permission.

TABLE 6.2
Percentage of Strategy Use and Errors

	Problem			
Strategy	MOD	MR	WT	WC
Algebra	82	86	72	64
Model	31	22	35	47
Ratio	18	14	15	42
Diagram	69	37	8	9
Errors				
Omission	7	21	24	12
Comission	18	49	42	14
Arithmetic	9	5	4	2
Algebra	6	8	8	0
Variable	1	6	14	2

Note. From Hall et al. (1989).

be beneficial by taking advantage of the computational efficiency of algebraic strategies and the sense-making function of informal strategies (Tabachneck, Koedinger, & Nathan, 1994).

A Cognitive Model

The use of different strategies to solve word problems was also assessed by Sebrechts at the Catholic University of America and three collaborators at the Educational Testing Service (Sebrechts, Enright, Bennet, & Martin, 1996). Their study was motivated by changing goals in mathematics education that have encouraged more open-ended problem solving assessment. In order to begin to characterize the cognitive basis for this emerging approach to measurement, they analyzed in detail the solutions to 20 problems that appeared on the Graduate Record Exam General Test. All problems were presented in an open-ended format to 51 undergraduates who represented a diverse range of educational interests.

Three broad classes of strategies (equation, ratio, simulation) occurred in 82% of the solutions. As was found by Hall et al. (1989), the popularity of the different strategies was influenced by the content of problems, which varied greatly in difficulty (6% to 82% correct). A particularly good predictor of problem difficulty was the appearance of a variable more than once in the equation-based representation, requiring students to engage in some minimal algebraic thinking. Many of the problems were nonalgebraic in that they could be represented using only one variable and solved through a series of arithmetic operations without any need to manipulate variables. Sebrechts et al. (1996) expressed the implications of these findings as follows:

> Thus, the application of algebraic concepts, which requires abstraction from a context and fosters generalization and formalization of the problem situation, characterizes some of the more difficult problems. According to the Curriculum and Evaluation Standards of National Council of Teachers of Mathematics (NCTM, 1989) the ability to represent quantitative situations with expressions that include variable quantities is a central competency that should be developed in the high school years if not earlier. The NCTM standards state that an "understanding of algebraic representation is a prerequisite to further formal work in virtually all mathematical subjects" (p. 150). Nevertheless, college students, who should be proficient in representing problems algebraically, found these relatively simple algebraic questions difficult. (p. 302)

This creates a paradox for instruction. On the one hand, Tabachneck et al. (1994) found that flexible strategy use helped students solve problems. On the other hand, if algebra word problems are given to students so they will learn how to use algebra, then providing problems that can be solved without algebra is counterproductive. For example, MacGregor and Stacey (1996) tested students in 10th and 11th grade on six problems of the following type:

> The three sides of a triangle are different lengths. The second side is 3 cm longer than the first side, and the third side is twice as long as the first side. The side lengths add up to 63 cm altogether. How long is the first side?

Although approximately 70% of the students wrote correct numerical answers for each problem on the final test, only 15 of the 90 students constructed a correct algebraic equation to solve any of the problems. In order to teach algebraic solutions, MacGregor and Stacey advocated the use of problems that discourage the search for arithmetic solutions, such as changing the perimeter of the triangle from 63 to 61.8 cm.

Sebrechts et al. (1996) also studied other variables that contributed to problem difficulty, which they interpreted within the context of the general model of cognitive activities shown in Fig. 6.6. When reading a problem a student must use linguistic knowledge to translate what is stated into the givens and goals of the problem. Although the problem goal and some constraints are explicit in the problem statement, other constraints and the relations among the problem elements are often implicit. Much of the challenge during the integration stage involves identifying these implicit relations and constraints, and organizing them into larger structures, using

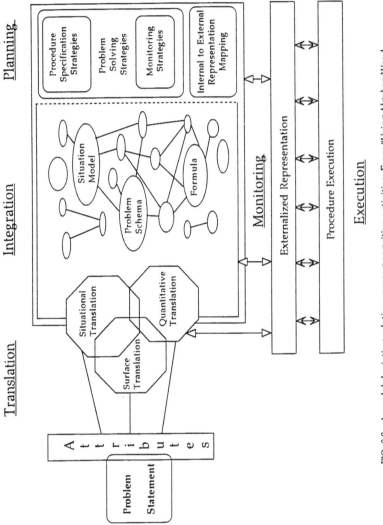

FIG. 6.6. A model depicting relations among cognitive activities. From "Using Algebra Word Problems to Assess Quantitative Ability: Attributes, Strategies, and Errors," by M. M. Sebrechts, M. Enright, R. E. Bennet, and K. Martin, 1996, *Cognition and Instruction, 14,* p. 323. Copyright 1996 by Lawrence Erlbaum Associates. Reprinted with permission.

mental schemas that are highly dependent on training and experience. It is also at this stage that students construct a model of the situation described in the problem. The chosen solution plan will depend on how the problem has been translated, the available schema, and the kinds of strategic knowledge a student has stored in memory. Once a sequence of steps has been planned the execution of the solution is carried out through a series of computations, as well as symbolic manipulations. The effectiveness of the plan and the accuracy with which actions are taken need to be monitored as the plan is implemented.

If a test is designed to evaluate quantitative ability, then it should minimize the role of linguistic attributes in determining solution difficulty. In fact, linguistic variables such as the number of arguments, predicates, connectives, and modifiers had low correlations with problem difficulty. Most students also understood the situation described in the problem statement. Only 11% of the errors indicated difficulty with situation comprehension, and the most common misinterpretations consisted of plausible alternatives. However, there was a substantial gap between correctly comprehending the situation and formulating a plan for solving the problem. The number of errors in formulating a strategy was related to SAT-M(athematics) scores, whereas procedural (computational) errors showed no significant relation with SAT-M. Sebrechts et al. (1996) concluded that their data "provide preliminary support for the view that solutions to the algebra word problems used here, as well as SAT-M scores, are primarily a measure of quantitative reasoning rather than computational ability" (p. 333).

The next section looks in greater detail at two important components in the integration stage of the model shown in Fig. 6.6—constructing a situation model and using problem schema to formulate a solution.

Situation Models

A common assumption in the study of strategies is that solving a word problem requires assembling quantitative constraints through understanding the situational context presented in the problem (Hall et al., 1989; Sebrechts et al., 1996). There are several advantages of constructing an accurate situation model of the problem. First, understanding the situation is a prerequisite to constructing an algebraic solution to the problem. Second, students can sometimes directly use their situation model, such as in the simulation strategy, to solve the problem. Third, understanding the situation can be helpful in formulating a recovery strategy (such as found by Koedinger and Tabachneck) when students suspect their solution is "off track."

Constructing a situation model in the service of understanding is not unique to algebra word problems. Text comprehension, in general, depends on constructing a model of the situation described in the text. In fact, recent efforts to improve instruction on mathematical word problems (Nathan et al., 1992; Staub & Reusser, 1995) have been influenced by theories of text comprehension in which a reader combines information in a text with prior knowledge to create a situation model of the events described in the text (Kintsch, 1988, 1994). Constructing a correct equation to represent a word problem depends on coordinating a situation model of the problem with a problem model that expresses the quantitative (algebraic) relations among the concepts described in the situation model. Figure 6.7 shows this correspondence for the following problem:

> A giant ant leaves San Francisco traveling east at 400 mph. One hour later a helicopter leaves Denver traveling west at 600 mph. How long will it take the helicopter to intercept the ant if the two cities are 1200 miles apart?

A computer-based learning environment called ANIMATE helps to coodinate the situation and problem models through an equation-driven animation of the situation (Nathan et al., 1992). ANIMATE is based on a psychological model of solving word problems; particularly on the work of Kintsch and Greeno (1985), Reusser (1988), and Cummins, Kintsch, Reusser, and Weimer (1988). The major theoretical claim is that comprehending a problem requires that a student make a correspondence between the formal equation representing the problem and his or her understanding of the situation described in the problem.

Students construct an equation by selecting from a palette of components those components that are part of the equation. For example, in a distance-rate-time problem (the only kind of problems included in the 1992 implementation), students select components specifying whether two distances should be added, subtracted, or equated; whether a distance needs to be represented as a product of rate and time; and whether one time is equal, greater than, or less than the other time. The chosen relations among the various distances, rates, and time are illustrated graphically in a network.

But the heart of ANIMATE is the simulation of the situation described by the student-constructed network. Students run the simulation by placing icons on the screen and by requesting a simulation when they believe they have entered enough information into the network. The program then attempts to run a simulation based on the constructed information. The simulation provides visual feedback regarding whether the relations among quantities and variables in the problem have been correctly specified (see Fig. 6.7). For instance, one icon may incorrectly start to move before the other, indicating an incorrect specification of the relation between the two times.

To assure that learning transferred to other testing environments, ANIMATE was used only for training. Nathan and his colleagues evaluated learning by comparing students' performance on a paper-and-pencil pretest and posttest. Test problems required that students construct equations to

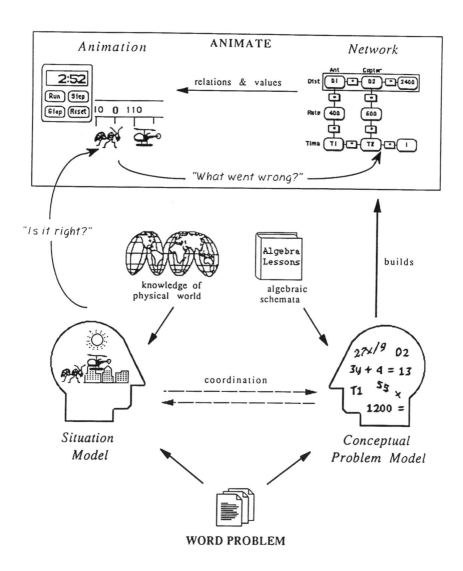

FIG. 6.7. A problem comprehension model proposed by Nathan, Kintsch, and Young (1992). From "A Theory of Algebra-Word-Problem Comprehension and its Implications for the Design of Learning Environments," by M. J. Nathan, W. Kintsch, and E. Young, 1992, *Cognition and Instruction, 9*. Copyright 1992 by Lawrence Erlbaum Associates. Reprinted with permission.

represent story problems, construct stories to represent equations of problems, and correct potentially flawed equations for problems. The results indicated that students who used the ANIMATE tutor improved significantly more on the posttest than students who only constructed networks of the mathematical relations or did not use the tutor.

Categorical Schema

At the beginning of this chapter two major differences between algebra word problems and arithmetic word problems were mentioned. The first is the use of algebra as an alternative, and sometimes necessary, way of solving the problems. The second is that the solution of algebra word problems typically begins with the categorization of the problem based on the situation described in the problem. When you initially read the ant problem in the previous section, you probably began by observing that it is a distance-rate-time problem in which two objects travel toward each other and meet. You then attempted to recall information about how to solve distance-rate-time problems, particularly problems in which two objects travel toward each other.

The important role that categorization plays in the solution of algebra word problems was first demonstrated by Hinsley, Hayes, and Simon (1977). They selected 76 problems from a high school algebra text and asked high school and college students to classify the problems by problem types, in which the meaning of problem types was unspecified. On the average, students identified 13.5 categories containing more than one problem, and there was considerable agreement among students about the identity of the categories. Examples included distance-rate-time, interest, ratio, triangle, area, mixture, and river-current problems.

Although the results showed that students are capable of categorizing algebra word problems, they did not show that the categories are used to formulate solutions. In fact, students may have had to formulate a solution before they could make a classification. This possibility would be very unlikely, however, if it could be shown that students can categorize a problem very early in the course of reading it. In a second experiment, problems were read to students one part at a time, and after each part they were asked to try to classify the problem. One half of the students were able to classify the problem correctly after hearing less than one fifth of the problem. The results verified the assumption that students can categorize problems before they have enough information to solve them.

The use of categories to guide the search for a solution was nicely demonstrated by Hinsley et al. (1977) in a third experiment that used a single, complex problem:

> Because of their quiet ways, the inhabitants of Smalltown were especially upset by the terrible New Year's Eve auto accident that claimed the life of one

Smalltown resident. The facts were these. Both Smith and Jones were New Year's Eve babies, and each had planned a surprise visit to the other on their mutual birthday. Jones had started out for Smith's house traveling due east on Route 210 just 2 minutes after Smith had left for Jones' house. Smith was traveling directly south on Route 140. Jones was traveling 30 miles per hour faster than Smith even though their houses were only 5 miles apart as the crow flies. Their cars crashed at the right-angle intersection of the two highways. Officer Franklin, who observed the crash, determined that Jones was traveling half again as fast as Smith at the time of the crash. Smith had been driving for just 4 minutes at the time of the crash. The crash occurred nearer to the house of the dead man than to the house of the survivor. What was the name of the dead man? (p. 102).

The problem is another example of a distance-rate-time problem but contains some irrelevant information (their houses were 5 miles apart as the crow flies) that suggests that it might be a triangle problem. Verbal protocols collected from six students who worked on the problem revealed that three of the six attended to the irrelevant triangle information. All three drew a triangle and identified the 5-mile distance as the hypotenuse of the triangle. The other three students classified the problem as a distance-rate-time problem. The knowledge associated with each of the two categories determined what the students attended to in the problem, what information they expected, what information they regarded as relevant, and even what errors they made in reading the text.

From their findings the authors concluded:

1. Students can recognize problem categories and agree considerably on the categories.
2. They can usually recognize the categories early in reading the text. Sometimes reading as little as the initial noun phrase is sufficient.
3. Students have information about the problem categories that is useful for formulating solutions. This information includes appropriate equations, diagrams, and procedures for identifying relevant information.

The categorical structure of word problems was further elaborated by Mayer (1981) who collected 1,100 story problems from 10 major algebra textbooks used in California secondary schools. He developed a taxonomy consisting of families, categories, and templates. The categories expanded on the categories identified by Hinsley et al. (1977). Related categories were grouped together into families, such as motion (distance-rate-time) and work problems, because they both related some amount (distance, task) to rate and time. Categories were partitioned into templates that showed variations of problems within a category. For instance, Mayer's classification included 12 templates for motion problems, 4 of which are shown in Table 6.3. These

TABLE 6.3
Problem Templates for the Motion Category

Name & Frequency	Description	Propositional Structure	Example Problem
Overtake (N = 23)	One vehicle starts and is followed later by a second vehicle that travels over the same route at a faster rate.	(RATE FOR A) = __ (RATE FOR B) = __ (TIME FOR A AND B) = __ (TIME FOR B TO OVERTAKE A) = UNK	A train leaves a station and travels east at 72 km/h. Three hours later a second train leaves on a parallel track and travels east at 120 km/h. How long will it take to overtake the first train?
Opposite Direction (N = 23)	Two vehicles leave the same point traveling in opposite directions.	(RATE FOR A) = __ (RATE FOR B) = __ (DISTANCE BETWEEN A & B) = __ (TIME) = UNK	Two trains leave the same station at the same time. They travel in opposite directions. One train travels 64 km/h and the other 104 km/h. In how many hours will they be 1008 km apart?
Round Trip (N = 13)	A traveler (or vehicle) travels from point A to point B and returns.	(RATE FROM A TO B) = __ (RATE FROM B TO A) = __ (TIME FOR ENTIRE TRIP) = __ (DISTANCE FOR ENTIRE TRIP) = UNK	George rode out of town on the bus at an average speed of 20 mph and walked back at an average speed of 3 mph. How far did he go if the entire trip took 6 hours?
Closure 1 (N = 12)	Two vehicles start at different points traveling toward one another.	(RATE FOR A) = __ (RATE FOR B) = __ (DISTANCE BETWEEN A AND B) = __ (TIME) = UNK	Two cyclists start at the same time from towns 36 miles apart. The cyclists move toward each other; one travels at 4 mph and the other at 8 mph. How long will it take for them to meet?

Note. From Mayer et al. (1984).

schematic categories influenced measures of performance such as what students remembered about the story problems. They remembered relevant information that is essential for solving the problem much better than irrelevant details (Mayer, Larkin, & Kadane, 1984).

Disadvantages of Categorization

As was seen in chapter 3, schemas are very useful for organizing memory and problem solving. A possible disadvantage, however, is that categorization might cause students to memorize stereotypic solutions to problems based on their categorization. They might memorize one equation for solving a distance-rate-time problem, another for solving a mixture problem, and a third for solving a work problem without understanding the meaning of the symbols in the equation. Sowder (1985) was one of the first math educators to voice this concern:

> Teaching problems by type is the antithesis of teaching problem solving. How many times have students said "But we don't know how to do that kind," as though already knowing how to do a particular type were the *only* way to solve a problem? It is clear that Mayer's focus on the usual word problems, and on studies in which subjects have had significant training in algebra, have led him in this direction. The heart of problem solving to most mathematics educators is "What do I do when I don't know what to do?" Teaching problems by type results in knowing exactly what to do, for problems of that type. Hence, to repeat the argument, that type of problem would then be an exercise (or "routine problem" to some of us), calling as it does on an already-learned algorithm. (p. 141)

I have a mixed reaction to this argument. I disagree with Sowder's argument because most college students can't solve these routine problems and therefore the problems may only be routine to math educators and researchers like myself who frequently work with word problems. I can solve routine problems without much thought and, therefore, am not doing any real problem solving. But most students struggle with these problems. As recently argued by a prominent group of math educators, problems are not inherently problematic or routine but depend on how students and teachers treat them (Hiebert et al., 1996). Thus, a group of second-grade children would be engaged in genuine problem solving if asked to find the difference between the height of two children who were 62 and 37 inches tall.

I agree with Sowder that we don't want students to rotely learn equations for routine stories. We would like them to analyze the problems into the mathematical relations that have been discussed in the preceding chapters. Too much emphasis on the story content can also obscure similarities in solutions to problems that belong to different categories. For example, students may fail to see how solutions to motion problems share some concepts with solutions to work problems because categorization typically can create artificial differences between problems that belong to different categories. Some of these difficulties are examined in the following chapters on transfer. The central question in these chapters is "How can we take advantage of a solution to a problem to solve problems that have a related solution, or can be solved by a related method?" This requires more than simply memorizing equations for a particular problem.

Summary

Constructing an equation to represent an algebra word problem makes use of the elementary schema that have been discussed previously, but also introduces the idea of using algebraic symbols to represent numbers. The change from an arithmetic to an algebraic perspective requires a new way of thinking about both the equals sign and the arithmetic operations in the equation. The equals sign must now be used to express a symmetric relation of equality, and the arithmetic operations are often the inverse of those used to carry out a sequence of operations in multistep arithmetic problems. The challenge of expressing algebraic relations can be seen in the misleadingly simple task of writing an equation to represent the statement that there are six times as many students as professors. In order to avoid reversal errors, students need to follow an operative strategy that makes the group of professors six times larger than it really is.

The difficulty of expressing algebraic relationships can cause students to rely on nonalgebraic methods. These methods include model-based reasoning that employs either simulation or a generate-and-test approach, a ratio strategy that expresses proportionality relations, and the use of diagrams. A flexible use of strategies can increase the number of correct solutions by taking advantage of the computational effectiveness of algebraic methods and the sense-making function of more informal methods. The disadvantage of flexibility—not learning the algebraic approach—can be avoided by including problems that are difficult to solve by a nonalgebraic approach.

A model of how students solve word problems should specify the cognitive operations required for a successful solution. When reading a problem a student must use linguistic knowledge to translate what is stated into the givens and goals of the problem. The integration stage involves identifying implicit relations and constraints, and organizing them into larger structures, using mental schemas that are highly dependent on training and experience. It is also at this stage that students construct a situation model of the problem. The selected solution plan will depend on how the problem has been translated, the available schema, and the kinds of strategic knowledge a student has stored in memory. Once a sequence of steps has been planned, the execution of the solution is carried out through a series of computations, as well as symbolic manipulations. A computer-based learning environment called ANIMATE provides an animation of a constructed equation, providing visual feedback of the operations represented in the equation. The model assumes that students have a correct situation model so they can recognize when an animation does not match the situation described in the problem. In fact, research results indicate that most errors are caused by the inability to formulate a mathematical model of the situation, rather than by an inability to understand the situation or solve an algebraic equation.

In contrast to the wide variety of situations described in arithmetic problems, a more limited number of typical situations occur in algebra problems. Students first recognize a problem as fitting a certain category such as a distance, work, mixture, or interest problem. They then use their schematic knowledge of how to solve problems in that category. Although the growth of schematic knowledge is often considered to be one aspect of acquiring expertise, it can result in a routine use of stereotyped equations in which students do not engage in real problem solving. Categorizing can also prevent students from perceiving how solutions learned for one class of problems might be helpful for solving problems in other categories. The next chapter on transfer takes a close look at this issue.

PART

III

TRANSFER

7

Abstracting Solutions

The three chapters in this section of the book discuss transfer of solutions to solve related problems. Table 7.1 shows an example problem and four test problems (Reed, 1987). The classification of the test problems shows what is meant by a related problem. The classification is based on whether the example problem and test problem share a common story context and a common solution procedure (equation). One would expect that students would do the best when the two problems share both. I label these problems as Equivalent and include them in my research as a measure of how well students have learned the solution to the example problem. It would be unfair to expect students to transfer a solution to modified problems if they haven't learned the solution to the example. Fortunately, students usually do fairly well in solving Equivalent problems.

Another relation between problems that has received much attention in examining transfer is what most researchers refer to as Isomorphic problems. Isomorphic problems have different story contexts but share a common solution. A practical issue is how different do the story contexts have to be in order to classify two problems as Isomorphic rather than as Equivalent. I consider the story context of algebra word problems to be different if the two problems fall into different categories in the taxonomies (Hinsley, Hayes, & Simon, 1977; Mayer, 1981) that were discussed in the previous chapter. For example, the Isomorphic problem in Table 7.1 would be classified as a motion problem in Mayer's (1981) taxonomy, although it can be solved the same way as the example. This chapter examines transfer to Isomorphic problems.

Chapter 8 examines transfer to Similar problems. These problems share a story context but require modifying the solution of the example to solve

TABLE 7.1
Examples of Relations Between Problems

Example Problem

A small pipe can fill an oil tank in 12 hours and a large one can fill it in 8 hours. How long will it
take to fill the tank if both pipes are used at the same time?

Test Problems/Solution Procedure

Story Context	Same	Different
Same	Equivalent	Similar
	A small hose can fill a swimming pool in 6 hours and a large one can fill it in 3 hours. How long will it take to fill the pool if both hoses are used at the same time?	A small pipe can fill a water tank in 20 hours and a large pipe can fill it in 15 hours. Water is used at a rate that would empty a full tank in 40 hours. How long will it take to fill the tank when both pipes are used at the same time, assuming that water is being used as the tank is filled?
Different	Isomorphic	Unrelated
	Tom can drive to Bill's house in 4 hours and Bill can drive to Tom's house in 3 hours. How long will it take them to meet if they both leave their houses at the same time and drive toward each other?	An airplane can fly from city A to city B at an average speed of 250 mph in 3 hours less time than it takes to return from city B to city A at 200 mph. How many hours did it take to return?

Note. From Reed (1987). Copyright © 1987 by the American Psychological Association. Reprinted
with permission.

the test problem. The question posed by the Similar problem in Table 7.1
is "Can students who have a solution to the example problem extend this
solution to include a case in which water is being used as the tank is filled?"
This requires a different skill than solving Isomorphic problems. Solving
Isomorphic problems requires recognizing that two apparently unrelated
problems are solved the same way by finding corresponding quantities in
the two problems. Solving Similar problems requires modifying the solution
of the example to solve a problem that is obviously related because of the
shared story context.

The final case is composed of problems that are Unrelated because they
share neither a story context nor a solution procedure. For this reason,

transfer to Unrelated problems is usually not very interesting. The exception is that there may be transfer between Unrelated problems that are solved by the same general method such as the use of a diagram. Novick (1990) used the term *Representational Transfer* to refer to transfer between two problems that have different solutions but share a common method of solution. Chapter 9 examines transfer of general methods.

The present chapter looks at the roles of story context and solution procedure in determining how people perceive problems. It begins by looking at how people sort problems into categories and how the relative emphasis on story context and solution procedure changes with increasing expertise. It then looks at how successfully using the solution of an Isomorphic problem depends on finding a correspondence between the quantities in the solution and the quantities in the test problem. Next, the role of abstraction in helping people recognize the common solution shared by Isomorphic problems is examined. And finally, the requirements for creating abstract solutions are examined to determine whether this approach might be helpful in teaching students to solve word problems.

Categorizing Problems

Ideally, teachers would like students to transfer a learned solution to other problems that are solved in the same way. Unfortunately, this does not always occur because two problems that have identical solutions may be described so differently that it is not obvious that they share a common solution. But this limitation can change as people become better problem solvers. As they become more expert about a particular subject matter, they become more capable of perceiving how problems are related even when they have different content. They become better at classifying problems based on their solutions and are less influenced by the specific story content. A study by Silver (1981) that used story problems was one of the first to demonstrate this finding.

Silver asked seventh-grade students to form groups of problems that were mathematically related and to explain the basis for categorizing them. He used 16 problems that could be represented by a 4 × 4 matrix. The four problems in each horizontal row were mathematically related, and the same mathematical procedure could be used to solve each. The four problems in each vertical column described a similar story content but required different procedures to solve them. The first two problems in Table 7.2 are mathematically related, because the same procedure is used to solve each. The third problem has the same story content as the first but requires a different mathematical procedure.

Although Silver asked his students to classify mathematically related problems, he expected that some might use story content as a basis of

TABLE 7.2
Examples of Related Structure and Related Content

Word problem	A farmer is counting the hens and rabbits in his barnyard. He counts a total of 50 heads and 140 feet. How many hens and how many rabbits does the farmer have?
Related structure	Bill has a collection of 20 coins that consists entirely of dimes and quarters. If the collection is worth $4.10, how many of each kind of coin are in the collection?
Related content	A farmer is counting the hens and rabbits in his barnyard. He counts six coops with four hens in each, two coops with three hens in each, five cages with six rabbits in each, and three cages with four rabbits in each. How many hens and how many rabbits does the farmer have?

Note. From Silver (1981). Reprinted with permission from the *Journal for Research in Mathematics Education.* Copyright © 1981 by the National Council of Teachers of Mathematics.

classification. Therefore, students were asked to solve 12 of the problems after they made their classification in order to determine whether there was any relation between their ability to classify and their ability to solve problems. Silver classified the students as good, average, or poor problem solvers on the basis of the number of problems they solved.

The results indicated that the better problem solvers formed categories on the basis of mathematical structure, and the poorer problem solvers formed categories on the basis of story content. The good problem solvers formed an average of 3.1 categories based on mathematical structure, compared to 1.8 categories for the average problem solvers, and 0.4 categories for the poor problem solvers. The opposite trend occured for story content. The poor problem solvers formed an average of 2.3 categories based on story content, compared to 0.6 categories for the average problem solvers, and 0.1 categories for the good problem solvers.

Similar results were obtained when students were asked to recall information about story problems. Good problem solvers were able to recall information about mathematical structure. Poor problem solvers rarely recalled this information, even when the solutions were discussed prior to their recall. However, they could often remember details about the story context and were sometimes better than the good problem solvers at recalling these details. The results suggest that an important source of individual differences in mathematical problem solving is the ability to categorize problems initially according to the mathematical procedure needed to solve them.

Differences in ability to categorize problems according to their mathematical structure also distinguish novices from experts in more advanced courses. Chi, Glaser, and Rees (1982) asked 8 novices and 8 experts to sort 24 physics problems into categories based on similarity of solutions. The novices were undergraduates who had recently completed a physics course. The experts were advanced Ph.D. students from the physics department. Each group formed about the same number of categories, but the problems in the categories differed for the two groups. Novices tended to categorize problems on the basis of common objects, such as spring problems and inclined-plane problems. Experts tended to categorize problems on the basis of physics principles that could be applied to solve them, such as the conservation of energy law or Newton's Second Law ($F = MA$). As in Silver's (1981) experiment with seventh graders, the better problem solvers were more sensitive to the formal structure of the problem.

A challenge for instruction on algebra word problems is that emphasizing traditional problem categories might prevent students from transfering isomorphic solutions across categories that differ in story content. A recent study by Blessing and Ross (1996) evaluated the possible harmful effects of instruction that focuses on problem types. One of the first aspects of their study that caught my attention was that their subjects were very good students—24 graduates of the Illinois Mathematics and Science Academy, a residential high school in Aurora, Illinois for academically gifted students. The study examined the possible constraining effects of problem types in the ability of these students (then at the University of Illinois) to solve word problems. Six problem types were chosen from the ones identified by Hinsley et al. (1977) and are commonly used in algebra textbooks: age, interest, mixture, motion, river current, and work. As pointed out by Mayer (1981), each of these types has a prototypical equation that was used to create appropriate content problems. Inappropriate content problems were created by using a prototypical equation for one category (such as a work problem) as the solution for another category (such as a motion problem). And finally, a neutral content was created for each prototypical equation by using stories that didn't fit any of the traditional content types.

The solutions were graded on a scale from 0 to 1, with partial credit given to solutions that were partially correct. The average score was .73 for problems with an appropriate content, .77 for problems with a neutral content, and .64 for problems with an inappropriate content. A statistical analysis revealed that the success rate was significantly lower for problems with an inappropriate content, confirming that problem type can have a detrimental effect, even for gifted students. The success on neutral content problems may have been due to students' ability to form an analogy to an appropriate problem type. For instance one participant wrote the following comments after solving a neutral "interest" problem in which the content was about flowers: "You always learn them as interest problems in math class so you always call them that, even if you use them differently. You don't group flowers as money but both problems are solved the same way" (Blessing & Ross, 1996, p. 805).

Mapping Quantities

In order to correctly use an isomorphic solution to solve a problem, one must be able to recognize corresponding quantities in the two problems. The claim that analogy involves a mapping of information is a general assumption that is shared by most theories of analogy, although factors that influence the mapping differ across theories (Hall, 1989; Holyoak & Thagard, 1989). One of the most influential theories of how people use analogous solutions is the structure-mapping theory proposed by Gentner (1983). She developed the theory to account for mapping knowledge from a base domain to a target domain that consisted of different objects, such as comparing an atom to the solar system. Because the objects differed, Gentner argued that it is the relations among the objects rather than the attributes of the objects that constrain the mapping. For instance, the relation between an electron revolving around the nucleus corresponds to the relation between a planet revolving around the sun.

An implication of the structure-mapping theory is that success in applying a solution to a problem should be determined by how well students can find corresponding quantities in the two problems. Reed (1987) tested this assumption for algebra word problems by measuring students' ability to solve problems and to find corresponding quantities in analogous problems. Students in one experiment received a solution to a mixture problem and to a work problem, and then had to construct equations for four variations of each of the two examples. The four variations consisted of two problems that were isomorphic and two problems that were similar to the example, as shown in Table 7.3 for the mixture problems. The example, one of the Isomorphic problems, and one of the Similar problems were previously shown in Table 7.1 for the work problems.

The results of the study showed that students were significantly better in constructing equations for Isomorphic test problems than for Similar test problems, and were significantly better on the work isomorphs than on the mixture isomorphs. A subsequent experiment demonstrated that the amount of transfer was related to students' ability to identify corresponding quantities in the example and test problems, as would be expected from the structure-mapping theory. Students were significantly better in generating matching quantities for Isomorphic problems than for Similar problems and were significantly better on the work isomorphs than on the mixture isomorphs.

Another demonstration of how the ability to map quantities determines success in solving problems appeared the same year. Ross (1987) tested students' ability to solve probability problems. Students were given an appropriate formula for each type of problem and an example solution. The following example was used to illustrate how to solve a permutation problem:

TABLE 7.3
Examples and Test Problems Used by Reed (1987)

Example	Isomorphic Mapping	Nonisomorphic Mapping
	Mixture	

		Nonisomorphic Mapping
		One alloy of copper is 20% pure copper and another is 12% pure copper. How much of each alloy must be mented together to obtain 60 pounds of alloy containing 10.4 pounds of copper?
		$Copper_1 + Copper_2 =$ Total copper $P_1 \times A_1 + P_2 \times A_2 =$ Total copper $.20 \times a + .12 \times (60 - a) = 10.4$
		An automobile radiator contains 16 quarts of a 20% solution of antifreeze. How much of the original solution must be drawn off and replaced with 80% antifreeze to make a solution of 25% antifreeze.
		$Antif_1 - Antif_2 = Antif_3 =$ Total $P_1 \times A_1 - P_2 \times A_2 + P_3 \times A_3 = P_4 \times A_4$ $.20 \times 16 - .20 a + .80 a = .25 \times 16$

Isomorphic Mapping		
Mr. Smith receives 5% interest from his checking account and 14% interest from treasury bonds. How much money is in each account if he averages a 12% return on $4,500?		
$Money_1 + Money_2 =$ Total money $P_1 \times A_1 + P_2 \times A_2 = P_3 \times A_3$ $.05 \times a + .14 \times (\$4,500 - a) = .12 \times \$4,500$		
A grocer mixes peanuts worth $1.65 a pound and almonds worth $2.10 a pound. How many pounds of each are needed to make 30 pounds of a mixture worth $1.83 a pound?		
$Money_1 + Money_2 =$ Total money $P_1 \times A_1 + P_2 \times A_2 = P_3 \times A_3$ $.05 \times a + .14 \times (\$1.65 \times a + \$2.10 \times (30 - a) = \$1.83 \times 30$		

Example		
A nurse mixes a 6% boric acid solution with a 12% boric acid solution. How many pints of each are needed to make 4.5 pints of an 8% boric acid solution?		
$Acid_1 + Acid_2 =$ Total acid $P_1 \times A_1 + P_1 \times A_2 = P_3 \times A_3$ $.06 \times a + .12 \times (4.5 - a) = .08 \times 4.5$		

Note. A refers to amount and P to percentage or price. Copyright © 1987 by the American Psychological Association. Reprinted with permission.

The IBM motor pool has to make sure the company cars are serviced. On a particular day there are 11 cars and 8 mechanics. The IBM mechanics randomly choose which car they will work on, but the choice is done by seniority. What is the probability that the three most senior mechanics, Al, Bud, and Carl will choose the cars of the Chairman, President and Vice-president, respectively?

The probability of Al selecting the Chairman's car is 1/11, the probability that Bud selects the President's car is 1/10, and the probability that Carl selects the Vice-president's car is 1/9. The probability that all three events occur is the product of these three probabilities.

Ross then systematically varied the correspondence between objects in the example solution and the objects in the test problems. One test problem had identical objects that had the same roles as the example—for instance, mechanics choosing which cars to service. Another problem had identical objects but reversed roles—for instance, the owners of the cars choosing among the mechanics. In the above problem, the probability of the first owner selecting Al would be 1/8, the probability of the second owner selecting Bud would be 1/7, and the probability of the third owner selecting Carl would be 1/6. A third (neutral) problem had similar content, but the objects did not have an obvious correspondence to the objects in the example, such as the assignment of computers to offices. Ross found that using the same objects with identical roles produced much better performance (74% correct) than the neutral condition (54% correct), but using the same objects with reversed roles produced the worst performance (37% correct).

Bassok, Wu, and Olseth (1995) found similar results using problems that differed in more abstract schematic structures. She used permutation problems in which either objects were assigned to people (such as computers to secretaries) or people were assigned to objects (such as students to prizes). Transfer was much better when the test problems had the same schematic structure as the examples. But the two schematic structures also differed in difficulty. Students did better on problems in which objects were assigned to people, reflecting that we typically think of people "getting" objects rather than objects "getting" people. In chapter 10 other examples of how our knowledge of the world influences (or sometimes fails to influence) problem solving are examined.

Abstract Schemas for Word Problems?

In one sense, the level of abstraction for Bassok's students was at the wrong level. Categorizing computers and prizes as objects, and secretaries and students as people, forms categories that are still based on story content rather than on the mathematical principles in which the assigned set in permutation problems can be either objects or people. In contrast, it was seen in chapter 3 that people are better at noticing that two solutions are isomorphic if they recognize the solutions as part of a more abstract schema that emphasizes structural relationships. Recall that Gick and Holyoak (1983) discovered that people were likely to form a more general schema if they read and compared two analogous stories before trying to solve an Isomorphic problem. Creating the convergence solution for the radiation problems was facilitated by realizing that a military problem and the oil fire problem also used convergence solutions, which made people think about the solution in general terms, abstracted from the specific situation described in each problem.

An issue raised by the Gick and Holyoak study is whether abstract schemas can be formed for more complex types of problems such as algebra word problems. It was seen in the previous chapter that people tend to classify algebra word problems according to the situations described in the problems rather than by more abstract criteria. Furthermore, students' ability to categorize complex problems according to their common solutions requires considerable expertise has also been discussed (Chi et al., 1982). This raises challenges to using the problem-comparison technique to facilitate noticing which word problems are isomorphic and applying isomorphic solutions. Research using this technique has been more successful in improving noticing (Cummins, 1992) than in improving applying (Reed, 1989) isomorphic solutions.

The design of Cummins' (1992) experiment was similar to the design of Silver's (1981) experiment in requiring students to classify problems that could be categorized either by common solution structures or by common story context. There were three different solutions: catch-up, dilution, and facilitation–interference. A catch-up problem is one in which there is less time than was anticipated to achieve some goal and a new rate has to be computed that will allow the goal to be achieved in less time. A dilution problem is one in which a higher rate and lower rate have to be averaged to accomplish the same amount as would have resulted from applying a medium rate for a certain period of time. A facilitation–interference problem involves increasing and decreasing a normal rate of performance by a constant to achieve a constant goal during different lengths of time. The three solution structures were crossed with four story contexts (travel, vat, interest, work) to create 12 different problem types. Cummins found that students who compared quantities and relations in one problem to quantities and relations in an Isomorphic problem did significantly better in later classifying problems according to their common solutions than did students who answered questions about individual problems. However, comparing Isomorphic problems did not result in a significant increase in students' ability to match problems to the equation needed to solve the problem.

My own research experience (Reed, 1989) has caused me to question whether it is possible to create abstract solution schemas for algebra word problems. I used three isomorphic mixture problems and three isomorphic distance problems to investigate whether constructing an analogical mapping between two isomorphs would help students solve a third isomorph. In the mixture problems (the nurse, interest, and grocer problems in Table 7.3), two quantities are added together to make a combined quantity. These problems are solved the same way but belong to different categories in Mayer's (1981) taxonomy. In the distance problems, two distances are added together to equal the total distance, but the two objects are either traveling toward each other, traveling away from each other, or succeeding each other. These problems belong to the same (motion) category in Mayer's taxonomy, but represent different templates and are characterized by different spatial relations (diverge, converge, succession) between two moving objects.

The students in my experiment attempted to construct equations for the series of three mixture problems and three distance problems. Providing an analogous solution helped students construct the equations. The percentage of correct solutions increased from approximately 10% for the first problem in a series to 50% for the second problem, which was accompanied by the solution to the first problem. However, a detailed comparison of the first two problems through mapping quantities did not increase the solution rate for the third problem. Furthermore, success on the third problem was uninfluenced by whether students compared the first two problems or elaborated each individual problem. These findings failed to support a schema abstraction hypothesis, as did two follow-up experiments that were designed to encourage schema abstraction.

I have suggested several explanations of why abstraction did not occur, but I want to focus on the lack of superordinate concepts to describe a more general schema. As mentioned previously, superordinate concepts such as central target, force, and multiple paths played an important role in the initial theoretical formulation of the convergence schema (Gick & Holyoak, 1983) and in subsequent instructional efforts to promote abstraction (Catrambone & Holyoak, 1989).

The creation of superordinate concepts has also been proposed by investigators working on artificial intelligence approaches to analogical reasoning. Winston (1980) suggested that finding an analogy between two situations may require matching quantities at more general levels than those provided in the statement of the problem. However, he cautioned that creating concepts that are too general will not sufficiently constrain the matches between two isomorphs. According to this hypothesis, abstraction requires creating concepts that are superordinate to the quantities in the Isomorphic problems but are not so general that they do not sufficiently constrain the solution. A constraint on creating an abstract solution is that it may be difficult to find such concepts.

Because the quantities of distance, rate, and time do not differ in Reed's (1989) distance problems, they do not have be replaced by superordinates. Only the described action has to be generalized to replace the specific actions of travel toward in the convergence problem, travel successively in the succession problem, and travel away in the divergence problem. Although the superordinate concept travel generalizes each of these actions, it is too general to constrain the spatial relations between the two objects that are traveling.

The lack of superordinate concepts is even more apparent in the mixture problems shown in Table 7.3. Although there are some identical quantities in specific pairs of problems (such as money in the interest and grocer problems), none of the specific quantities can be generalized under a superordinate concept that applies to all three problems. Thus, volume is an important quantity in the nurse problem, weight in the grocer problem, and interest rate in the interest problem. Also note that quantities such as money that are shared between a specific pair of problems would facilitate analogical mapping for that pair, but would reduce the need to create superordinate concepts in a more abstract schema. The moral may be that it is difficult to create more abstract schemas for story concepts.

Instructional Implications

The fact that algebra word problems can be categorized by type creates a dilemma. On the one hand this is what students typically do (Hinsley et al., 1977) and this is how algebra books have traditionally been organized (Mayer, 1981). An advantage of creating a schema for the different types of problems is that it allows students to organize their knowledge so that, after categorizing the problem, they can direct their attention to relevant parts of the problem and retrieve relevant equations for solving it (Hinsley et al., 1977). The disadvantage is that students can become overly dependent on story content and not be able to transfer solutions to problems that are solved in similar ways but have different story content. As expressed by Schoenfeld (1992), problem types, therefore, have a shady reputation among many mathematics educators:

> However, the straightforward suggestion that mathematics instruction focus on problem schemata does not set well with the mathematics education community, for good reason. As noted in the historical review, IP (information processing) work has tended to focus on performance but not necessarily on the basic understandings that support it. Hence, a reliance on schemata in crude form—"When you see these features in a problem, use this procedure"—may produce surface manifestations of competent behavior. However, that performance may, if not grounded in an understanding of the principles that led to the procedure, be error prone and easily forgotten. Thus, many educa-

tors would suggest caution when applying research findings from schema theory. (p. 352)

It should be emphasized that the level of schematic abstraction in this quote is problem types such as mixture problems, river-crossing problems, et cetera. In fact, "word problems by type, such as coin, digit, and work" are listed in the NCTM standards (1989, p. 127) as one of the topics that should receive decreased attention, which raises the question of whether they should receive any attention. I believe that traditional word problems should not be eliminated from the curriculum, but that they are a starting point rather than an ending point. There is nothing wrong with categories, per se. In fact, the categories such as interest problems, distance-rate-time problems, mixture problems, and work problems are problems that can (and should) be related to real-world activities, which is the topic of chapter 10. Furthermore, there is some domain-specific content that has to be learned in order to solve problems in each of these categories. Students need to learn basic equations such as *Distance = Rate × Time* and *Amount of Work = Rate of Work × Time worked* in order to solve problems in a specific domain. Also note that a quantity such as *Rate* may be used differently across categories. It refers to how far one travels per unit of time in a distance problem, and the proportion of a task that is completed per unit of time in a work problem.

Medin and Ross (1989) proposed that people have overlooked the importance of specific examples because of the tendency to equate intelligence with abstract thought. But reliance on specific examples is not necessarily bad:

> At first thought, the idea of having knowledge tied to particular contexts and examples appears to be a limitation. We do not deny that there are situations where transfer of training is limited by context-bound knowledge. On the other hand, specificity has its virtues. In particular, we argue that specificity may make access to and application of relevant knowledge easier, may permit graceful updating of knowledge, may protect the cognitive system from incorrect or inappropriate inferences, and may provide just the sort of context sensitivity that much of our knowledge should, in fact, have. (pp. 190–191)

Reimann and Schult (1996) also cautioned against too much emphasis on abstraction in their review of the case-based reasoning literature in artificial intelligence. They distinguished between three forms of representing and using examples. One extreme is a direct mapping from the example to the current problem. Another extreme is applying knowledge that is generalized (decontextualized) from the examples. They advocated an intermediate approach that they labeled *derivational analogy*. It works by taking into account the rationale for the example solution when trying to relate it to a new problem-solving task. This requires an elaborated representation of the example—the kind that was produced by the better problem solvers in their self-explanations of example solutions (Chi, Bassok, Lewis, Reimann, & Glaser, 1989), as discussed in chapter 3.

Reimann and Schult argued that acquiring general knowledge structures is rarely done spontaneously by learners and that such knowledge may be difficult to apply. A challenge, therefore, is to show students how various domain-specific quantities are related to more general methods of solution. To take an example from physics, consider an artificial intelligence program called FERMI that connects specific physics problems with more general solution methods (Larkin, Reif, Carbonell, & Gugliotta, 1988). For instance, a general method such as decomposition can apply to many different situations such as pressure drops for water pressure, potential drops in electric circuits, and centers of mass of objects. FERMI is able, through the assistance of a knowledgeable programmer, to relate the domain-specific knowledge associated with each of these situations to a general method, decomposition. Domain-specific quantities in the different problems inherit the general procedures by directly linking each specific quantity (such as pressure drop) to a general method that can compute a value for that quantity.

The vastly different content of these topics makes it unlikely that students will be able to combine them into a common solution category through schema abstraction. Even the analogical mapping between potential drops and pressure drops is not obvious (Gentner & Gentner, 1983) and the relation of both of these topics to centers of mass seems even more tenuous. Rather than hope that students will spontaneously recognize that a common method applies to each of these situations, teachers need to design instruction that will help them learn this relation.

Finding these deeper structural relations is also important for the isomorphic word problems discussed in this chapter. For example, consider the following two problems:

1. Mary can paint a house in 5 days, Joan in 3. How long does it take them if they work together?
2. Pipe A fills a swimming pool in 12 hours, pipe B in 9. If both pipes are used, how long does it take the pool to fill?

What counts most is the underlying mathematical structure, which says that the things you can combine are rates:

The % of the job X does in a certain amount of time +
  The % of the job Y does in that amount of time =
    The % of the job both get done in that amount of time.

Thus, for problem 1,

(Mary + Joan's) rate = Mary's rate + Joan's rate
= 1/5 job/day + 1/3 job/day = 8/15 job/day
    so it takes 15/8 of a day.

As Schoenfeld (personal communication, August 1, 1997) explained it:

> This same relationship can be used not only for all of the variants of problem 1, but for all of the variants of problem 2 as well. And—no kidding—I and any mathematician see these as all being essentially the same problem. These differ fundamentally from, say, mixture problems—where the rules that govern the ways terms can be combined are completely different. In short: The deep structural relationship among the objects in a problem determines whether mathematicians will see problems as being the same—and this is ultimately what teachers would like students to understand.

Summary

One use of analogy to solve problems is to recognize that two problems that differ in story content nonetheless have identical solutions. As demonstrated across many different problem domains, weaker solvers tend to classify problems by story content and better solvers tend to classify problems by mathematical structure when instructed to categorize problems by common solution procedures. Story content can be a particular limitation for algebra word problems because of the tendency to view categories such as distance-rate-time problems, mixture problems, work problems, et cetera as having unique solutions that are unrelated to the solutions of problems in the other categories.

Gentner's structure-mapping theory of analogy claims that our ability to recognize analogy, such as between an atom and the solar system, depends on how well we can map objects and relations in one domain onto the objects and relations in another domain. Research with algebra word problems has shown that students' ability to identify corresponding quantities between an example and a test problem is a good predictor of how well they can use the example solution to solve the test problem. In addition, success in solving probability problems depends on whether objects in the test problem have the same roles as objects in the example, again illustrating that the ease of finding corresponding objects constrains transfer.

A question raised by these findings is to what extent is the mapping of objects and relations mediated by schema abstraction in which two problems are identified as belonging to the same abstract schema. Encouraging schema abstraction by requiring students to compare quantities and relations across Isomorphic problems has been successful in helping them categorize word problems by common solutions. It has been less successful in enhancing their ability to use an example solution to solve an Isomorphic problem. A limiting factor may be that isomorphic word problems typically do not share superordinate concepts that could describe the abstraction.

An instructional implication is that greater time should be spent in showing students how problems with different story content may share a common solution. The amount (and type) of instruction will depend both on the expertise of the problem solvers and transparency of the mapping between problems. Although categories of word problems may limit transfer, they also have value. Students tend to organize schematic knowledge around categories such as distance-rate-time problems, interest problems, work problems, and motion problems. The challenge for instruction is to recognize the unique quantities in each of these categories, while at the same time encouraging students to look for common solutions across categories.

8

Adapting Solutions

In the previous chapter the distinction was made between Isomorphic problems that had identical solutions, but different stories, and Similar problems that had identical stories, but different solutions. Both types of problems require the two basic operations for the successful use of analogy—finding a good analogous problem and mapping the objects and relations in the analogous solution to the test problem. However, the relative difficulty of these two operations differs across the two types of problems. It was seen that the most challenging requirement in solving Isomorphic problems is realizing that two apparently different problems share the same solution. Students often do fairly well in finding corresponding objects and relations in the two problems after they realize that the problems are isomorphic. In contrast, the most challenging requirement in solving Similar problems is adapting those relations that are not identical to the ones in the analogous solution.

This chapter begins with the issue of selecting a helpful solution. Because students often judge similarity of problems on the basis of story content, it is natural for them to use story content when selecting a helpful analogy. If given a homework problem that requires mixing two solutions, they are likely to look for example problems that involve mixing two solutions. But what if they find two examples, one of which is more complex than their homework problem and one of which is less complex than their homework problem. Which should they choose as being more helpful?

The chapter then turns to the second operation, mapping objects and relations. The difficulty here is that some of the relations between the two problems are not identical and students often have difficulty modifying these relations. Because of this difficulty, different instructional interventions to improve students' ability to adapt a solution to fit a similar problem are discussed. One approach provides an elaborate solution to an example and a set of rules for adapting the solution. Some of the limitations of this approach and how rules can be made more effective are then considered.

In conducting this research I have attempted not only to evaluate different forms of instruction but to test some simple assumptions about how students combine examples, rules, and their prior knowledge to adapt solutions. A model based on a particular set of assumptions has made fairly accurate predictions about how different types of instruction influence students' success in applying a simple solution to more complex problems. However, the model has been less successful in predicting students' success in applying a complex solution to simpler problems. An implication may be that students have general heuristics that help them simplify solutions and, therefore, are less dependent on supplemental rules.

The final section of this chapter provides several illustrations of how work in artificial intelligence on case-based reasoning is being applied to the classroom. The objective of this work is to provide a rich set of examples (cases) in a computer-based learning environment that students can access when solving problems. Assumptions such as the importance of a clear goal structure in organizing solution steps has been supported by psychological research.

Selecting Helpful Solutions

The question was raised in the introduction of whether a solution to a simpler problem or a solution to a more complex problem would be more helpful in solving a similar problem. Unlike some questions, the answer to this one doesn't seem intuitively obvious so I tried to find the answer in a study published by Reed, Ackinclose, and Voss (1990).

In this study students had to first decide, for each of six problems, which of two examples they would prefer to use as an analogous problem to solve a test problem. Consider the following three problems of increasing complexity (inclusiveness):

1. A group of people paid $238 to purchase tickets to a play. How many people were in the group if the tickets cost $14 each.
2. A group of people paid $306 to purchase theater tickets. When 7 more people joined the group, the total cost was $425. How many people were in the original group if all tickets had the same price?
3. A group of people paid $70 to watch a basketball game. When 8 more people joined the group, the total cost was $120. How many people were in the original group if the larger group received a 20% discount?

The first problem is less inclusive than the second (test) problem because it has missing information, and the third problem is more inclusive than the second problem because it has excess information. Students were twice as successful in constructing equations for the test problems when given a more inclusive solution than when given a less inclusive solution, but failed to show a preference for the more inclusive problem when initially asked to choose between two analogous problems. Showing students the solutions of the two analogous problems didn't increase the selection of the more inclusive solution, and the amount of mathematical experience (introductory psychology students vs. mathematics majors) didn't influence selections.

However, more encouraging results came from a study in which students made their selections as they were solving the test problems. In the Reed et al. (1990) study students made their selections *before* they solved the problems, so could not use feedback from their problem solving experiences to reevaluate their selections. In a subsequent computer-implemented study students were shown solutions to the simple and complex work problems, and then asked to solve test problems that ranged over four complexity levels from the simple problem to the complex problem (Reed, Willis, & Guarino, 1994). They could refer back to either solution at any time while working on the test problems. Evidence for good monitoring skills included our findings that students referred significantly more often to the complex solution than to the simple solution, and students' use of the complex solution increased as the complexity of the test problems increased.

But even in this study, room for improvement can be found. A good strategy would be to always select the simple example when a test problem was equivalent to the simple example, and always select the complex example when a test problem was equivalent to the complex example. But when solving a test problem that was equivalent to the simple example, students referred back to the complex example on 35% of the occasions that they reviewed a solution, and when solving a test problem that was equivalent to the complex example, students referred back to the simple example on 28% of the occasions. An implication of the findings from both of these studies on selecting examples is that students would benefit from direct training on choosing good analogies. A computer tutor that can monitor their selections and advise them on making good choices would be an effective first step toward increasing students' skill in using analogous solutions. The instructional implications of these findings are addressed later in the chapter, including recent work on providing computer-based support.

Mapping Quantities

After selecting an analogous solution, it is necessary to map the objects and relations in the solution to the test problem. In the previous chapter a study by Reed (1987) was reported that tested the hypothesis that the extent of

transfer between two problems is related to students' ability to find corresponding quantities between the two problems. You may recall that students did better in mapping quantities and solving Isomorphic problems that had identical solutions, but different stories, than in solving Similar problems that had identical stories, but different solutions. The solutions to the Similar problems were not very different but required some adaptation to apply the example solution to the test problem.

Table 8.1 shows the instructions given to students before their ability to generate quantities in the test problems that corresponded to quantities in an example problem was evaluated. Notice that the instructions included an example in which two problems differ in the specification of the distance between the girl and the fulcrum. The first problem states that Laurie sits 6 feet from the fulcrum and the second problem states that Mary sits 4 meters from Tom. Her distance from the fulcrum must therefore be specified as a function of Tom's distance from the fulcrum. The example shows the corresponding quantities, in which only the distance between the girl and the fulcrum has to be modified.

Students in that experiment had to map information from an example to four test problems for both a mixture example and a work example. As for the fulcrum problem in Table 8.1 the quantities in the example were listed in the left column, and students had to generate corresponding values in the right column. As might be expected, students were fairly successful in generating a corresponding value in Similar problems if the value did not have to be adapted, but usually had a great amount of difficulty in adapting values. For instance, compare the nurse problem, which asks how many pints of a 6% and a 12% boric acid solution are needed to make 4.5 pints of an 8% solution, to the alloy problem, which asks how much of a 20% and a 12% copper alloy are needed to make 60 pounds of an alloy containing 10.4 pounds of copper (see Table 7.3). The amount of acid in the mixture is .08 × 4.5 pints, but the amount of copper in the mixture is stated directly (10.4 pounds). None of the 45 college students gave this answer, and most listed the product of two numbers such as 60 pounds × 10.4 pounds.

Novick and Holyoak (1991) used a hint paradigm to examine in greater detail why using analogous solutions is so difficult. College students first studied the solution to a word problem that required finding the least common denominator and later were asked to solve a Similar test problem that also required finding the least common denominator. Table 8.2 shows the solution to the initial (garden) problem and the transfer (marching band) problem. The hints either simply encouraged them to use the analogous example or, in addition, provided information about the matching information. One group received a retrieval hint that told them it is important to use the solution to the example to solve the test problem. Another group received an object-mapping hint that identified corresponding objects in the

TABLE 8.1
Concept Mapping Instructions

Concept Matching Instructions

This experiment is concerned with matching the concepts in two related word problems. Below is a completed example. The problem on the left is a fulcrum problem and the concepts below it (weights, distances, and their products) are used to solve it. On the right is a variation of the problem and the example shows how the concepts correspond. Laurie weighs 40 pounds and sits 6 feet from the fulcrum. The product of her weight and distance is 40 pounds x 6 feet. Mary weighs 65 kg and sits (4 - d) meters from the fulcrum. The product of her weight and distance is 65 kg x (4 -d) meters. Notice that each of these concepts is matched in the example. The corresponding concepts are matched for Bill and Tom.

The last two questions ask how the two problems are similar and dissimilar. They refer to the concepts in the problem, as is illustrated by the answer to each question. In the problems which follow, try to identify the concepts in the problem on the right that correspond to the concepts listed on the left; then answer the last two questions. You will be given the answer to the first question to help you begin.

Laurie weighs 40 pounds and is sitting 6 feet from the fulcrum of a seesaw. Bill weighs 50 pounds. How far from the fulcrum must Bill sit to balance the seesaw?	Mary and Tom are sitting 4 meters apart on a seesaw. Mary weighs 65 kg and Tom weighs 80 kg. How far from the fulcrum must Tom sit to balance the seesaw?
Let d be Bill's distance from the fulcrum.	Let d be Tom's distance from the seesaw.

Concepts	*Matching Concepts*
1. 40 pounds	1. 65 kg
2. d feet	2. d meters
3. 50 pounds x d feet	3. 80 kg x d meters
4. 6 feet	4. (4 - d) meters
5. 50 pounds	5. 80 kg
6. 40 pounds x 6 feet	6. 65 kg x (4 - d) meters

7. How are the two problems similar?

Both problems are examples of fulcrum problems. The weights and distances in the first problem correspond to the weights and distances in the second problem.

8. How are the two problems dissimilar?

In the first problem we are told that Laurie sits 6 feet from the fulcrum. In the second problem we have to represent Mary's distance from the fulcrum as a relation to Tom's distance. Since Mary and Tom are sitting 4 meters apart, and Tom sits d meters from the fulcrum, Mary sits 4 - d meters from the fulcrum.

Note. From Reed (1987). Copyright © 1987 by the American Psychological Association. Reprinted with permission.

TABLE 8.2
Least Common Denominator Problems

Garden Source Problem

Problem

Mr. and Mrs. Renshaw were planning how to arrange vegetable plants in their new garden. They agreed on the total number of plants to buy, but not on how many of each kind to get. Mr. Renshaw wanted to have a few kinds of vegetables and ten of each kind. Mrs. Renshaw wanted more different kinds of vegetables, so she suggested having only four of each kind. Mr. Renshaw didn't like that because if some of the plants died, there wouldn't be very many left of each kind. So they agreed to have five of each vegetable. But then their daughter pointed out that there was room in the garden for two more plants, although then there wouldn't be the same number of each kind of vegetable. To remedy this, she suggested buying six of each vegetable. Everyone was satisfied with this plan. Given this information, what is the fewest number of vegetable plants the Renshaws could have in their garden?

Solution Procedure

Since at the beginning Mr. and Mrs. Renshaw agree on the total number of plants to buy, 10, 4, and 5 must all go evenly into that number, whatever it is. Thus the first thing to do is to find the smallest number that is evenly divisible by those 3 numbers, which is 20. So the original number of vegetable plants the Renshaws were thinking of buying could be any multiple of 20 (that is, 20 or 40 or 60 or 80 etc.). But then they decide to buy 2 additional plants, that they hadn't been planning to buy originally, so the total number of plants they actually end up buying must be 2 more than the multiples to 20 listed above (that is, 22 or 42 or 62, or 82 etc.). This means that 10, 4, and 5 will now no longer go evenly into the total number of plants. Finally, the problem states that they agree to buy 6 of each vegetable, so the total number of plants must be evenly divisible by 6. The smallest total number of plants that is evenly divisible by 6 is 42, so that's the answer.

Marching Band Target Problem

Members of the West High School Band were hard at work practicing for the annual Homecoming Parade. First they tried marching in rows of twelve, but Andrew was left by himself to bring up the rear. The band director was annoyed because it didn't look good to have one row with only a single person in it, and, of course, Andrew wasn't very pleased either. To get rid of the problem, the director told the band members to march in columns of eight. But Andrew was still left to march alone. Even when the band marched in rows of three, Andrew was left out. Finally, in exasperation, Andrew told the band director that they should march in rows of five in order to have all the rows filled. He was right. This time all the rows were filled and Andrew wasn't alone any more. Given that there were at least 45 musicians on the field but fewer than 200 musicians, how many students were there in the West High School Band?

Note. From Novick and Holyoak (1991). Copyright © 1991 by the American Psychological Association. Reprinted with permission.

two problems, such as the number of band members in a row or column corresponds to the different kinds of plants. A third group received a number-mapping hint, such as the numbers 12, 8, and 3 in the band problem correspond to the numbers 10, 4, and 5 in the garden problem. A fourth (control) group did not receive any hints. The rates of successful transfer were 19% for the no-hint group, 35% for the retrieval hint, 37% for the object-mapping hint, and 50% for the number-mapping hint. Novick and

Holyoak concluded that although the number-mapping hint resulted in a significantly higher amount of transfer, the fact that only half of these students were successful shows that adapting solutions is very difficult even when students are given information about corresponding numbers in the two problems.

If it's any consolation, computer-based problem solvers also have difficulty adapting solutions. One of the more detailed formulations of analogical mapping between problems is the ACME (Analogical Constraint Mapping Engine) program developed by Holyoak and Thagard (1989). The program, which combines a symbolic representation of knowledge with a connectionist constraint satisfaction, is successful in mapping isomorphic relations but is unsuccessful in adapting solutions (Holyoak, Novick, & Melz, 1994). However, this weakness makes the program a fairly accurate model of Reed's (1987) and Novick and Holyoak's (1991) subjects who performed well in mapping isomorphic concepts, but were unable to modify a solution to incorporate nonisomorphic concepts.

So, what can instructors do to help students adapt solutions? The rest of the chapter focuses on research that has compared different instructional conditions to determine if students' ability to adapt solutions can be improved.

Providing Rules for Adapting Solutions

As the previous discussion just showed, students do fairly well in using that part of an example that corresponds to the test problem. Their difficulty is not knowing what to do on the part of the test problem that does not correspond to the example. Reed and Bolstad (1991) reasoned that students' ability to construct equations for word problems could be greatly improved by giving them a list of rules to supplement the example. This study was influenced by early theoretical work in artificial intelligence that combined schema and rule-based approaches by attaching procedures to slots in a schema (Bobrow & Winograd, 1979). This approach was called *procedural attachment* in chapter 4 and this method was also used in the FERMI model discussed at the end of the chapter 7 (Larkin, Reif, Carbonell, & Gugliotta, 1988).

To evaluate the effectiveness of combining an example with a set of rules Reed and Bolstad (1991) compared three different methods of instruction. In the Example condition students received an elaborated solution to the following problem:

Ann can type a manuscript in 10 hours and Florence can type it in 5 hours. How long will it take them if they both work together?

In the Procedures condition students were given the correct equation for the problem along with a set of rules that specified how to enter values into

the equation. The purpose of the rules was to show how different mathematical values could be substituted for each quantity in the equation. The rules for representing time were:

1. Time refers to the amount of time each worker contributes to the task. If this value is stated in the problem, enter it into the equation. For example, if one person works for 5 hours, enter 5 hours into the equation for that worker.
2. Time is often the unknown variable in these problems. Be sure to represent the correct relative time among the workers if they do not work for the same time. If one worker works 3 hours more than the value (h) that you are trying to find, enter $h + 3$ for that worker.

In the Example & Procedures condition students received both the example solution and the set of rules. After studying the instructional material all students attempted to construct equations for eight test problems that differed from zero to three transformations from the example. A transformation modified either *rate* (expressed relationally for the two workers), *time* (one worker labored longer), or *tasks* (part of the task had already been completed). Each of these is illustrated in the test problem that differs by three transformations from the example:

John can sort a stack of mail in 6 hours and Paul is twice as fast. They both sort 1/5 of the stack before their break. How long will it take John to sort the remainder if he and Paul work together, but Paul works 1 hour longer?

The four transformation levels and three instructional methods enabled an evaluation of the predictions of a simple mathematical model for each of these 12 conditions. Because both the example and procedures provided students with the basic equation for solving these problems, it was assumed that the probability of generating a correct equation is equal to the probability of correctly generating the values for the five quantities in the equation: the rate and time of work for each of the two workers and the number of tasks to complete. Students generated these values by either matching information presented in the example (m), following the rules (r), or using their general knowledge (g) about the problem. The parameters m, r, and g specify the probability of generating the correct value from each of these sources of knowledge.

It was assumed that students in the Example and the Example & Procedures groups relied on the example for those quantities in the test problem that did not have to be modified. When they did have to adapt quantities, it was assumed that they relied on rules in the Example & Procedures condition and on their general knowledge in the Example condition. In the Procedures condition they relied on the rules to generate each quantity in the equation because they did not have an example. The parameter estimates were .96 for correctly matching information presented in the example, .65 for correctly following a procedure, and .45 for using general (prior) knowledge. The model accounted for 94% of the variance as determined by the square of the multiple regression coefficient.

Although the predictions produced by the model were pleasing, the effectiveness of the Examples & Procedures condition was disappointing. The generalization gradient for this group was not as steep as for the Examples condition but the overall performance of these two groups was not significantly different (42% vs. 34% correct). However, both groups did significantly better than the Procedures group, which generated correct equations for only 15% of the problems.

Providing Applied Rules

This large discrepancy between the effectiveness of an example and the effectiveness of a set of procedures motivated the goal of a study by Reed and de la Pena (1996): To test a possible reason for the differences. One possible answer concerns the degree of elaboration of the solution. The example solutions used by Reed and Bolstad (1991) were more elaborate than a list of rules, and included a greater emphasis on underlying principles and a table for organizing information. As pointed out by Riesbeck and Schank (1989), a disadvantage of rules is that they capture "what to do" knowledge, but usually not "why it works" or "what it means" knowledge, making it more difficult to represent understanding at a deep level in a rule-based system. For example, rules for learning how to operate a device can often be more readily understood if supplemented with additional material such as examples, diagrams, or metaphors (Kieras & Bovair, 1984; Mayer, 1989; Smith & Goodman, 1984).

A second possible answer is that a worked-out example shows how (implicit) rules are applied. In some situations, conceptual elaboration may not be necessary; merely using an example to show students "what to do" could be sufficient for greatly improving their performance. This could occur when a skill does not need to be supported with much conceptual elaboration (Anderson & Fincham, 1994) or when students can provide their own elaboration by thinking critically about the solution (Chi, Bassok, Lewis, Reimann, & Glaser, 1989). The result is that it is often difficult to predict when, or what kind of, elaboration in a solution will be helpful. Catrambone (1996) recently found for algebra word problems that some forms of elaboration (providing labels to highlight subgoals) significantly improved students' ability to construct equations, but other forms of elaboration (describing possible representations for the different terms in the equation) had little effect.

Reed and de la Pena (1996) evaluated the two interpretations of why the example was much more effective than the rules by comparing both methods to a new instructional condition that they labeled Applied Procedures. The Applied Procedures condition uses the procedures from Reed and Bolstad's second experiment, but applies them to an example without conceptual elaboration. If conceptual elaboration is not necessary in this situation, then the Applied Procedures condition should be as effective as the Example & Procedures condition, which includes an elaborated example. Both of these conditions provide a complete set of procedures and an illustration of how some of the procedures are applied to an example.

The Applied Procedures had a very different organization than the elaborated Example used by Reed and Bolstad (1991). First, the rules were grouped according to the three different kinds of concepts in the equation; rate of work, time of work, and number of tasks. Second, each of these concepts was represented by a pair of rules; one of which was explicitly applied to the example. Third, the Applied Procedures instruction was not as elaborate as the Example instruction, which emphasized conceptual principles and included a table for organizing values by these principles. Although the organization was very different, both forms of instruction showed how to construct an equation for a particular problem.

Reed and de la Pena (1996) studied five instructional conditions in two experiments to compare the instructional effectiveness of Applied Procedures with the instructional conditions tested by Reed and Bolstad. One group of students received the Procedures, a second group received the Applied Procedures, a third group received an Example, a fourth group received an Example & Procedures, and the fifth group received an Example and Applied Procedures. A major theoretical objective of the study was to extend the predictions of the Reed and Bolstad (1991) model to the two new instructional conditions that included the Applied Procedures.

Figure 8.1 shows the percentage of correct equations for the five instructional groups across the four levels of transformation from a simple example. The results show that the three instuctional conditions that included both an example and procedures were equally effective in enhancing trans-

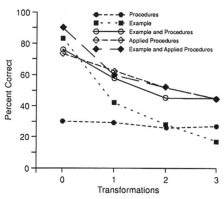

FIG. 8.1. Generalization gradients for adapting a simple solution. From Reed and de la Pena (1996).

fer. These findings demonstrate that showing how procedures are applied to an example can dramatically boost the success of the procedures. They are consistent with the assumption that Applied Procedures can be as successful as an elaborated Example & Procedures, indicating that a rule-base approach was effective in this case if students could see applications of the rules.

Figure 8.2 shows the percentage of correct equations for the five instructional groups across the four levels of transformation from a complex example. Most notable are the flat generalization gradients for all five instructional groups and the fairly similar performances for all but the Procedures group. Particularly noteworthy is the finding that students did not need to be given procedures to successfully adapt the complex example. The major new contribution of this experiment is the finding that students can generalize instruction about complex values to generate simple values. In contrast, the steep gradients obtained for the simple example indicates that students could not generalize instruction about instantiating simple values to generate complex values.

Reed and de la Pena (1996) used the model proposed by Reed and Bolstad (1993) to try to predict the generalization gradients in Figs. 8.1 and 8.2, based on the assumption that the same parameter (m) could be used for matching information in the example whenever the instruction included either the elaborated example or the application of the procedures to an example. This model was very successful in predicting the generalization gradients in Fig. 8.1 for the simple example. It was fairly successful in predicting generalization gradients in Fig. 8.2 for the complex example, but there were some systematic discrepancies in the predictions. The problem was that students did better than the model predicted when they had a complex example. Reed and de la Pena attempted to explain this discrepency by proposing that students utilize adaptation heuristics to directly modify an example, but these heuristics are primarily useful for simplifying a complex

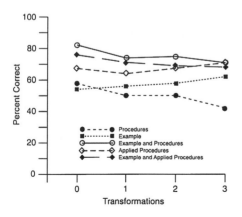

FIG. 8.2. Generalization gradients for adapting a complex solution. From Reed and de la Pena (1996).

solution so it will apply to a simpler problem. The next section illustrates how such heuristics can be helpful.

Heuristics for Adapting Solutions

How could a student take a solution to the complex problem:

> Jill can complete an audit in 12 hours and Barbara is three times as fast. They both complete 1/8 of the audit before being interrupted. How long will it take Jill to complete the audit if she and Barbara work together but Barbara works 2 hours longer?

and adapt it to the simple test problem:

> Bob can paint a house in 12 hours and Jim can paint it in 10 hours. How long will it take them to paint a house if they both work together?

Let's first consider instantiating values for rate. Calculating Bob's rate is done the same way as calculating Jill's rate in the example (taking the reciprocal of time worked). Calculating Jim's rate is not identical to calculating Barbara's rate, but it is identical to calculating Jill's rate. The first adaptation rule applies to the generalization of rate. It states that:

> IF a rule shows how to instantiate a value of a concept and the same rule applies to another instance of that concept THEN apply the same rule to that instance.

Instruction for the complex problem illustrates how to calculate Jill's rate. Generalizing to the simple problem requires recognizing that this same procedure can be used to calculate both Bob's and Jim's rate.

The second adaptation rule allows for the generalization of time. The solution to the complex problem indicated that Jill's time is the unknown variable, h hours. This same value can be used to represent both Bob's time and Jim's time in the simple problem. The second rule states:

> IF a rule shows how to instantiate a value for a concept and another instance of that concept has the same value THEN instantiate the same value for that instance.

One might argue that students could simply use the same procedure (as specified in the first adaptation rule) to represent time for both Bob and Jim. But instantiating the same value is more specific than reapplying the same rule (using an unknown variable to represent a quantity, in this case). Reapplying the same rule does not make it explicit that the *same* unknown variable represents the time worked by both workers. Students occasionally include more than one unknown variable in an equation, resulting in an incorrect generalization.

The third adaptation rule generalizes an arithmetic procedure and, therefore, is not as domain-independent as the first two adaptation rules. It states that:

> IF a rule shows how to instantiate a value by using an arithmetic procedure THEN allow for the possibility that a variable in that procedure may have a value of 0.

In the complex example students are shown that the number of tasks can be calculated by subtracting the fraction (f) of the task completed from one task. Generalization to the simple example requires realizing that, because none of the task has been completed, one can use a procedure such as $1 - f$ to instantiate the value for tasks by letting $f = 0$.

The three adaptation rules specify when to reuse the same rule, when to reuse the same value, and when to use 0 in an arithmetic procedure. These adaptation rules are sufficient for showing how students could generalize the solution of the complex problem to solve simpler problems, producing the flat generalization gradients in Experiment 2. The steep generalization gradients in Experiment 1 occurred because of the difficulty of generalizing rules for producing simple values to produce more complex values that require adding, subtracting, multiplying, or dividing pairs of values.

Although I have emphasized how adaptation rules can be successfully used, we must remember that adaptation rules are heuristics, not algorithms. Strategies such as reusing the same value or reapplying the same procedure from another part of the solution are not always going to work. Reed and de la Pena's (1996) finding that students did very well in adapting the complex solution should not obscure the fact that adaptation is often quite difficult, even when adapting complex solutions to fit simpler problems (Reed et al., 1990).

One constraint on the successful use of adaptation rules is determining when to use them. Reed et al. (1985) found that many of the incorrect equations in a transfer task contained matching errors in which the equation for a simpler test problem had the identical structure as the equation in the example. Such errors of omission occur when students fail to modify the solution. When evaluating the success of adaptation rules it is also necessary to consider the "false alarm" rate in addition to the "miss" rate. For instance, their students were very successful in reusing the same procedure and the same value at appropriate places in constructing the equation for the simple problem. But would they refrain from using these adaptation rules when they were inappropriate? If an equation had two unknowns, would they refrain from using the same variable to represent both unknowns?

The challenge is that the condition for using the rules is stated so generally (such as reuse the same procedure or same value when appropriate) that students need to learn when the rules are appropriate. Ohlsson (1996) recently argued that performance errors typically result from overly general rules, so learning a skill requires specializing the rule by incorporating more information about the task environment into their applicability conditions. As learning continues, the condition side of the rule becomes more specialized and the rule will be invoked in fewer (hopefully appropriate) instances.

A second constraint on the effective use of adaptation rules is selecting the correct one after deciding that the solution needs to be modified. There are many methods for modifying a solution, as documented by Kolodner (1993) in her book on case-based reasoning. Even simply deleting part of the solution, can be a challenge as was illustrated for the fulcrum problem studied by Reed et al. (1990). The percentage of correct solutions increased from 3% on the pretest to 47% after students saw the complex solution. Although the complex example was very helpful for one half of the students, the remainder failed to construct a correct equation even though they only had to delete part of the example's solution to solve the simpler problem.

Instructional Implications

In addition to research in psychology, work on case-based reasoning in artificial intelligence is being used to develop computer instruction in which reasoning from examples plays a key role. Case-based reasoning focuses on the use of analogy to solve real-world problems and the use of computational modeling to develop hypotheses about how people use examples to solve problems (Kolodner, 1997). This work is particularly concerned with providing plausible hypotheses about how the encoding and retrieval of analogs interacts with memory, reasoning, and learning.

But work on case-based reasoning also has a more applied goal—the design of learning environments. Kolodner pointed out that several kinds of software tools might be helpful, including tools for comparing and contrasting cases, tools for generating and testing ideas derived from cases, tools for explaining what is important, and tools for simulating adaptations. Two major centers are designing this kind of software. The Institute of the Learning Sciences at Northwestern, headed by Roger Schank, is creating computer environments, called Goal-based Scenarios, to support self-paced learning. Janet Kolodner's EduTech group at the Georgia Institute of Technology is working with teachers to develop classroom activities for science and technology education.

Another computer-based learning environment that emphasizes case-based problem solving is CACHET, a memory assistant for chess end-games (Reimann & Schult, 1996). Initially the learner watches examples of successful end-games and elaborates on what happens on the board. After having studied worked-out examples, the learner is asked to play end-games. Suboptimal moves trigger the presentation of supporting cases, if available. Problems solved by students can be entered into the case library, which are then analyzed and stored appropriately by the program. A general objective in learning from examples is to help students (a) close gaps in examples because intermediate steps have been left out, (b) think about conditions and effect of their actions, (c) organize a sequence of solution steps into a hierarchically organized goal structure, (d) reason about the relation between the selected actions and domain knowledge, and (e) reason about alternative routes to the solution.

The importance of organizing solution steps into a hierarchically organized goal structure is supported by Catrambone (1995). If students simply memorize a series of steps for solving a problem, then they will often fail on a test problem that has the same goal structure but requires different steps for achieving the goals. Emphasizing subgoals is useful because they group steps together and show what the steps accomplish. They can also help guide the learner about which steps need to be modified in the old solution to achieve the same subgoals in the new solution.

Catrambone's (1995) research demonstrated that labeling subgoals and visually isolating steps belonging to a common subgoal helps students transfer solutions to similar problems. Students in his experiments solved statistics problems in which they used a formula for the Poisson distribution to calculate the probability of a specified event. A subgoal for using the formula required finding the total frequency of the events. Labeling that part of the solution as *Total number of briefcases owned* for an example problem involving briefcases helped students solve similar problems that required using a different method for finding the total frequency.

Labeling parts of a solution also helped students solve algebra word problems (Catrambone, 1996). Table 8.3 shows three parts of a solution that focus on elaboration, labels, and the equation. Catrambone studied students' ability to use this solution to solve similar test problems. To supplement the equation, one group received both labels and elaboration (as shown in Table 8.3), a second group received only labels, a third group received only elaboration, and a fourth group received neither.

Table 8.4 shows how well students did in solving the transfer problems, and in correctly specifying components in the equation that had either the same structure (old representations) or a different structure (new representations) from those provided in the solution. There was a significant effect of providing labels, but not of providing elaboration, both for correct solutions and for correct components. These results, like those of Reed and de la Pena (1996) discussed previously, show that it is not always obvious what kinds of elaboration will be effective. The labels of basic components

TABLE 8.3
Solution Showing Elaboration and Labels

Mary can rebuild a carburetor in 3 hours and Mike can rebuild one in 4 hours. How long would it take Mary to rebuild a carburetor if she and Mike work together, but Mike works for 1/2 hour more than Mary?

(Elaboration)

The following equation can often be used to solve these problems:

$$(\text{Rate}_1 \times \text{Time}_1) + (\text{Rate}_2 \times \text{Time}_2) = \text{Tasks Completed}$$

where $(\text{Rate}_1 \times \text{Time}_1)$ is the amount of work completed by the first worker $(\text{Rate}_2 \times \text{Time}_2)$ is the amount of work completed by the second worker, and Tasks Completed is the total work completed by both workers. The Rate of a worker can be represented as a constant, a function of a constant, a variable, or a function of a variable. Similarly, the Time a worker works can be represented as a constant, a function of a constant, a variable, or a function of a variable. The particular representation used depends, of course, on the givens in the problem and the question that is being asked by the problem.

(Labels)

1/3 = Mary's rate
t = time Mary spent rebuilding carburetor
1/4 = Mike's rate
t + 1/2 = time Mike spent rebuilding carburetor

(Equation)

$(1/3 * t) + (1/4 * (t + 1/2)) = 1$
$7/12 * t = 1 - 1/8$
$t = 7/8 * 12/7 = 3/2$ hours = time Mary spent rebuilding carburetor

---

Note. From Catrambone (1996).

in the equation are fairly low-level subgoals, compared to the higher level subgoals specified in the elaboration (such as finding the amount of a task completed by a worker by multiplying her rate of work by her time of work).

A key issue here may be that the transfer problems required modifying how the basic components were represented in the equation, so emphasizing the lower level subgoals would be a good instructional strategy in this case. If this interpretation is correct, then the elaboration should be effective when the transfer problems require using different steps for achieving higher order subgoals. For instance, if the problem simply stated that one of the workers completed 1/4 of the task, then it would not be necessary to calculate this value by multiplying rate × time. As shown by Catrambone (1995) for the Poisson problems, students without subgoal instruction frequently did not know what to do when given a subgoal value (total frequency) that they previously had to compute.

In conclusion, this chapter contains several ideas that have instructional implications. One idea is that learning a complex solution has some benefits because, once learned, it facilitates transfer to other (simpler) problems.

TABLE 8.4
Effect of Elaboration and Labels on Adapting Solutions

	Elaboration		No Elaboration	
	Label (n = 20)	No Label (n = 20)	Label (n = 20)	No Label (n = 20)
Proportion of problems solved correctly	.70	.42	.57	.33
Proportion correct old representations	.92	.81	.84	.69
Proportion correct new representations	.73	.52	.68	.51

Note. From Catrambone (1996).

The design of case-based learning environments, with tutoring advice on searching for relevant cases, can also help students select a good example. The finding that transfer is related to students' ability to find corresponding quantities between two problems also has instructional implications. Exercises that require students to compare similarities and differences between problems and generate matching quantities (as shown in Table 8.1) may help promote analogical transfer. Practice on learning specific rules (representing that one worker labors more hours than the other) and general heuristics (deleting part of a complex solution) provides students with the tools for adapting solutions.

Summary

Solutions sometimes have to be adapted, such as basing a solution on an example in which two workers labor for the same number of hours when the two workers in the test problem labor for a different number of hours. Although most of the research on adapting solutions has focused on how well students adapt a provided solution, some research has looked at how well they select a good example to adapt. Although it is easier to modify a complex solution to fit a simpler problem than to modify a simple solution to fit a more complex problem, students showed no preference when allowed to choose between a solution that was more complex than the test problem and a solution that was less complex than the test problem. However, they made better choices in an interactive computer environment in which they could refer back to a complex solution or a simple solution as they worked on test problems. Evidence for good monitoring skills included the findings that students referred back significantly more often to the complex solution, and their use of the complex solution increased as the complexity of the test problems increased.

Students typically find it difficult to adapt solutions, often relying too much on the example solution without making the necessary adjustments. One approach for determining which variables constrain successful transfer is to provide increasingly specific hints about the relation between two problems. A hint that identified corresponding numbers in two least common denominator problems was more successful than a hint that identified corresponding concepts in the two problems, but only one half of the students solved the problems with the most helpful hint, confirming the difficulty of adapting solutions.

An instructional approach for improving students' ability to adapt solutions is to provide them with a set of rules to supplement example solutions. The rules tell students what to do when a problem differs from an example, such as how to represent the time relations between two workers who do not work the same number of hours. Generalization gradients show students' success in adapting solutions as a function of the number of changes between the example and test problem. These gradients can be fairly accurately predicted by knowing how many components in an equation can be constructed by using either the example or the set of rules. An exception is that students do better than predicted when they have to adapt a complex solution to fit a simpler problem. A possible explanation is that they may be using general heuristics that allow them to simplify solutions.

Providing a set of rules for constructing equations was a much less effective instructional technique than providing a solution to an example problem. Two interpretations for this difference are that an example is effective because it either shows how rules are applied or allows for conceptual elaboration of the rules. Results that showed applied rules were as effective as an elaborated example suggested that the former interpretation was more appropriate for this particular case. Another instructional technique that is important for helping students adapt solutions is to emphasize subgoals in the solution. Labeling subgoals helped students solve statistics problems and algebra word problems by grouping steps and showing what the steps accomplish. In general, helping students select a good example, map corresponding quantities to a test problem, and modify noncorresponding quantities can facilitate their ability to adapt solutions.

9

Representing Solutions

Transfer may occur at a more general level than transferring the details of a specific solution. Sometimes you may notice that the general method you used to solve a previous problem may also apply to the problem you are now trying to solve. Novick (1990) referred to the transfer of general methods as *representational transfer* to distinguish it from the *analogical transfer* of specific solutions. Analogical transfer is concerned with the transfer of specific steps in the solution, such as modifying the equation for a work problem in which two workers work the same amount of time to fit a problem in which one worker works longer than the other worker. Representational transfer is concerned with the transfer of a general method. The method may be a very general one, such as use of a diagram, or a more specific one, such as use of a Venn diagram.

Representational transfer, like analogical transfer, can be broadly divided into noticing that two problems can be solved by the same general method and applying that method to a test problem. It was discussed previously that noticing similarities among problems can be studied by asking people to sort problems into categories based on identical solutions (Silver, 1981) or common principles (Chi, Glaser, & Rees, 1982). This technique can also be used to investigate whether people can categorize problems according to general solution methods (Schoenfeld & Hermann, 1982). Applying general methods can be studied by pointing out the analogous problem and then measuring students' success in using the same method to solve a test problem. Novick and Hmelo (1994) used this technique to study whether students would transfer the use of an appropriate diagram from one problem to another problem that had a different solution, but could be solved by using the same diagram.

As shown by Novick and Hmelo's experiments, constructing diagrams is a good example of a general method for solving problems. After looking at the studies of perceiving and using a common solution method, this chapter focuses on the use of diagrams in problem solving. Research on the use of diagrams has often examined how diagrams make it easier for students to make inferences about the problem situation, although these inferences can be difficult when it is necessary to mentally animate objects in the diagram. Finally, the chapter returns to the discussion of transfer by considering the transfer of mental models in which perception and action play a more important role than symbolic structures.

Categorizing Problems

Chapter 7 on abstracting solutions began with a discussion of categorization based on identical solutions and common principles. Categorization can also be based on general methods of solution, as illustrated in a study by Schoenfeld and Hermann (1982) and elaborated by Schoenfeld (1985). As in previous studies, this one contrasted the categories formed by experts and by novices, but in addition, examined whether the categories created by novices would become more influenced by common solution methods after they completed a short course on mathematical problem solving.

As an example of a common solution, consider the relation between a problem that requires proving that any two distinct nonparallel lines must intersect at a unique point, and a problem that requires showing that if a function has an inverse, it has only one. Although these problems are about different situations, the method of solution in both cases is based on a uniqueness argument—that there is only one object (a point and a function, respectively) with specific properties. Other examples of general methods included in Schoenfeld's set of problems involved discovering patterns, using analogy, constructing diagrams, arguing from contradiction, and examining special cases. In contrast, a problem that asks how many straight lines can be drawn through 37 points in a plane has the same geometric content as the problem about intersecting lines but requires a different method of solution.

Each participant in Schoenfeld and Hermann's (1982) experiment sorted 32 problems into categories that were "similar mathematically in that they would be solved the same way." The expert group consisted of nine faculty members from the mathematics departments at Colgate University and Hamilton College. The experimental group consisted of 11 students at Hamilton College who had enrolled in a month-long course on mathematical

TABLE 9.1
Percentage of Strongly Clustered Pairs in Which Both Problems Share the Same Representation

| | Measure 1 (all pairs) | | | | Measure 2 (noncoinciding pairs) | | | |
| | Story Content | | Solution Method | | Story Content | | Solution Method | |
Test Group	%	n	%	n	%	n	%	n
Experts	59	22	82	22	25	12	67	12
Experimental, pretest	81	26	58	26	58	12	8	12
Control, pretest	91	23	57	23	82	11	9	11
Combined, pretest	76	21	62	21	67	9	11	9
Experimental, posttest	58	24	79	24	9	11	55	11
Control, posttest	83	24	58	24	64	11	9	11

Note. From Schoenfeld and Hermann (1982). Copyright © 1982 by the American Psychological Association, Reprinted with permission.

problem solving. Although various problem solving techniques were presented in the course, there was no discussion of classifying problems based on solution methods. The control group consisted of eight students from a course on structured programming. Students in both the control and experimental groups sorted the problems immediately preceding, and immediately following, their courses.

Table 9.1 shows how the story content and solution method influenced the classifications. Measure 1 is based on all pairs of problems and Measure 2 is based on only those pairs in which the story content and solution method do not coincide. The pretest sortings confirmed previous results that experts emphasize the solution methods, whereas the novices emphasize story content. Students in the control group continued to emphasize story content following their course on structured programming. But students in the experimental group were able to use solution methods as a basis for classification following their course on mathematical problem solving. In fact, their posttest classifications were similar to the ones made by the experts.

Schoenfeld and Hermann's findings demonstrate that a problem-solving course that focuses on heuristic strategies, with an emphasis on understanding, can influence students' perceptions of problems. This is particularly impressive because, as discussed by Schoenfeld (1985), finding common solution methods across problems is typically not taught in mathematics courses. In contrast, principles of physics are well agreed on and often form the basis for organizing instruction.

Representational Transfer

As mentioned previously, successful transfer depends not only on noticing that two problems share a common representation, but on being able to apply the method to solve a test problem. Novick (1990) became interested in studying representational transfer after noticing that although many psychologists were studying the transfer of specific solutions, studying the transfer of representations was mostly ignored. Because problem solvers often do not construct appropriate diagrams to represent problems, Novick and Hmelo (1994) examined whether students would transfer the use of an appropriate diagram from one problem to another problem that had a different solution, but could be solved by using the same diagram.

Figure 9.1 shows three different kinds of diagrams. The network diagram consists of nodes joined by links. In the example problem, a couple had to plan a trip that involved visiting islands (nodes) joined by bridges (links). The test problem required figuring out which pairs of people (nodes) at a cocktail party shook hands (links) with each other. The example for the hierarchy diagram was a categorization problem in which a mother was trying to group the words her young child knew into categories such as zoo animals, farm animals, and pets. The test problem involved representing different paths that a rat could take through a maze. The example for the part–whole representation consisted of a set membership problem in which the solver had to determine the number of children who collected only rocks, the number who collected only shells, and the number who collected both. These kind of problems can be represented by the Venn diagrams shown in Fig. 9.1. The test problem was a geometry problem in which the angles of two intersecting lines could be represented as either parts or wholes.

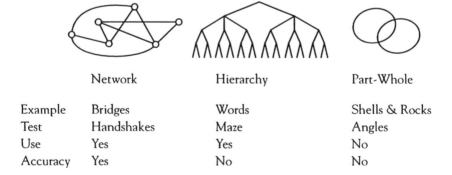

	Network	Hierarchy	Part-Whole
Example	Bridges	Words	Shells & Rocks
Test	Handshakes	Maze	Angles
Use	Yes	Yes	No
Accuracy	Yes	No	No

FIG. 9.1. Representational transfer of network, hierarchical, and part–whole representations. Adapted from Novick and Hmelo (1994).

Novick and Hmelo (1994) compared students' ability to solve test problems under three conditions. Participants either did not previously see any examples in the control condition, saw a relevant example in the no-hint condition but were not told of its relevance, or saw and were informed about the relevant example in the hint condition. The complete lack of spontaneous transfer (noticing the common method of solution) was shown by the lack of difference between the control and no-hint groups. When not informed that a previously studied example would be helpful, students did not change their representations and improve their performance.

The results for the hint group varied across the three representations. The network representation was the most successful. Students who were told to use the relevant example (bridge problem) were more likely to use a network representation to solve the handshake problem and were more successful. The results were mixed for the hierarchical representation: More people used a hierarchy to solve the maze problem, but they were not more successful. A possible reason is that people who didn't draw a hierarchy typically drew the maze, and drawing the maze was as helpful as drawing a hierarchy to represent the maze. The part–whole problem was the least successful: Neither the frequency of use nor the accuracy increased for solving the geometry problem. A limitation in this case is that students were not able to identify correspondences between the shells and rocks in the example problem and the angles in the geometry problem. Figure 9.1 summarizes these findings.

You may have noticed that there are some similarities between these initial results on representational transfer and the results on analogical transfer that were discussed in chapter 7. Spontaneous transfer of either an isomorphic solution or a more general method was poor because of the difficulty of noticing the similarity between two problems that had different physical descriptions, such as the attack-dispersion and radiation problems (Gick & Holyoak, 1980) or the bridges and handshake problems (Novick & Hmelo, 1994). Second, even when people are told to use an analogous problem, transfer of a particular solution depends on how easily people can find correspondences between objects in one problem and objects in the other problem (Gentner, 1983; Reed, 1987). This also limited transfer of the part–whole method from the shells and rocks problem to the geometry problem. A difference between analogical transfer and representational transfer is that successful transfer of a representation does not guarantee greater success in solving the problem if the transferred representation is not an improvement over the representation that is normally used to solve the problem. This is illustrated by the finding that encouraging people to represent the maze as a hierarchy did not result in more correct solutions.

In conclusion, the research on general strategies demonstrates that employing strategies such as the construction of diagrams can be useful. However, the challenge is to know when and how to apply each of these strategies. It would be helpful, therefore, if we had a better understanding of why a particular strategy is effective. The next section examines the case of diagrams.

When Are Diagrams Helpful?

In an article titled "Why a Diagram Is (Sometimes) Worth Ten Thousand Words," Larkin and Simon (1987) specified the possible advantages of a diagram over text when both descriptions are informationally equivalent. By informationally equivalent they meant that all of the information in one representation is inferable from the other, and vice versa. The fundamental difference between the information in the text and information in the diagram is that a diagram can explicitly show topological and geometric relations among the components of the problem.

Thus, even when diagrammatic and text representations contain equivalent information, computational demands can differ in accessing the information. Related information in diagrams is often located at adjacent locations, making it easier to recognize patterns, search for information, and make inferences. For example, consider a set of points presented either in a table of x and y coordinates or as geometric points on a graph. Visual patterns such as smooth curves, maxima or minima, and discontinuities are more readily recognized in the diagram. Diagrams are typically better representations not because they contain more information, but because they support more efficient computations.

Koedinger and Anderson (1990) proposed a detailed model of how diagrams help people construct proofs in geometry. They argued that experts are able to plan their proofs by focusing on key steps that depend on their ability to divide diagrams into perceptual chunks. The perceptual chunks cue relevant schema knowledge that allows skilled problem solvers to initially skip less important steps while planning the solution. Although Koedinger and Anderson agreed with Larkin and Simon (1987) that diagrams facilitate the search for relevant solutions, they suggested that perceptual inferences may not be inherently easier than symbolic inferences. Rather, perceptual inferences may appear easier because people practice them more than symbolic inferences.

A recent dissertation by Lobato (1996) illustrates the challenge of teaching students to make correct perceptual inferences. She studied part of an experimental curriculum that spent considerable time on teaching the concept of slope. The instruction included a week of activities in which staircases, both real and computer generated, were used to quantify slope as a vertical change (rise) divided by a horizontal change (run). Students were also taught how to find the slope of a line on a graph. A subsequent test showed that students did well on the instructional tasks (80% correct on lines and 87% correct on staircases) but showed relatively low levels of transfer. Only 40% of the answers were correct for calculating the slope of a playground slide and only 33% of the answers were correct for calculating the slope of a roof.

Figure 9.2 shows that many incorrect responses were caused by students' difficulty in identifying which parts of the diagram should be the rise and the run. Although Lobato was disappointed with the lack of transfer, she argued that researchers typically overlook real transfer because they define transfer according to a normative model in which transfer is only recognized

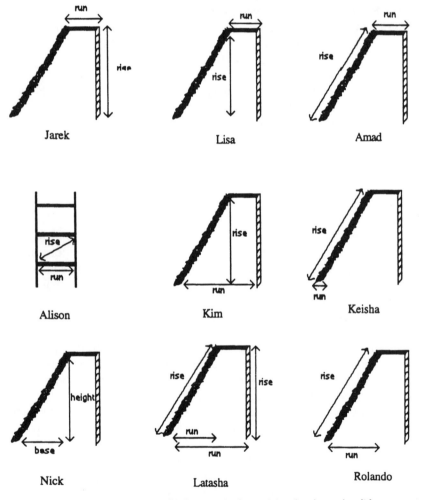

FIG. 9.2. Incorrect perceptual inferences in determining the slope of a slide. From Lobato (1996). Reprinted with permission.

if it leads to correct answers. However, students may show considerable transfer by using their previous experiences to make sense of a novel problem. Through interviews, Lobato sought to find out how students created "sameness" between a problem and their previous experience. For instance, those students who thought the length of the horizontal platform on the slide provides the *run* measurement perceived a similarity to the horizontal lengths of the steps in the staircase. Studying how students' perception of sameness can sometimes result in the transfer of nonnormative information can help us construct a curriculum that focuses their attention on making correct perceptual inferences.

Mental Animation

Constructing correct perceptual inferences can be particularly challenging when they require animation of components presented in a static display. Hegarty (1992) created mechanical problems that require people to infer the motion of components in a pulley system from their knowledge of the configuration and the movement of the components. Figure 9.3 shows an example of a problem in which people have to respond *true* or *false* as quickly as they can to either a static statement or a kinematic statement. Her reaction time and eye-fixation data support the view that, for kinematic statements, people attempt to run a mental model of the system by applying a set of causal rules to determine the states of successive components. However, the mental animation process is constrained by working memory limitations and by the lack of mechanical knowledge for some people.

Mental animation can also be helpful in solving word problems. A study by Trismen (1988) illustrates how using mental animation can help students solve a challenging problem without using algebra. Figure 9.4 shows the problem and I encourage you to try to use the diagram and mental animation to solve it. If you need help, read further to obtain a hint.

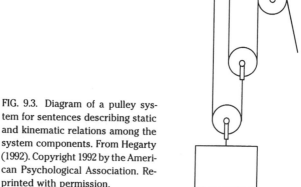

FIG. 9.3. Diagram of a pulley system for sentences describing static and kinematic relations among the system components. From Hegarty (1992). Copyright 1992 by the American Psychological Association. Reprinted with permission.

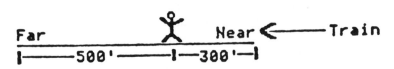

A man is standing on a bridge as shown above. A train is approaching as indicated by the arrow. If the man runs at a speed of 10 mph toward the train, he will reach the near end of the bridge just as the train does. If he runs at a speed of 10 mph away from the train, he will reach the far end of the bridge just as the train overtakes him. What is the speed of the train (in mph)?

FIG. 9.4. The bridge problem. From Trismen (1988). Reprinted with permission from the *Journal for Research in Mathematics Education*. Copyright 1988 by the National Council of Teachers of Mathematics.

Only 8 of the 87 high-school students who worked on the problem were able to solve it without a hint. The remaining students received the following hint:

Which of the following statements is true?

1. If the man runs away from the train, he will have run less than 300 feet when the train reaches the near end of the bridge.
2. If the man runs toward the train, he will have run 200 feet during the time it takes the train to reach the near end of the bridge.
3. If the man runs away from the train, he will be 100 feet from the far end of the bridge when the train reaches the near end.
4. No matter which way he runs, the man will run 300 feet during the time it takes the train to reach the near end of the bridge.
5. In order to meet at the far end of the bridge, the man must run 500 feet during the time the train crosses the bridge.

Of the 79 students who received the hint, 44 answered the hint correctly and 15 of those students immediately answered the problem correctly.

These results demonstrate that although diagrams can help support spatial inferences, the inferences may still be challenging. Most of the students needed the hint and, even with the hint, still found the problem difficult. Part of that difficulty is that the solution presented by Trismen (which is a good solution, but not the only one) requires "mental animation" of the objects in the diagram. A first step is to imagine the man running at 10 mph away from the train and realizing that he will be 300 feet closer to far end of the bridge when the train reaches the near end of the bridge (as stated in Hint 4). Because the man and the train reach the far end at the same time, the man has to cover the remaining 200 feet in the same time that it takes the train to travel the total 800 feet across the bridge. The train must therefore travel four times as fast as the man, or 40 mph.

This mental animation of the problem raises the more general issue of the role of imagery in solving problems. Shepard (1978) suggested several reasons why mental imagery and spatial visualization can facilitate problem solving. One reason is that it provides an alternative approach that differs from more traditional approaches. Constructing equations is the more traditional approach for solving word problems because this method is typically taught in algebra classes. There is nothing wrong with this method if students can apply it correctly, but imagery can provide an alternative method for some problems such as the bridge problem. Shepard argued that images precede language development and can result in more intuitive solutions. The algebraic solution of the bridge problem depends on knowledge of algebra that may be lacking in some students. As was seen in chapter 6, knowing multiple strategies is an advantage in solving word problems (Koedinger & Tabachneck, 1994). Those students who are able to solve the problem by making spatial inferences therefore have an advantage over students who rely solely on algebra.

Another reason for using imagery in this case is that the richness of imagery suggests new relations that are not immediately apparent in the verbal statement of the problem. Imagining the man running 300 feet toward the far end of the bridge has the advantage that we now know the location of both the man and the train, which greatly simplifies the problem. An algebraic solution requires solving two equations because both the speed and location of the train are unknowns in the initial statement of the problem. Imagery may also help reveal structural symmetries and invariances. As recognized by those students who chose the correct hint, it doesn't matter whether the man runs 300 feet at 10 mph toward the near end or far end of the bridge—in both cases the train will arrive at the near end. Recognizing this invariance leads to the relatively simple solution based on imagery.

Transfer of Mental Models

Some of the tasks in the previous section would seem to better fit a framework in which students construct a mental model of the task than a framework in which students create symbolic structures. In contrast to the emphasis on mapping symbols (concepts and numbers) in chapters 7 and 8, Greeno, Smith, and Moore (1993) formulated a theory of transfer in which direct perception and actions receive greater emphasis than the creation of symbols. Their approach does not rule out the use of abstract symbolic representations but places greater importance on transformations of activity that are influenced by perceptual similarities between two tasks. For example, when reading text, readers construct mental models that simulate the physical objects, persons, and events that the texts describe. Inferences are made on the basis of these simulations, as was illustrated in the solution of the bridge problem.

Greeno, Smith, and Moore (1993) hypothesized that these mental models mediate transfer between problems:

> The mental model constructed in initial learning may provide information about how to solve the transfer problem if objects or events in the two models have similar properties. Similar properties can include spatial relations, such as objects that move similarly in relation to each other, or functional roles, such as causal interactions or properties that avoid some consequence. The most important difference between this hypothesis of mental models and the more common hypothesis of abstract symbolic schemata is that properties needed for analogical problem solving may be properties of simulated events or objects, rather than being denoted by symbols. (p. 149)

In the mental model view of transfer, transfer depends on reenacting simulations in a way that makes their behavior available for application in a new situation. An interesting application of this idea was to results obtained by Bassok and Holyoak (1993). Greeno and his colleagues suggested that the cause of the obtained asymmetrical transfer was the relative ease with which one can view a continuous process. Information about a continuously changing process, such as velocity, could be represented in a mental model with a variable quantity that changes continuously over time, or with a mental model in which a variable model changes over discrete intervals of time. In contrast, information about a discrete process, such as annual salary increments, is more difficult to perceive as a continuous process. This interpretation leads to the prediction that less transfer should occur from continuous situations to discrete situations than from discrete situations to continuous situations, a prediction that was later confirmed by Bassok and Olseth (1995).

However, the mental model approach faces the same challenge of how to promote transfer that is faced by the symbolic approaches. Consider the case of two standard distance-rate-time problems. In a round-trip problem, a person drives the same route on both legs of a round trip. In a catch-up problem, one driver catches up with another driver who has left earlier. Both problems are solved by equating distances—the distance between locations in the round trip or the distance traveled by the two drivers in the catch-up problem. The equation for each problem involves the same symbols, but the actions taken by the driver(s) differ in the two problems. Thus, mentally simulating the two different situations may not reveal that identical equations can be used to represent the two problems.

In some cases, it may be possible to create an intermediate level of abstraction that provides a link between specific situations and the equations that model those situations. White (1993a) argued that initially emphasizing either equations in a top-down approach or specific situations in a bottom-up approach has limitations:

> Understanding the form, evolution, and application of scientific models should be a primary goal of science and engineering education. The most effective means for achieving this goal is not, I argue, the top-down approach of traditional curricula, in which students are first presented with formulas, such as $V = IR$ and $E_k = 1/2\ mv^2$, and then with examples of how they apply in a variety of real-world contexts. Such formulas are often too abstract to be meaningful to students; the semantic distance between the formulas and their real-world applications is too great, and thus, the relationship between formulas and the physical world they model is often not clear to students. On the other hand, neither do I advocate the bottom-up approach proposed by situated cognition theorists, who argue that knowledge structures that are widely applicable (which they term generalizations) should be gradually induced from exposure to many real-world instances (Brown, Collins, & Duguid, 1989). I argue that this process of gradual generalization is slow and inefficient. Further, it is unnecessary because students can make sense of abstractions if they are presented in the right form and at the right level of abstractness. Instead, I propose a middle-out approach in which students are introduced to new domains via causal models represented at an intermediate level of abstraction. (p. 178)

White uses this approach in her ThinkerTools computer microworlds that enables sixth-grade students to learn the principles underlying Newtonian mechanics through interactive simulations (White, 1993b). Figure 9.5 shows an example problem in which the goal is to make the dot navigate the track and stop on the target. The speed and direction of the dot's motion are represented dynamically by the motion of the dot itself, and by the small dots (wake) on the screen. The positions of the arrows that point at the dot show the x and y components of the dot's velocity. In addition, there is a more abstract representation of the dot's velocity components in the datacross that shows the horizontal and vertical components of velocity by the amount of "mercury" in two crossed thermometers. When a student applies an impulse to the dot, the effect can be seen simultaneously on all four types of representation (the motion of the dot, the wake, the arrows, and the datacross). Although White emphasized the intermediate level of abstraction (for instance, the dot could represent a spaceship with a rocket engine or a billiard ball controlled by a stick), her system might also be viewed as an environment in which multiple levels of abstraction are tightly linked together.

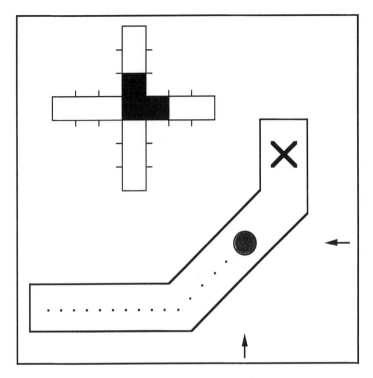

FIG. 9.5. A problem in the ThinkerTools microworld. From White (1993b). Reprinted with permission.

The ThinkerTools software has been very successful in helping sixth-grade students understand Newtonian mechanics in real-world, problem solving contexts. After interacting with the microworld, students were given a transfer test composed of noncomputational questions that typically revealed students' misconceptions. The ThinkerTools students did significantly better on the transfer test than high school physics students who had been taught about force and motion using traditional methods.

The three chapters in this section of the book illustrate the many facets of transfer. In this chapter, representations were considered that had a strong perceptual component, whether constructing a general solution method such as a matrix representation or using visual imagery to mentally animate a specific problem. Notice, however, that many of the same theoretical issues reoccur across chapters. The issue of what level of abstraction is most appropriate to represent objects in the ThinkerTools software echoes the issues raised in chapter 7 about the appropriateness of superordinate concepts to represent isomorphic word problems at a more abstract level. Calculating the slope of a slide by finding rise and run in a diagram is concerned with mapping concepts (rise and run) across problems that were discussed in chapter 8. Likewise, the concern expressed by Lobato (1996) of finding what does transfer in the face of disappointing normative results is of value in our attempts to increase all kinds of transfer. In the next chapter two other aspects of transfer are considered—how does classroom learning transfer to solving problems outside the classroom, and how does experience outside the classroom influence problem solving in the classroom?

Summary

Representational transfer is the transfer of general methods rather than the transfer of the detailed steps of a solution. Representational transfer shares some of the same theoretical concerns as analogical transfer, such as how to recognize the similarity of two problems that are solved by the same general method and how to apply the method when the problem changes. Schoenfeld and Hermann found that novices emphasize story content when classifying mathematical problems, but experts emphasize common solution methods. However, novice students benefited from a course on mathematical problem solving, as revealed by their posttest classifications, which were similar to the categories formed by the experts.

Novick's work on representational transfer examined how different kinds of diagrams—such as networks, hierarchies, and Venn diagrams—are transferred across problems. As was previously found for the transfer of isomorphic solutions, the transfer of a general method can be limited by a failure to notice the similarity between two problems. Telling students to use the solution method of an example problem had mixed results. Success in solving the problems was determined by how well students could see a correspondence between the two problems and whether they already had a solution method that worked well.

Identifying why a diagram is helpful enables instructors to determine when to encourage the use of diagrams in solving problems. Larkin and Simon emphasized that diagrams typically represent related information at adjacent locations, making it easier to infer relevant information. Koedinger and Anderson argued that experts at constructing geometry proofs are able to divide diagrams into perceptual chunks that can cue relevant schema knowledge Some diagrams require mental animation of the objects in the diagram, allowing people to infer what happens in a pulley system, or to solve mathematical problems by discovering new relations that simplify the solution. Shepard showed that visualization aids problem solving by allowing people to make new discoveries and bypass more symbolic approaches.

Greeno, Smith, and Moore formulated a theory in which the construction of mental models plays a major role in transfer. Perception and action replace symbolic structures as the key components of mental models. Thus, transfer between continuous and discrete actions is determined by the ease with which people can convert one form of representation to the other. Forming appropriate mental models is a goal of designers of computer microworlds in which students interact with objects. White argued that initially interacting with generic objects at an intermediate level of abstraction has an advantage over starting with either abstract principles or specific situations. Her ThinkerTools microworld successfully uses this approach to teach the principles of mechanics to sixth-grade students.

IMPORTANT TOPICS
IN THE NCTM STANDARDS

10

Wor(l)d Problems

This last section of the book focuses on topics that the NCTM standards recommended for increased attention. One of the objectives of the NCTM standards is to promote the transfer of knowledge learned in the classroom to problems outside the classroom. Therefore, it is not surprising that one of the recommended topics for increased attention is the use of real-world problems to motivate and apply theory (NCTM, 1989). This issue is examined in this chapter. Chapter 11 looks at estimating answers to word problems and using estimates to measure students' understanding of functional relations between two variables. Chapter 12 discusses curriculum reform and examines how research and the NCTM recommendations are influencing the design of instruction.

At various times educators and cognitive scientists have criticized word problems as being too artificial to transfer to real-world situations. For instance, Brown, Collins, and Duguid (1989) stated the following in their influential article "Situated Cognition and the Culture of Learning":

> Math word problems, for instance, are generally encoded in a syntax and diction that is common only to other math problems. . . . By participating in such ersatz activites students are likely to misconceive entirely what practitioners actually do. As a result, students can easily be introduced to a formalistic, intimidating view of math that encourages a culture of math phobia rather than one of authentic math activity. (p. 34)

This chapter begins by examining their view of situated cognition and then looking at recent research studies that have investigated how students solve problems that represent real-world constraints.

The relation between problem solving inside the classroom and problem solving outside the classroom has been investigated in several different ways. One approach looks at how story content influences strategy selection and the accuracy of answers. For instance problems about familiar situations (buying objects in a store) might be solved differently than problems about unfamiliar situations because of children's experience with these situations. Another approach examines how real-world constraints influence the reasonableness of an answer. One constraint is whether the numerical format of the answer makes sense, such as concluding that it will require 2.3 buses to transport children on a school outing or that each child at a party should receive 1.8 balloons. Another constraint is that the implicit assumptions of standard solutions may be unreasonable, such as assuming that a runner will need only twice as much time to run twice as far. Some mathematics educators have convincingly argued that instructors need to teach students to use a mathematical modeling approach to problem solving that considers such realistic constraints in formulating solutions.

Another way in which real-world problem solving differs from typical classroom problem solving is that people often have to formulate the problem and collect relevant data for solving it. The real world is not as nicely packaged as typical word problems in which the problem and relevant data are clearly stated in a short paragraph. The Cognition and Technology Group at Vanderbilt (CTGV) addressed this gap in instruction by designing authentic problem-solving adventures in which students have to solve a complex, multistep problem through careful planning that requires finding relevant data embedded in a story. We will take a look at the efforts of this group after looking how real-world constraints influence the solution of more elementary problems. And finally, I want to present my views on the role of "traditional" word problems in curriculum reform.

Situated Learning

Brown, Collins, and Duguid begin their situated cognition paper by arguing that the assumption that conceptual knowledge can be abstracted from situations inevitably limits the effectiveness of education. By ignoring the situated nature of cognition, education defeats its own goal of providing usable, robust knowledge. Table 10.1 summarizes the main differences that the authors perceive to separate students' activities from the activities of just plain folks (JPFs) and practitioners. Students reason with laws that involve symbols to solve well-defined problems that have fixed conceptual meaning. But solving real-world problems often requires causal modeling of situations in which problems are ill-defined and meaning is socially constructed.

TABLE 10.1
Just Plain Folks, Student, and Practitioner Activities

	JPFs	*Students*	*Practitioners*
reasoning with:	causal stories	laws	causal models
acting on:	situations	symbols	conceptual situations
resolving:	emergent problems and dilemmas	well-defined problems	ill-defined problems
producing:	negotiable meaning & socially constructed understanding	fixed meaning & immutable concepts	negotiable meaning & socially constructed understanding

Note. From Brown et al. (1989). Copyright © 1989 by the American Education Research Association. Reprinted by permission of the publisher.

The authors consider conceptual knowledge to be similar to a set of tools. Concepts, like tools, can only be fully understood through using them in different situations. People who use tools actively build an increasingly rich understanding of the tools and of the world in which they use the tools.

The effect of situational constraints on finding a solution to an emergent problem made a dramatic impact on me when I found myself in the following situation. My wife was in charge of food for a picnic for several hundred people. My son and I were picking up a large order of roasted chicken at a grocery store when my key to our van broke in the door lock. The only solution I could think of was to call my wife to drive out with her key, but I knew we had too tight a schedule. Fortunately, my son had a more situation-oriented solution. He used his pocket knife to remove the broken key from the door lock and noticed that there was a Home Depot near our car. They were able to create a duplicate key that rescued us from our dilemma. Brown et al. (1989, p. 36) stated that "instead of taking problems out of the context of their creation and providing them with an extraneous framework, JPFs seem particularly adept at solving them within the framework of the context that produced them." Well, at least those people who are more experienced at using tools than I am.

Brown, Collins, and Duguid recommended that learning should occur through a "cognitive apprenticeship" and provided two examples of how this approach can be used in the classroom. The first example is Schoenfeld's (1985) teaching of problem solving in which he provides college students with the experience of solving problems in the way that mathematicians solve problems. Students bring problems to class so they can engage in spontaneous mathematical thinking and see mathematics as a sense-making pursuit, rather than watch the instructor write down a solution to a

previously solved problem. The class therefore has the opportunity to formulate and practice working with various mathematical strategies.

The second example is Lampert's (1986) teaching of multiplication in
which she tries to relate problem solving to everyday knowledge. For example,
she teaches multiplication in the context of coin problems, which her fourth-
grade students can relate to their own experiences. Initial problems ask
questions such as "How would you make 82 cents using only nickels and
pennies?" During the second phase students create stories for multiplication
problems. The third phase of instruction gradually introduces students to
the standard algorithms that are used to solve these problems. Her approach
follows procedures that are characteristic of cognitive apprenticeship:

- By beginning a task embedded in a familiar activity, it helps students
  learn how their current knowledge can be used to solve more unfamiliar
  tasks;
- By exploring alternative ways to find solutions, it demonstrates that
  heuristics and algorithms are not absolute but need to be assessed with
  respect to a particular task;
- By allowing students to generate their solutions, it allows them the
  opportunity to create, discuss, and evaluate their activities as a
  collaborative process.

Although these techniques are commendable, cognitive psychologists
continue to debate the basic premise of situated learning—that what is
learned is specific to the situation in which it is learned. Anderson, Reder,
and Simon (1996) argued that this claim is overstated and that there is more
evidence for transfer than would be expected if problem solutions never
generalized across situations. By transfer, the authors meant not only transfer found in laboratory studies, but transfer between school and real-world
activities:

> Particularly important has been situated learning's emphasis on the mismatch
> between typical school situations and "real world" situations such as the work-
> place, where one needs to deploy mathematical knowledge. Greater emphasis
> should be given to the relationship between what is learned in the classroom
> and what is needed outside of the classroom, and this has been a valuable
> contribution of the situated learning movement. However, while it is important
> to have our consciousness raised about this issue, the claims from the situated
> learning camp are often inaccurate. (p. 5)

In the rest of this chapter some of the experimental evidence for how
successful people are in applying school knowledge to real-world problems
is reviewed.

Effect of Problem Content

A classic study of the relation between real-world knowledge and school knowledge investigated how problem context influenced the strategies used by a group of third graders from a poor area in Brazil (Carraher, Carraher, & Schliemann, 1987). This study was motivated by the results of an earlier investigation that showed unschooled children working as market vendors solved problems about a market context more easily than problems encountered in school (Carraher, Carraher, & Schliemann, 1985). The study of the third graders also showed that problem context influenced success rate. The children were much more successful in solving word problems (such as winning marbles) and store problems (such as the cost of buying two items) than in solving arithmetic problems (such as adding two numbers) that were not embedded in a story context. Furthermore, the children were more likely to use mental computations to solve word and store problems, and written computations to solve the arithmetic problems.

The finding that the Brazilian children did better on word problems than arithmetic problems is perhaps surprising to many of us. Would the same results be found for children in the United States? To find out, Baranes, Perry, and Stigler (1989) replicated the Carraher et al. (1987) study, except for a few minor changes such as changing the monetary units to U.S. ones. In contrast to the children in Brazil, the U.S. children solved 7.0 of the 10 arithmetic problems, 7.0 of the 10 word problems, and 6.9 of the 10 store problems. They performed mental computations less often than the Brazilian children, and the proportion of mental and written computations did not differ across the three problem contexts.

There was one area, however, in which real-world content had a significant impact on the results. In a second experiment, Baranes, Perry, and Stigler contrasted eight word problems that involved time with eight word problems that involved money. Some of the numbers in the problems could be more easily mapped onto our money system (7×25 and $75/3$) and some of the numbers could be more easily mapped onto an analog clock (8×15 and $45/3$). Children who received time problems were more successful with "time" numbers than with "money" numbers, and children who received money problems were more successful with "money" numbers than with "time" numbers.

Baranes et al. (1989) concluded their article by emphasizing the importance of school-taught strategies:

> In reading the studies showing how school-taught strategies are not used outside school, one often wonders whether the implication is that schools might just as well not teach algorithms at all. This is definitely not implied by the results we have reported. We have shown that although in some cases the school-taught algorithm is simply not the strategy of choice, in other cases it

would be a welcome strategy if only it were truly available. Providing contextual cues may help children to access alternative strategies for problem solving, and this seems to be a good tactic. But it also seems that algorithms should be taught, though much better than they are now. (p. 317)

The Mathematical Modeling Perspective

We began with problems that could be solved by using standard arithmetic algorithms and learned that the type of problem influenced strategies and success rate for the Brazilian children. Although this was not true for American children, American children were helped by problems that contained numbers that were appropriate for the story content. But some problems can not be solved by the straightforward application of algorithms because applying these algorithms would require making unreasonable assumptions about the situation described in the problem.

Greer (1993) discussed this issue in his article "The Mathematical Modeling Perspective on Wor(l)d Problems." A challenge for mathematics education, according to Greer, is that using only problems with stereotypic solutions does not provide children with training on how to discriminate between cases in which routine solutions are or are not appropriate. His study of one hundred 13- and 14-year-olds from two schools in Northern Ireland confirmed his suspicions. Table 10.2 shows examples of nonroutine problems that would require unreasonable assumptions to apply proportional reasoning in a straightforward way. Each of these problems was paired with a routine problem in which proportional reasoning provided an accurate model of the situation. The routine problems asked questions such as how long it would take a barge (rather than a runner) to travel 3 miles, or how many birthday cards (rather than Christmas cards) would be sold

TABLE 10.2
Examples of Nonroutine Problems

A man wants to have a rope long enough to stretch between two poles 12 meters apart, but he only has pieces of rope 1.5 meters long. How many of these would he need to tie together?

An athlete's best time to run a mile is 4 minutes and 7 seconds. About how long would it take him to run 3 miles?

The flask is being filled from a tap at a constant rate. If the depth of the water is 2.4 cm after 10 seconds about how deep will it be after 30 seconds? (This problem was accompanied by a picture of a tapered flask.)

A girl is writing down names of animals that begin with the letter C. In one minute she writes down 9 names. About how many will she write in the next 3 minutes?

A shop sells 312 Christmas cards in December. About how many do you think it will sell altogether in January, February, and March?

Note. From Greer (1993).

during the 3 months following December. Students were given minimal, nondirective instructions and received only one problem (routine or nonroutine) from each pair.

The students made virtually no errors in solving routine problems, but made few adjustments for realistic constraints in solving the nonroutine problems. The one exception was the recognition that the sale of Christmas cards was not uniform across months. Comparable findings occurred in a study of fifth graders at three different schools in Flanders (Verschaffel, De Corte, & Lasure, 1994). As predicted, the students showed a strong tendency to exclude real-world knowledge and realistic considerations in their solutions of nonroutine problems. Only 120 of the 750 reactions (17%) to the problems could be considered as realistic, either because the students wrote a realistic answer or made qualifying comments regarding their answer.

One of the questions raised by Greer in discussing his findings is whether teachers are aware of the issues raised in his paper. For preservice teachers, the answer is that more needs to be done to increase their awareness (Verschaffel, De Corte, & Borghart, 1996). A study of 332 preservice teachers in three teacher training instites in Flanders revealed that the student-teachers showed a strong overall tendency to exclude realistic considerations. Only 48% of their answers could be considered as realistic responses. After answering the questions, they were asked to grade answers from pupils with 1 point for a completely correct answer, .5 points for a partly correct answer, and 0 points for a completely incorrect answer. They assigned a score of 0 to 47% of the realistic answers, compared to 18% of the nonrealistic answers. Verschaffel, De Corte, and Borghart (1996) concluded that "if we want to connect problem solving in school mathematics to the experiental world of children—as strongly advocated in most current reform documents related to mathematics education—we will also have to stimulate and help (student-)teachers to construct the proper concepts, skills, and beliefs that are needed for realistic modeling of problem situations" (p. 394).

Instruction on Modeling

To counteract the tendency to ignore real-world constraints, Greer (1993) recommended that the straightforward application of arithmetic procedures for solving problems be taught as only one of a number of candidates for modeling of a situation. Students need to learn to consider each presented situation on its own merits, including the reasonableness of any proposed solution. This modeling approach offers several advantages:

- It addresses the problem of the stereotyped nature of word problems in which success can often be achieved through superficial methods rather than actually thinking about the situation described in the problem.

- It addresses the concern raised by educators who believe that the unrealistic nature of school problems makes it difficult to transfer this knowledge to real-world problems.
- It introduces the modeling perspective at an early stage so students will be able to use this approach in subsequent mathematics courses.

Verschaffel and De Corte (1997) responded to this challenge by designing instruction that would hopefully encourage fifth-grade students to be more sensitive to real-world constraints when formulating solutions. Their experimental group consisted of 19 fifth-grade boys from a boys' school in a small Flemish town. Two control classes consisting of 18 and 17 sixth-grade boys from the same school were used for comparison. Students in the school were being taught with standard word problems and realistic modeling of problems had not been addressed. Prior to instruction all three groups took a paper-and-pencil pretest that consisted of five routine and five pairs of nonroutine problems that were similar to the ones used by Verschaffel et al. (1994). Table 10.3 shows three examples of nonroutine problems. One member of each pair (a learning item) resembled the problems used during instruction and one member (a near-transfer item) had a problem content that differed from the instructional problems.

TABLE 10.3
Examples of Learning (A) and Near-Transfer (B) Items

1A	1180 supporters must be bused to the soccer stadium. Each bus can hold 48 supporters. How many buses are needed? (Carpenter, Lindquist, Matthews, & Silver, 1983)
1B	228 tourists want to enjoy a panoramic view from the top of a high building. In the building there is only one elevator. The maximum capacity of the elevator is 24 persons. How many times must the elevator ascend to get all tourists on the top of the building? (Verschaffel, 1995)
2A	At the end of the school year, 66 school children try to obtain their swimming diploma. To get this diploma one has to succeed in two tests: swimming 100 meter breaststroke in 2 minutes and treading water during 1 minute. 13 children do not succeed in the first test and 11 fail on the second one. How many children get their diploma? (Verschaffel, 1995)
2B	Carl and Georges are classmates. Carl has 9 friends he wants to invite for his birthday party, and Georges 12. Because Carl and Georges have the same birthday, they decide to give a joint party. They invite all their friends. All friends are present. How many friends are there at the party? (Nelissen, 1987)
3A	Some time ago the school organized a farewell party for its principal. He was the school's principal from January 1, 1959, until December 31, 1993. How many years was he the principal of that school? (Verschaffel, 1995)
3B	This year the annual rock festival Torhout/Werchter was held for the 15th time. In what year was this festival held for the first time? (Verschaffel, 1995)

Note. From Verschaffel and De Corte (1997). Reprinted with permission from the *Journal of Mathematics Education.* Copyright © 1997 by the National Council of Teachers of Mathematics.

The routine problems that were typically taught in the school were replaced with nonroutine problems for students in the experimental class. Each teaching unit focused on a nonroutine problem that was similar to one of the learning items on the pretest. The first unit involved interpreting the outcome of a division problem in which there is a remainder. The second involved the union of two sets in which the number of shared members is unknown. The third contained problems in which it is not immediately clear whether the result of adding or subtracting two numbers gives the appropriate answer or an answer that is one more or one less than the correct one. The fourth involved tying rope together to produce a rope of a specified length. The fifth contained proportional reasoning problems that required discriminating when solutions based on direct proportional reasoning are or are not appropriate.

Not only the problems but the teaching method differed for students in the experimental class. The most important difference was the central role of interactive learning through small-group and whole-class discussions. The purpose of this change was to create cognitive conflicts between stereotyped responses and responses that were sensitive to realistic constraints. The subsequent discussion and reflections would hopefully create a change toward a modeling perspective.

At the end of the experimental program a parallel version of the pretest was administered as a posttest in all three classes. In one of the control classes students were given a 15-minute introduction to the idea that routine solutions are sometimes inappropriate when considered in terms of realistic constraints. These students were then explicitly warned that the (post)test contained several questions in when such routine solutions were not appropriate.

Consistent with previous research, Verschaffel and De Corte found a strong tendency to exclude realistic considerations on the pretest, but the instruction in the experimental class was effective in significantly improving realistic responses on the posttest. The increase was from 9% to 60% on the five learning items and from 6% to 41% for the five near-transfer items. Particularly encouraging was the significant improvement on the transfer items. When tested 1 month later, students gave 40% realistic responses to parallel versions of the near-transfer items and 39% realistic responses to a new set of far-transfer items. In contrast, the relatively small and nonsignificant increase in realistic responses on the posttest for the two control classes demonstrated that merely warning students (in one of the classes) to not always apply routine solutions was insufficient.

As might be expected, the success of the experimental instruction varied across both problems and individuals. The biggest gain occurred for deciding what to do with remainders, and the smallest gains occurred for deciding whether an answer is one more or one less than a calculated result and discriminating between situations in which direct proportional reasoning is or is not appropriate. The biggest gain for students occurred for the more able math students who were more actively involved in group and class discussions. To enhance the active involvement of all students Verschaffel and De Corte (1997) suggested assigning roles during group work.

An analysis of videotapes revealed some problems with the attempt to create a new classroom culture in the experimental class:

> Indeed, interventions aimed at establishing new social and sociomathematical norms in line with the mathematical modeling perspective outlined in the beginning of this article too rarely occurred and too often remained implicit. Of course, the teacher initiated some discussion, raised questions, made remarks, and gave feedback with a view to changing pupils' beliefs and to inducing new classroom norms (about what counts as a good problem, a good solution strategy, a correct answer, and a proper explanation, or about what can be expected from the pupils and the teacher in a mathematics class). But most of these discussions, questions and comments were rather unsystematic and inconspicuous, and they rarely elicited serious thought and reflection among the pupils. (p. 596)

This quote should remind us of the remaining challenges, whereas the initial success should encourage us to try to overcome these challenges.

Plans for Multistep Modeling

Previous chapters examined how knowledge of elementary problems can be combined to solve more complex, multistep problems. The discussion of multistep problems in chapter 5 focused on planning—a cognitive process that becomes even more important when problems are embedded in a rich scenario that requires finding relevant information to solve a problem with numerous subgoals. In most word problems presented in school, the relevant information is contained in a short text, usually consisting of several sentences that do not contain irrelevant, distracting information. One limitation of this approach is that even if students learn to solve these kinds of problems, their knowledge may remain "inert" and not be activated when they have to use this knowledge to solve real-world problems.

The Cognition and Technology Group at Vanderbilt (CTGV) faced this challenge by designing problem-solving adventures on video disks that require students to identify problems in a real-world context (CTGV, 1990). Their first series involves a person named Jasper Woodbury and is intended for the fifth and sixth grade. The adventure requires solving a complex mathematical problem involving approximately 15 subgoals. In the first adventure, Jasper sets out for Cedar Creek in a small motorboat to look at an old cruiser for possible purchase. His major goal, however, is to get home before sunset without running out of gas. Students are encouraged to generate subproblems that represent possible obstacles to his goal and invent strategies for solving the subproblems. Throughout the story are relevant data. For instance, the time of the sunset is broadcast on the weather channel and there is a map that can be used for calculating the distance between Cedar Creek and Jasper's home dock. Every effort was made to insure authenticity of the stories, such as using speeds and gas mileage figures that are realistic for the boats in the stories.

Goldman, Pellegrino, and Bransford (1994), three of the principal members of CTGV, listed several goals of the Jasper Woodbury series. One goal is to generate excitement about mathematics among middle-school students and help them develop powerful skills for formulating and solving problems. A second goal is to help students see how topics that are traditionally taught as separate subjects in the classroom are actually integrated in the real world. Solving real problems often involves using mathematic, scientific, geographic, and economic concepts together. A third goal is to motivate students to become proficient in the basic skills of mathematics.

The Jasper series is based on seven design principles that were motivated by the NCTM curriculum standards (NCTM, 1989). The principles follow the recommended emphasis on complex, open-ended problem solving that requires communication and reasoning. The design also connects mathematics to other topics and to the world outside the classroom, and uses powerful computer-based tools such as spreadsheets and graphing programs for exploring relationships. The design principles are:

- *Video-based presentation format.* The video format can make the characters, settings, and actions more interesting, particularly for students with below-average reading skills.
- *Narrative format.* Embedding the problems in a well-formed story creates a more meaningful context for problem solving.
- *Generative learning format.* Students actively participate in the learning process by determining the resolution of the story.
- *Embedded data design.* The mathematical problems are not explicitly stated at the beginning of the video, and the needed numerical information is incidentally presented throughout the story. Students are able to look back at the video for the data they need.
- *Problem complexity.* The first episode of the series contains a problem comprised of more than 15 interrelated steps. In the second episode, multiple solutions need to be considered in order to find the optimum one.
- *Pairs of related videos.* The Jasper series consists of pairs of similar episodes. For example, the first two episodes deal with trip planning

and require the use of distance, rate, and time concepts, although the specific details of the two trips differ. Students can be helped in analyzing what is specific to each episode and what can be generalized.

- *Links across the curriculum.* The maps provided for the trip planning can be linked to geography or other famous trips that required route planning, such as Charles Lindbergh's solo flight across the Atlantic.

These design principles have been carefully formulated by members of the CTGV, but are they successful? Goldman, Pellegrino, and Bransford (1994) reported that observations, anecdotes, and personal reports indicate that reaction to the Jasper series is extremely positive. Attitude data demonstrate that students of all abilities enjoy solving the problems, a finding that is consistent with the reports of teachers who have observed their students working on these problems. But there are many challenges for developing more systematic tests; for example, paper-and-pencil tests that measure how well students can generate appropriate questions and explain why one would carry out certain calculations in order to solve the problem.

Role of "Traditional" Problems in Curriculum Reform

The problems described in this chapter fit the goal of the NCTM standards to relate mathematical problem solving to situations outside of the classroom. However, the content of this chapter (as did chapters 6 and 7) raises the question of whether the research on "traditional problems" has been a waste of time. This is a particularly important issue because some statements by prominent people in the field of mathematics education would seem to dismiss this work, as exemplified in the following quote from Kaput (1995) on the integration of ideas in an algebra course:

> Integration has traditionally taken the form of algebra applications in the form of "word problems" rather than in the larger senses described above. And, since these researchers by and large shared the curricular assumption that ability to use algebra is reflected in ability to solve such problems, much research, far too extensive to be cited here and extending well into the psychological sciences, focused on learning how to solve word problems of various types. This research helps only indirectly in the current reform effort, because the current reform no longer shares this curricular assumption. (p. 81)

However, as discussed in the final chapter, word problems are playing an important role in curriculum reform. This is not surprising because of the emphasis on problem solving in the reform movement. In fact, I would guess that Kaput and others do not object to word problems, per se, but rather to how they have been used in the traditional curriculum. To quote the first paragraph in Kaput's (1995) article on reforming algebra courses:

> School algebra in the U.S. is institutionalized as two or more highly redundant courses, isolated from other subject matter, introduced abruptly to post-pubescent students, and often repeated at great cost as remedial mathematics at the post secondary level. Their content has evolved historically into the manipulation of strings of alphanumeric characters guided by various syntactical principles and conventions, occasionally interrupted by "applications" in the form of short problems presented in brief chunks of highly stylized text. All these are carefully organized into small categories of very similar activities that are rehearsed by category before introduction of the next category, when the process is repeated. (p. 71)

As a teacher of introductory statistics, I am sympathetic to this argument. Most courses and textbooks on this topic are organized around chapters that successively describe various statistical tests such as chi-square, t tests, correlation, and analysis of variance. It is obvious, therefore, which test to use on homework problems. A variety of experimental designs (if included at all) are described in the last chapter, so students will have to select the appropriate statistical test for each design. I always promise myself that I will spend more time on this section, never spend enough time, and am always disappointed by how poorly students do in selecting the appropriate test for each of the described experiments. Following instruction on various "types" of statistical or algebra word problems, the problems should be mixed together and include some problems in which the type is not obvious. A good example is the Smalltown problem described on page 92 in which it is not immediately obvious whether it is a distance-rate-time or a triangle problem.

I also agree that problems should be elaborated so they do not consist of highly stylized text. Elaboration provides the opportunity to mention information that could be related to coursework in other areas, such as an investor might choose to invest money at different rates of interest because higher rates are often more risky investments than lower rates. Students should be able to extend their knowledge about routine problems to answer questions about the real-world problems that were discussed in this chapter or in other chapters. For instance, students who are given a solution to the water tank problem in Table 7.1 (p. 102) should be able to apply it to answer the question about the sinking ship on page 71.

Routine problems can also form the basis for solving the big problems that are part of curriculum efforts like those created by the CTGV. For instance, the Jasper series assumes a certain level of proficiency in solving routine problems in order to be successful in solving the bigger problems embedded in a scenario. In the Journey to Cedar Creek adventure, a student has to be able to calculate how far the boat can travel before refueling in order to determine whether it is necessary to stop for fuel. The tutors developed by Derry, Marshall, and Reusser, discussed in chapter 5, could be used to help students learn to solve multistep problems before they face the more challenging kinds of questions posed in the Jasper series. A combination of both approaches would hopefully provide a high level of competency in solving standard problems that could then be applied to identify and solve problems in a rich, narrative context.

Figure 10.1 shows one of my favorite examples of a multistep problem (Randhawa, 1994). There are several reasons why I like this problem. First, students have to use their knowledge of both arithmetic and geometry to solve it; knowledge that is accumulated from solving simpler, routine problems. Second, there are many steps, so considerable planning is necessary to fit together the component calculations. Third, because some of the component calculations can be done in parallel, students in a group can be assigned various tasks. One student can calculate the total area of the house, while a second student calculates the area of the windows, and a third student calculates the cost of a gallon of discounted paint. And finally, it is a real-world problem that I can imagine having to solve.

In conclusion, instructors should begin with routine problems but do a better job in teaching students how to solve these problems. It seems to me to be overly idealistic to expect students to solve more challenging problems if they are still struggling with routine problems. If this first goal can be reached, then instructors will be in a better position to teach students when the assumptions for creating routine solutions are unreasonable, how to relate problems that belong to different categories, and how to combine information

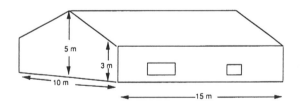

5. You are going to paint the house shown below with one coat of paint. It has a 1m by 2m picture window at the front and six smaller windows measuring 1m by 1m on the sides and the back. The roof will not be painted.

A rule of thumb that painters use is one litre of paint for 9.3m² of surface.

The regular price for a 1-litre can is $10.95 but now on sale at 25% discount.

The regular price for a 4-litre can is $27.95.

If you cannot use any unused portion of the paint in a can for anything else, what will be the lowest cost to paint the house?

FIG. 10.1. A multistep real-world problem. From Randhawa (1994). Reproduced with permission from the author.

from several routine problems to solve the big problems. The examples of problems in this chapter, however, are needed to go beyond routine problems and provide enhanced instruction that will be beneficial for making connections between the classroom and the world outside the classroom.

Summary

One of the claims in some formulations of the situated learning perspective is that classroom instruction on traditional word problems does not capture what people do outside the classroom. According to this claim, students reason with laws that involve symbols to solve well-defined problems that have fixed conceptual meaning. But solving real-world problems often requires causal modeling of situations in which problems are ill-defined and meaning is socially constructed. Examples of instruction that place greater emphasis on real-world problem solving are courses that help fourth graders reason with familiar coin problems and college students experience solving problems that they bring to class.

However, some cognitive psychologists have challenged the assumption that there is poor transfer between classroom and real-world problem solving. Conflicting results occurred between a study in Brazil and a study in the United States on whether students benefit from familiar situations (store problems). The American study found that students did not do better on the store problems, but they did benefit from numbers that could be easily mapped onto the monetary system.

There has been increasing research interest in how to help students recognize that a standard algorithm, such as proportional reasoning, does not apply because it would require making unrealistic assumptions. These studies have shown that students (and prospective teachers) often make no adjustment for unrealistic constraints when solving these nonroutine problems. Fortunately, direct instruction on solving nonroutine problems looks promising. Students who received such instruction performed well on transfer problems, whereas students who were merely warned about applying routine solutions to nonroutine problems did not significantly inrease the number of realistic responses.

Another example of successful instruction has been the work of the CTGV. This group has developed problem-solving adventures on videodisks that require students to identify problems in a real-world context. Students have to discover relevant data in the story in order to solve a variety of subproblems that lead to obtaining a goal. The subproblems are often standard word problems such as distance-rate-time problems. Such standard problems are relevant for real-world problem solving, but as illustrated in this chapter, they should be embedded in instruction that promotes transfer to real-world situations. Standard problems, therefore, provide a beginning but not the final goal of instruction.

11

Estimation and Functions

The emphasis thus far has been on solving problems by calculating an exact answer. The topic now shifts to investigate how well people can estimate answers to word problems. Many situations in our daily lives require an estimate: Do I have enough cash to pay for these books? How much paint do I need for this room? How long will it take me to drive to the dentist's office? (Sowder, 1992)

There are a number of reasons why it is important to provide reasonable estimates to problems, and estimation has been receiving increased emphasis in mathematics education. One reason estimation is important is that people often don't know how to calculate an exact answer to a problem. Second, even when they know a correct procedure, they may not take the time to use it if an approximate answer is sufficient. For example, a person may estimate how long it will take to reach a destination without calculating an exact answer. Third, estimation provides a means to evaluate the reasonableness of an answer following calculation (De Corte & Somers, 1982).

Estimation can also provide teachers or researchers with a measure of how well students understand a procedure. A dramatic example of how students may learn a procedure by rote with little conceptual understanding is illustrated by performance on the National Assessment of Educational Progress test (Carpenter, Corbitt, Kepner, Lindquist, & Reys, 1980) . When asked to estimate the answer to the fraction addition problem $12/13 + 7/8$, 7% of the 13-year-olds selected the response 1, 24% selected the correct answer 2, 28% selected 19, 27% selected 21, and 14% selected *I don't know*. Carpenter and his colleagues suggested that because students actually did better on questions that required an exact answer, many students had little understanding of fraction addition even if they had correctly learned the procedure.

Although the ability to provide accurate estimates is a useful skill, there has been surprisingly little research on the accuracy of estimates to word problems. There has been much more research on computational estimation that measures people's ability to provide a reasonable answer to a numerical problem, such as 98×43, without using some external device to compute an exact answer (Sowder, 1992). Although computational estimation can be an important component in providing an accurate estimate to a word problem, it is of little use if people don't have an understanding of the problem, which is the focus of this chapter.

This chapter begins by looking at estimation problems in which the understanding of a weighted average is a key for successful estimation. The discussion then turns to various instructional efforts to help students give more accurate estimates, including situations in which there is a systematic variation in a variable, such as the proportion of the more concentrated acid in a mixture of two concentrations. This enables a consideration of whether students' estimates are within the correct range of values and whether they follow a correct pattern such as increasing when the proportion of a higher concentration or higher temperature increases. Finally, the discussion will focus on whether such estimates are guided by an integrated representation such as a weighted average formula or whether the estimates are guided by functional principles such as range and monotonicity.

Weighted Average Problems

The term *weighted average* refers to an arithmetical combination of two numbers in which one number receives a higher weight or emphasis than another in determining the answer. For instance, if you travel at two different speeds and want to find your average speed, you would weight the two speeds by the amount of time you spent traveling at each speed. The ability to appropriately weight two numbers can be a useful skill for estimating the answer to many word problems.

Several examples should make this idea more clear. Table 11.1 shows three algebra word problems that represent three different categories according to both students' classifications (Hinsley, Hayes, & Simon, 1977) and Mayer's (1981) taxonomy. A standard solution follows each problem, and the solutions do not appear to be related to each other. However, there is more than one way to solve a problem and the relation among the solutions becomes more apparent if the problems are solved as weighted average problems. Table 11.2 shows the weighted average solutions.

Both the average-speed problem and the tank problem require differentially weighting two numbers when combining them to formulate an answer. In the average-speed problem, the slower speed has greater influence on

TABLE 11.1
Standard Solutions for Algebra Word Problems

Average-Speed Problem

Flying east between two cities that are 300 miles apart, a plane's speed is 150 mph. On the return trip, it flies at 300 mph. Find the average speed for the round trip.

Solution: The average speed is calculated by dividing the total distance by the total time. The plane took 1 hr to travel 300 miles at 300 mph and 2 hr to travel 300 miles at 150 mph. Altogether, it took 3 hr to travel 600 miles. Its average speed was 600 miles/3 hr or 200 mph.

Work Problem

A small pipe can fill an oil tank in 8 hr, and a large pipe can fill it in 4 hr. How long will it take to fill the tank if both pipes are used at the same time?

Solution: The small pipe fills 1/8 of the tank in 1 hr since it requires 8 hr to fill the entire tank. The large pipe fills 1/4 of the tank in 1 hr. The two pipes together fill 1/8 + 1/4 = 3/8 of the tank in 1 hr and the entire tank in 8/3 hr.

Mixture Problem

A nurse mixes a 4% boric acid solution with a 10% boric acid solution. How many pints of each are needed to make 18 pints of a 6% boric acid solution?

Solution: The total amount of boric acid in the mixture must equal the total amount of boric acid in the two component solutions. The amount of acid is calculated by multiplying the percentage of acid by the quantity of solution. The problem requires adding p pints of 4% acid to 18 - p pints of 10% acid to produce 18 pints of 6% acid. The equation is:

$$0.04 \text{ x } p \text{ pints} + 0.10 \text{ x } (18 - p) \text{ pints} = 0.06 \text{ x } 18 \text{ pints}$$

Solving for p yields $0.04p + 1.8 - 0.10p = 1.04$

$$-0.06p = -0.72$$

$$p = 12 \text{ pints of 4% acid}$$

$$18 - p = 6 \text{ pints of 10% acid}$$

Note. From Reed (1984). Copyright © 1984 by the American Psychological Association. Reprinted with permission.

the answer because more time is spent traveling at the slower speed. In the tank problem, the faster pipe has greater influence on the answer because it will fill more of the tank. A third example in which students must differentially weight two numbers is a mixture problem. For instance, mixing a 4% and a 10% boric acid solution to create a 6% boric acid solution will require more of the 4% solution because the desired concentration is closer to 4% than to 10%. As can be seen by the examples, a weighted average conception is a sophisticated problem schema at a high level of abstraction.

TABLE 11.2
Weighted Average Solutions for Algebra Word problems

Average-Speed Problem

Flying east between two cities that are 300 miles apart, a plane's speed is 150 mph. On the return trip, it flies at 300 mph. Find the average speed for the round trip.

Solution: It is necessary to consider how long the plane flies at each speed in order to calculate the average speed. Since the plane flies twice as long at 150 mph as it does at 300 mph, 150 mph contributes twice as much to the average speed. The answer is calculated by multiplying 150 mph by 2/3 and 300 mph by 1/3.

Average speed = 2/3 (150 mph) + 1/3 (300 mph) = 200 mph

Work Problem

A small pipe can fill an oil tank in 8 hr, and a large pipe can fill it in 4 hr. How long will it take to fill the tank if both pipes are used at the same time?

Solution: The large pipe will fill 2/3 of the tank, and the small pipe will fill 1/3 of the tank when both are used at the same time because the large pipe is twice as fast. Since it takes the large pipe 4 hr to fill the entire tank, it takes 2/3 of 4 hr or 8/3 hr to fill 2/3 of the tank. It takes the small pipe 8 hr to fill the entire tank and 8/3 hr to fill 1/3 of the tank. It therefore takes 8/3 hr to fill the tank using both pipes.

Mixture Problem

A nurse mixes a 4% boric acid solution with a 10% boric acid solution. How many pints of each are needed to make 18 pints of a 6% boric acid solution?

Solution: The relative amounts of the 4% and 10% solutions is determined by how close each is to 6%. Since 6 is twice as close to 4 (6 - 4 = 2) as it is to 10 (10 - 6 = 4), twice as much of the 4% solution is required. The nurse can make 18 pints of a 6% solution by mixing 12 pints of the 4% solution and 6 pints of the 10% solution.

Note. From Reed (1984). Copyright © 1984 by the American Psychological Association. Reprinted with permission.

I was interested in whether college students (one half of whom had taken a college algebra course) could give accurate estimates to the problems and how the numbers in the problems would influence their estimates (Reed, 1984). I wrote three questions for each of the three categories and placed each set of questions on a single page so a student could compare his or her answers across the questions. The instructions indicated that the students should estimate the answer without writing down the solution. They were told to guess the answer if they could not solve the problem mentally.

Table 11.3 shows the questions and the percentage of students who gave the correct answer. One reason for placing the three average-speed questions on a single page was to determine whether students would realize that

TABLE 11.3
Percent Correct Answers for Estimation Problems

Average-Speed Problem

---

1. Flying east between two cities, a plane's speed is 150 mph. On the return trip, it flies 300 mph. Find the average speed for a round trip. (9% correct)
2. Flying east between two cities that are 300 miles apart, a plane's speed is 150 mph. On the return trip, it flies 300 mph. Find the average speed for the round trip. (22% correct)
3. A plane flies 150 mph for 2 hr and 300 mph for 1 hr. Find its average speed. (46% correct)

Work Problem

---

1. One pipe can fill an oil tank in 6 hr, and another pipe can fill it in 6 hr. How long will it take to fill the tank if both pipes are used at the same time. (95% correct)
2. One pipe can fill an oil tank in 8 hr, and another pipe can fill it in 4 hr. How long will it take to fill the tank if both pipes are used at the same time. (54% correct)
3. One pipe can fill an oil tank in 10 hr, and another pipe can fill it in 2 hr. How long will it take to fill the tank if both pipes are used at the same time. (49% correct)

Mixture Problem

---

1. How many pints of a 50% acid solution should be added to 10 pints of a 20% acid solution to produce a 30% acid solution. (22% correct)
2. How many pints of a 50% acid solution should be added to 10 pints of a 20% acid solution to produce a 35% acid solution. (10% correct)
3. How many pints of a 50% acid solution should be added to 10 pints of a 20% acid solution to produce a 40% acid solution. (17% correct)

Note. From Reed (1984). Copyright © 1984 by the American Psychological Association. Reprinted with permission.

all three questions had the same answer. The percentage of students who gave the correct answer of 200 mph was 9% for Problem 1, 22% for Problem 2, and 46% for Problem 3, all of which differed significantly from each other. The percentage of students who incorrectly responded with the simple average of 225 mph also differed significantly across the three problems: 68% for Problem 1, 52% for Problem 2, and 15% for Problem 3. Thus, making explicit that the plane spent different amounts of time traveling at the two different speeds greatly changed the number of responses from a simple to a weighted average.

There were also large differences in the percentage of correct responses across the three tank problems: 95% of the students correctly responded when the two pipes had the same rate, but this number dropped to about 50% correct when the two pipes had different rates. One third of the students gave the simple arithmetic average of 6 hours when the pipes had different rates. As was the case for the average-speed problems, the format of the problem greatly influenced whether students would simply average the two numbers.

The results of the mixture problems were surprising because they did not correspond to this trend. I thought a problem in which the desired amount was an arithmetic average (35%) of its two components (20% and 50%) would be a simpler problem than one in which the desired amount was a weighted average (30% or 40%) of the two components. As shown in Table 11.3 this did not occur.

One question raised by these results is how would they change if students were allowed to use paper and a pencil to calculate the answers. The answer is that the results are essentially the same. In another variation of this experiment, the procedure was exactly the same but students were given paper and pencil and allowed to make calculations whenever they thought it would help them improve their answer. Very few students took advantage of this opportunity and were usually incorrect when they wrote and tried to solve equations. The findings from this experiment, therefore, closely replicated the data in Table 11.3 (Reed, 1984, Experiment 4).

Effect of Computer Animation

The substitution of a simple average for a weighted average seemed to me to be particularly counterintuitive in the case of the tank problems. Why would one third of the students say that it would take 6 hours to fill the tank when simultaneously using one hose that would fill it in 4 hours and another hose that would fill it in 8 hours? I thought that I could easily correct this misconception by designing a computer animation program that would show tanks being filled by either a single hose or a pair of hoses. This turned out to be more of a challenge than I expected, so let me share my results and the reasons why I encountered (and tried to correct) some difficulties (Reed, 1985).

College students in this study received a pretest in which they estimated answers to speed, tank, and mixture problems, then viewed a computer simulation of the events, and finally answered estimation questions on a posttest that had the same questions as the pretest. In the tank simulation students first saw four cases of how long it would take to fill a tank with a single pipe that required either 8, 6, 4, or 2 hours (1 hr equaled 2 sec of simulation time). They then saw a simulation of four cases involving two pipes—one requiring 8 hours and the other requiring either 8, 6, 4, or 2 hours. Students changed 42% of their answers on the posttest but approximately one half of the changed estimates were less accurate than on the pretest.

I tried several modifications of the simulation program before finding one that significantly improved the accuracy of the estimates. One change was to simultaneously present two simulations so students could make a direct comparison. One member of each pair showed a single pipe (such as an 8-hr pipe) and the other member showed that pipe combined with a second pipe (an 8-hr and a 6-hr pipe). The purpose of these paired comparisons was to eliminate the need to remember previous instances, as required by the sequential comparisons. This change helped, but still did not result in significant gains. The second change was to require students to estimate an answer after viewing each simulation, such as the time required when both an 8-hour and a 6-hour pipe are used. These estimates were not scored for accuracy, but were intended to encourage students to attend more closely to the paired comparisons. A simulation program that included both of these modifications resulted in a significant improvement in the accuracy of the estimates on the posttest.

Students in this experiment also observed a point traveling at two different speeds on a round trip. Before answering questions on the pretest they received a hint that the average speed was not the arithmetic average of the initial and return speeds, because the time spent traveling at each of the two speeds had to be considered. The purpose of the simulation was determine whether viewing the time spent traveling at each speed would improve their estimates. Variations of this program typically produced better, but not significantly better, estimates of average speed on the posttest.

One version that I thought would be successful included a second reference point that traveled at the arithmetic average of the two speeds. For example, if the simulation showed an initial speed of 20 mph and a return speed of 10 mph then the reference point would travel in both directions at 15 mph. By viewing how much sooner the reference point completed the trip, students could determine how much to adjust their estimate away from the average speed. Unfortunately, the reference point did not provide much additional help until its function was changed.

Reed and Saavedra (1986) compared three very different instructional approaches to determine whether students' conception of average speed could be improved. One method took the animation program a step further by using the reference point to simulate the estimate. If a student estimated that the average speed was 14 mph for the 20–10 example, they would discover that they overestimated because the reference point (traveling at a simulated 14 mph) would return before the point traveling at the two different speeds. The visual feedback provided by the reference point greatly improved students' estimates on transfer problems and was much more successful than alternative methods of instruction, such as viewing graphs, such as the one in Fig. 11.1, or calculating answers to problems.

Although I was pleased with the success of the animation program, I must admit that I was not successful in trying to develop a deeper understanding of the counterintuitive concept that the average speed can never be more than twice the slower speed. If you averaged 10 mph in getting to some

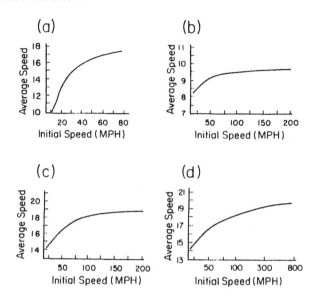

FIG. 11.1. Graphs that show how the initial speed influences average speed when the return speed is either 10 mph (a, c, d) or 5 mph (b). From Reed and Saavedra (1986).

location, your average speed could not exceed 20 mph. The best possible case would occur if you returned at an infinite speed that required no time at all. Because speed is calculated by dividing distance by time, doubling your distance with no increase in time can only double your speed. Reed and Saavedra (1986) tried to show this concept in the asymptote of the graphs (see Fig. 11.1) and explain it in the choice of computational examples, but these forms of instruction were much less successful than the simulation program.

Learning Functional Relations

I have generally been unsuccessful in using graphs to improve students' estimation skills. This lack of success has surprised me. I initially thought that the simplest way to improve students' ability to accurately estimate a sequence of answers that follows some monotonic function would be to show them a graph of the function.

My lack of success has included relatively simple functions, such as linear ones. As pointed out by N. H. Anderson (1983), many scientific phenomena can be described by linear functions. For example, because *distance = velocity × time*, distance increases as a linear function of time when velocity is held constant. Velocity determines the slope of the function so one can generate a variety of linear functions relating distance to time, each characterized by a different slope or velocity.

A less familiar example of a linear function shows the concentration of a mixture when the proportion of the two components are systematically varied. For instance, the concentration of a mixture created by mixing a 20% acid solution with a 50% acid solution would increase as a linear function of the proportion of the 50% solution. Reed and Evans (1987) attempted to improve students' estimation skills for mixture problems by showing them a graph of this function. Points on the graph were even linked to specific examples by giving students the answer to each of five examples and then plotting that answer on the graph. Figure 11.2 shows the graph after students had seen three examples in which different proportions of 20% and 50% solutions were combined to form a 10-pint mixture.

Reed and Evans were much more successful in improving estimation skills when students were directly taught the principles that were thought to be important in developing an understanding of the task. The first principle in Table 11.4 refers to the range of values, the second principle refers to the monotonic characteristics of the function, and the third principle refers to the linearity of the function. Students did significantly better in improving their estimates to the test questions shown in Table 11.4 after studying the principles than after studying the construction of a graph.

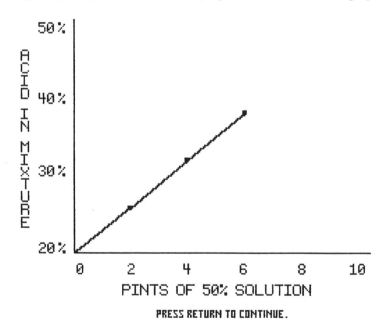

FIG. 11.2. Graph that shows the linear increase in concentration of a mixture as the proportion of the more concentrated component increases. From Reed and Evans (1987). Copyright 1987 by the American Psychological Association. Reprinted with permission.

TABLE 11.4
Principles and Test Questions for Functional Relations

Read the following principles, and then try to answer the test questions.

There are three principles that should help you become a better estimator. Try to follow these principles when you make your estimates. We will illustrate the principles with an example that combines a 25% acid solution with a 45% acid solution to make a 10-pint mixture.

1. If two solutions are mixed together, the concentration of the mixture will be between the concentrations of the two solutions. For example, if a 25% solution is mixed with a 45% solution, the concentration of the mixture will be between 25% and 45%.

2. The concentration of the mixture increases as the proportion of the highest concentration increases. For example, a mixture consisting of 6 pints of the 45% solution and 4 pints of the 25% solution will have a higher concentration than a mixture consisting of 4 pints of the 45% solution and 6 pints of the 25% solution.

3. Identical changes in the proportion of the two solutions produce identical changes in the concentration of the mixture. For example, to make a 10-pint mixture, increasing the 45% solution from 2 pints to 3 pints produces the same increase in the concentration of the mixture as increasing the 45% solution form 7 pints to 8 pints.

Test questions
Estimate the concentration of a mixture when:

1. 1 pint of a 20% concentration is mixed with 9 pints of a 75% concentration.
2. 3 pints of a 20% concentration is mixed with 7 pints of a 75% concentration.
3. 5 pints of a 20% concentration is mixed with 5 pints of a 75% concentration.
4. 7 pints of a 20% concentration is mixed with 3 pints of a 75% concentration.
5. 9 pints of a 20% concentration is mixed with 1 pint of a 75% concentration.

Note. From Reed and Evans (1987). Copyright © 1987 by the American Psychological Association. Reprinted with permission.

Although the principles were found to be helpful, Reed and Evans thought that the instruction could be further improved by basing the principles on a familiar analogy. The principles were explained by referring to the temperature, rather than the concentration, of a mixture. For instance, the first principle now stated:

1. If two solutions are mixed together, the temperature of the mixture will be between the temperatures of the two solutions. For example, if a 25°C solution is mixed with a 45°C solution, the temperature of the mixture will be between 25°C and 45°C.

It was hypothesized that the principles would be much easier to understand in a more familiar situation. Students may not know that the concentration of a mixture is between the concentrations of its two components, but they should know that the temperature of a mixture is between the temperatures of its two components. The results were consistent with our hypothesis. Students gave fairly accurate estimates about the temperature of mixtures before they read the principles, and gave very accurate estimates about temperature after reading the principles. They also gave very accurate estimates about the concentration of mixtures if the principles were explained in terms of temperature and the students were then told that the same principles apply to estimating the concentration of mixtures. The more direct approach of explaining the principles in terms of concentration, as shown in Table 11.4, was much less effective in producing accurate estimates of concentration.

In analyzing these results Reed and Evans (1987) were interested not only in the accuracy of the estimates, but in how consistent they were with the principles that were being taught. Table 11.5 shows the findings for both accuracy and consistency. To make these findings more interpretable, the procedure is briefly summarized as follows: The test booklet contained four pages consisting of a pretest, a statement of the principles, and two posttests. Each test consisted of two series containing five questions, such as the ones shown in Table 11.4. The ranges of the series were 10–40 and 60–80 for Test 1, 20–60 and 80–90 for Test 2, and 5–20 and 40–75 for Test 3.

The principles and test questions for students in the Acid group all referred to the concentration of an acid solution. The same numbers were used for students in the Temperature group but the units were changed from % concentration to °C for the pretest, principles instruction, and posttest. However, the units for the transfer test were *% concentration* so this test was identical to the transfer control test given to students in the Acid group. Because it was unlikely that students would spontaneously notice the isomorphism between the acid and temperature tasks (based on the findings discussed in chapter 7), they were informed that the principles were the same for the two tasks.

For subjects in the Acid group, the average absolute deviation from the correct answer declined from 12.6 on the pretest to 8.3 on the posttest. As

TABLE 11.5
Accuracy and Consistency for Acid and Temperature Tasks

Group and Trial	Accuracy (perfect = 0)	Range (perfect = 10)	Monotonicity (perfect = 8)	Linearity (perfect = 3)
Acid				
1. Pretest	12.6	7.1	3.9	1.26
2. Posttest	8.3	8.7	5.4	1.60
3. Transfer control	7.3	8.8	5.3	1.82
Temperature				
1. Pretest	3.1	9.4	6.5	2.19
2. Posttest	1.4	10.0	7.4	2.55
3. Transfer	0.9	10.0	7.6	2.77

Note. From Reed and Evans (1987). Copyright © 1987 by the American Psychological Association. Reprinted with permission.

can be seen from Table 11.5, there were also moderate gains in how well the estimates satisfied each of the three principles. But the posttest results were not as impressive as the pretest results for the Temperature group. Changing the units from *% concentration* to *°C* created a familiar situation that students already understood fairly well. Furthermore, they continued to improve on the posttest and showed excellent transfer to the acid questions when told that the same principles apply to mixing acid.

One interesting aspect of these findings is that students in the Temperature group did much better than students in the Acid group on the final test even though both groups received the identical test, and only students in the Acid group were shown examples about mixing acid during instruction. The results are interesting because theories of analogy usually predict (and find, Reed, 1989) that transfer should be better when the examples and test problems share the same story content. But as illustrated by Reed and Evans (1987), changing to a more familiar domain can be advantageous when students better understand the principles of that domain and the analogy is made explicit.

Estimation Strategies

I have been talking about instruction for improving estimation skills without discussing the strategies that students use to estimate the answers. As argued by N. H. Anderson (1987), it is difficult to interpret the data in Table 11.5 without knowing more about the kinds of strategies that the students used to produce the estimates. For instance, if people used a weighted average strategy, they would automatically produce answers that satisfied the principles of range, monotonicity, and linearity without necessarily understanding these principles that specify the functional relations among the answers. The discussion begins, therefore, by contrasting two different strategies that are related to the two general concepts that have already been mentioned—the concept of a weighted average and the concept of a linear function.

According to the weighted average formulation, the concentration of a mixture is an average of the concentration of its two components, weighted by how much each component is used. If $C1$ and $P1$ are the concentration and proportion of the lower concentration, and $C2$ and $P2$ are the concentration and proportion of the higher concentration, then the concentration of the mixture is:

$$\text{Concentration} = C1 \times P1 + C2 \times P2 = 20\% \times .3 + 40\% \times .7 = 34\%$$

for an example in which 3 pints of 20% solution is mixed with 7 pints of a 40% solution.

Another way to estimate an answer is to use an interpolation strategy. Because $P1 = 1 - P2$, the weighted average equation can be rewritten as:

$$\text{Concentration} = C1 + P2 \times (C2 - C1) = 20\% + .7 \times (40\% - 20\%) = 34\%$$

for the same example. The interpolation strategy utilizes the principles of a linear function that we have been discussing. It shows that the concentration increases as a linear function of $P2$, with the slope determined by the range $(C2 - C1)$.

Reed, Francis, and Actor (1988) attempted to identify the strategies used by students in an estimation task that followed the same format used by Reed and Evans (1987). Students were told to estimate the answer without writing down the solution, but they could solve the problem mentally if they knew a procedure. The questions for the acid mixture consisted of five cases in which 20% acid was mixed with 60% acid and five cases in which 80% acid was mixed with 90% acid. The amount of the lower concentration increased (in 2-pint increments) from 1 to 9 pints for the five questions in each series. The questions for the temperature mixtures had the same format except a 10°C solution was mixed with a 40°C solution for one series of questions and a 60°C solution was mixed with an 80°C solution for the other series. At the bottom of the two estimation pages (acid and temperature) students described how they did the task and wrote down a formula if they used one. Approximately one half of the students answered the temperature questions first and one half answered the acid questions first.

Estimation accuracy was measured by calculating the absolute deviation from the correct answer. The average absolute deviation was 7.0 for the temperature questions and 16.7 for the acid questions, replicating the advantage for temperature found by Reed and Evans (1987). The significant domain effect was accompanied by a significant Domain × Order interaction. As expected, estimating the acid concentrations first did not influence the accuracy of the temperature estimates. However, the accuracy of the acid estimates greatly improved when preceded by the temperature estimates. The absolute deviation was 23.0 when the acid questions occurred first and 10.2 when the temperature questions occurred first, demonstrating some spontaneous transfer from the temperature task (in contrast to my previously mentioned expectations).

A combination of self-reports and response patterns were used to classify students' strategies according to the taxonomy shown in Table 11.6. Students were classified as using the *formula strategy* if they correctly produced the weighted average formula when asked to give a formula if they used one. Students were classified as using an *incorrect formula* if the use of a systematic, incorrect procedure could be identified. Typical examples included multiplying the concentrations by volumes, without converting vol-

TABLE 11.6
Frequency and Accuracy of Estimation Strategies for the Acid and Temperature Tasks

	Acid		Temperature	
Strategy	number	Deviation	Number	Deviation
Formula	8	0.4	11	1.3
Incorrect formula	4	55.1	4	24.8
Interpolation	20	4.0	36	2.5
Guessing	24	23.5	8	23.2
Mixed	4	9.9	3	14.7

Note. From Reed, Francis, and Actor (1988).

umes to proportions, or simply adding the two concentrations and ignoring volumes.

A large number of students reported that they did the estimation task by guessing. The responses of these students ranged from very good guesses that satisfied the range and monotonicity principles to (apparently) random responding. Therefore, response patterns were used to distinguish between the interpolation and guessing strategies. In order to be classified as *interpolation*, at least 8 of the 10 answers had to satisfy both the range and monotonicity constraints. These answers had to be between the concentration (or temperature) of the two components and decline as the proportion of the higher concentration (or temperature) declined. Some students, of course, explicitly mentioned these constraints but others followed the constraints without stating them. Response patterns that failed to satisfy these criteria were classified as *guessing*. The final category (*mixed* strategies) was used when students apparently used different strategies on the two series of questions.

Table 11.6 shows that students' superior performance on the temperature questions was caused by their greater use of the interpolation strategy, rather than simply guessing. There was also a slightly greater use of the weighted average formula on the temperature questions, although this difference was not significant. Both of these strategies gave fairly accurate estimates. This was particularly true for those students who reported using a weighted average formula, indicating that they were successful in performing the mental calculation required by the formula. It should be noted, however, that the problems did not require difficult calculations, which likely contributed to its successful use.

Converging evidence that students use principles such as range and monotonicity to constrain their estimates comes from a study by Dixon and Moore (1997). They evaluated whether students' estimates were guided by explicit knowledge of principles, or by a more integrated representation like the weighted average formula. College students were asked to judge the correctness of unseen math strategies based only on provided answers to a series of temperature-mixture problems. The experimenters manipulated the discrepancy of incorrect answers from the correct answers and whether the answers violated a principle. The assumption is that if people are using an integrated representation, only the discrepancy of the answer from the correct answer should influence correctness judgments. However, if students have direct knowledge of the principles, then violation of a principle should influence correctness judgments. For instance, if students have an understanding of range, they should be very accurate in rejecting an answer that is close to the correct answer but falls outside the correct range. The findings supported the claim that students use their knowledge of principles when judging the correctness of answers. The amount-wrong manipulation had a very consistent effect on the accuracy of judgments when the hypothetical answers did not violate principles. However, this manipulation had little or no effect on judging hypothetical answers that violated principles because the answer could be judged wrong solely on the basis of the principle violation.

Relation Between Qualitative and Quantitative Reasoning

A question raised by these finding is the role that knowledge of principles plays in the selection of mathematical strategies. Are principles used merely to constrain the answers in a qualitative sense or are they used to select mathematical procedures for solving the problems? Ahl, Moore, and Dixon (1992) investigated this question in a study in which they referred to the use of qualitative reasoning as intuitive knowledge—a type of reasoning that occurs without calculation. They were influenced by the distinction that Inhelder and Piaget (1958) made between qualitative and quantitative proportions, including their claim that a qualitative grasp of proportions precedes children's ability to manipulate numerical proportions. One implication of such a claim is that asking students to perform a qualitative reasoning task might enhance their subsequent performance on a quantitative reasoning task by activating their intuitive knowledge.

Ahl et al. (1992) tested this hypothesis by designing a qualitative and a quantitative version of a temperature-mixture task, based on drawings of containers containing water. In the quantitative condition the use of numerical strategies was encouraged by the presence of numerical values for temperatures and amount, and by instructions to use math. Either 1, 2, or 3 cups of water was added to 3 cups of water that was either 40 or 60 degrees in temperature. The added water was either 20, 40, 60, or 80 degrees. In the qualitative condition, students saw the amount of water in each container, but the amount was not stated explicitly. The temperature of the water was described as "cold" (20°), "cool" (40°), "warm" (60°), or "hot" (80°). Students marked their answers on pictures of unscaled thermometers. They were also instructed to write the number that represented the temperature for the quantitative problems.

College students gave fairly accurate answers to both versions of the task. However, the performance of fifth and eighth graders in the quantitative version was much better when they performed the qualitative version first. Twenty three of the 65 students who did the quantitative version first simply added the two temperatures, whereas only 9 of the 71 students who did the quantitative version second followed this procedure. This order effect shows that increasing the memory availability of intuitive knowledge increases the correspondence between intuitive and analytic knowledge. In contrast, there was no order effect on the qualitative reasoning task. Performing the quantitative task first was not beneficial.

These findings suggest that intuitive knowledge of the principles involved in qualitative reasoning influences the choice of numerical solutions to problems. Dixon and Moore (1996) explored the relationship between the development of intuitive understanding and the use of quantitative procedures for students in 2nd, 5th, 8th, 11th grade, and in college. The qualitative version of the task was presented first and used to measure students' understanding of principles such as range and monotonicity (called "crossover" in this study). Students then performed the quantitative version in which they were instructed to use math.

Performance on the two versions of the task were very different. In the intuitive condition even second graders quickly estimated the answer, and none of the participants appeared to use math. In the quantitative version, participants took considerable time to select a strategy, and 78% of the participants attempted some math. A particularly interesting finding is that students did much better in the intuitive version. Although they made marks on thermometers that were not numbered in the intuitive condition, the experimenter converted their marks to numerical responses. The average absolute error was 4 degrees in the intuitive version, compared to 16 degrees in the numerical version. The qualitative estimates were fairly close to the correct answers, even when they violated some of the principles. In contrast, incorrect math strategies often produced answers that were not even close to the correct answer.

But how are principles and math strategies related? Dixon and Moore (1996) found that understanding a principle is a necessary, but not a sufficient, prerequisite for generating an appropriate math strategy. Very few participants used a math strategy that was consistent with a principle that they did not understand. On the other hand, students did occasionally use math strategies that violated principles that they understood. The findings, therefore, suggest that participants perform a mapping process between their qualitative understanding of the task and their understanding of different math strategies. They may use their understanding of the principles to search for math strategies that are consistent with the principles. The previous finding of Ahl et al. (1992) on the asymmetrical transfer from the qualitative to the quantitative version of the task is consistent with the idea that knowledge of principles constrains the selection of a math strategy, rather than the math strategy constraining the knowledge of principles.

The idea that qualitative knowledge can constrain quantitative reasoning is a general one in mathematics education. In their chapter on alternative perspectives of knowing mathematics, Putnam, Lampert, and Peterson (1990) pointed out that many researchers emphasize connections among various kinds of knowledge as an important component of understanding. The claim that conceptual knowledge constrains but does not completely determine procedural knowledge can be found in a number of theories including theories of young children's early counting behavior (Gelman & Meck, 1983; Greeno, Riley, & Gelman, 1984). Because an important component of understanding is establishing connections among different types of knowledge, it is not surprising that this is one of the objectives of the NCTM Standards.

Summary

There are a number of reasons why it is important to provide reasonable estimates to problems. One reason that estimation is important is that people often don't know how to calculate an exact answer to a problem. Second, even when they know a correct procedure, they may not take the time to use it if an approximate answer is sufficient. Third, estimation provides a means to evaluate the reasonableness of an answer following calculation.

Estimation can also provide teachers or researchers with a measure of how well students understand a procedure or concept. An example is the concept of a weighted average in which two numbers must be differentially weighted to produce the answer. Many standard word problems such as speed, work, and mixture problems can be represented as weighted average problems, and students' estimates reveal their understanding of how this concept applies to the different kinds of problems. Attempts to increase students' understanding of weighted average have compared instruction based on graphs, computational problems, and animation of the events. Animation has been effective in improving estimates when appropriate visual feedback is provided in the animation.

Estimation paradigms have also been used to measure students' understanding of functional relations, such as knowing how the acidic concentration of a mixture changes as the proportion of the more concentrated acid increases. Understanding functional relations includes knowing such principles as the concentration of the mixture will be between the concentration of the components (range) and the concentration of a mixture will increase as the proportion of the more concentrated component increases (monotonicity). Although instruction on these principles has been effective in improving estimates, the most effective instruction has been combining the principles with a familiar example. Explaining the principles in the context of mixing water at different temperatures has been more effective than explaining principles in the context of mixing acid, showing that transfer across domains is sometimes more effective than transfer within a domain.

A comparison of estimation strategies has revealed that the greater accuracy in producing estimates in the temperature domain is caused by greater use of an interpolation strategy that is guided by knowledge of principles such as range and monotonicity. In contrast, students' estimates of acidic concentration often did not follow a systematic pattern. Use of a weighted average formula occurred less often than the use of an interpolation strategy and did not differ in frequency of use across the two domains. There is evidence, however, that understanding the principles of functional relations can improve students' choice of a computational procedure for calculating answers. Understanding principles has been shown to be a necessary, but not a sufficient, prerequisite for the use of an effective math strategy. A possible causal relation between understanding principles and selecting an effective math strategy is suggested by the asymmetrical transfer between a qualitative (principle-based) and a quantitative (computational-based) reasoning task. Performing the qualitative task first improved performance on the quantitative task, but performing the quantitative task first did not improve performance on the qualitative task.

12

Curriculum Reform

The emphasis in the preceding chapters has been on research that has focused on particular topics related to mathematics education. Some of the educational implications of these studies have been occasionally discussed, but this book would be incomplete without saying more about the curriculum reform efforts that were mentioned in chapter 1. This final chapter is concerned with new curriculum that is consistent with the NCTM Standards. Is it working? Are students developing a deeper understanding of mathematics? Are they losing their ability to perform basic computations? I will try to answer these questions by reviewing the evaluation of several programs that have implemented curriculum changes.

In chapter 1, linking instruction with theory was discussed by giving an overview of work done at Northwestern by Fuson, Hudson, and Pilar (1997), which used a theoretical model to guide the design of instruction. That discussion emphasized the model rather than the instruction, so this chapter begins by looking at the instruction-side of the program. A second program is the Purdue Problem-Centered Mathematics Project, which is based on the constructivist belief that students learn mathematics most effectively if they construct meanings for themselves, rather than simply listen to the instructor (Cobb, Yackel, & Wood, 1992). From this point of view, learning is seen as involving extensive interaction and exchange of ideas between students and teachers. A third program is the Cognitively Guided Instruction program at the University of Wisconsin, which tries to help teachers to better understand their students' thinking (Carpenter & Fennema, 1992). All three of these programs focus on instruction at the lower elementary grades and use research on elementary word problems (discussed in chapter 4) in the design and evaluation of instruction.

The chapter then focuses on two programs that are producing curriculum changes at the high school level, College Preparatory Mathematics and the Interactive Mathematics Program. These programs are newer, more extensive, and have not been as carefully evaluated as the research done at the lower elementary grades. The chapter then concludes with a presentation of my impression of where we currently stand in the curriculum reform movement.

Phases of Classroom Mathematical Problem-solving Activity

Figure 1.2 (p. 9) in chapter 1 provided a framework for linking theoretical ideas with classroom instruction (Fuson et al., 1997). The brief summary in that chapter focused on the right (theoretical) side of the figure, the Conceptual Phase Model. Let me now say a bit more about the left (instructional) side of the figure—the Phases of Classroom Mathematical Problem-solving Activity (PCMPA). Fuson and her colleagues designed the instruction based on the Conceptual Phase Model, following an iterative procedure over several years that has alternated between instructional design and evaluation.

The instruction involves six learning progressions along which children move during the academic year. Because of individual differences in where children fall on each progression, teachers must monitor each child's progress. The first progression is *types* of word problems. It was shown in chapter 4 that there are different types of problems such as Change, Compare, and Combine problems. These problems vary considerably in difficulty depending on the type of problem and the unknown variable. In contrast to traditional instruction in which not all types are taught, the PCMPA instruction includes coverage of all types, progressing from the easier to the more difficult problems.

A second progression monitors children's ability to *create* as well as to solve word problems. Children initially tell stories that do not have an adequate mathematical expression, but can invent adequate word problems by the end of the first grade. However, creating problems that match a particular problem type or a specified schematic drawing takes longer. A third progression requires students to *explain* their solution. With time and support from the teacher, children who are initially very shy improve in their ability to tell what they are doing. The fourth progression is *math tools*, beginning with objects, fingers, and drawings. More complex tools such as graphs and equations are not introduced until later, but this can occur as early as the seventh week of first grade. The fifth progression is *solution methods*, which range from abbreviated counting to full modeling of the situation. This sixth progression is one of increasing the *size of numbers* in the problem. Beginning with small numbers allows the children to focus on the situation and on the relations among the small numbers without the added complexity of having to make or count larger numbers of objects.

Considerable care has gone into systematically varying the content of the problems. The challenge is to balance consistency (in order to promote understanding of a new concept or linguistic term) with variety (in order to encourage understanding the situation and inhibit rote learning). Variation, therefore, has to be carefully linked to the learning ability of the students. It includes the type of problem, the language used in the problem, and the situation. Although transfer was previously discussed in chapters 7–9, algebra word problems were used in the examples. Fuson reminds us that a concern with transfer should occur early in the instructional process.

A goal of the PCMPA framework is to provide a solid base for algebraic thinking at the elementary school level. The instruction should easily progress from using equations and graphs to understanding functions and variables. As discussed in chapter 6, the transition to algebra is very difficult for most students. The instruction also promotes an approach to solving problems by understanding the situation that should carry into middle-grade mathematics, resulting in fewer instances of students looking for keywords or numbers (see chapter 4) as the key to the solution.

Problem-centered Instruction

Purdue's Problem-centered Instruction Program is included because it has been one of the most carefully evaluated instructional programs. Purdue's program, like many other curriculum reform efforts, is based on a constructivist approach to learning (Wood & Sellers, 1996). Less emphasis is placed on the teacher telling students what to do and more emphasis is placed on students working on problems. A typical mathematics lesson in a problem-centered class generally begins with children working in pairs for 20–25 minutes, followed by whole-class discussion for another 15–20 minutes. Table 12.1 shows examples of the instructional activities.

Wood and Sellers (1997) reported the results of a longitudinal study that tracked three groups of students in Grades 1 to 4. The basic format of the assessment tests remained consistent across all grade levels although the specific content was appropriate for the grade level being assessed. One of the tests was a standardized achievement test—the Indiana Sequential Test of Educational Progress or ISTEP—that consisted of a Computation subtest and a Concepts and Applications subtest. The Computation subtest contained addition/subtraction and/or multiplication/division problems presented in traditional vertical-column format. The Concepts and Applications subtest contained items that required students to associate numbers with specific representations such as bundled sticks or multibase blocks.

TABLE 12.1
Example of Activities in Problem-Centered Instruction

Balances. These are a *series* of activities using a pan balance format developed to enhance students' learning of numerical relationships, including those known as Thinking Strategies. Concepts of place value, addition/subtraction, and multiplication/division are also included. The balance format is used continuously throughout the second-grade year. These are open-ended activities and emphasize student invention. Pupils' use a variety of solution methods. These activities were informed by the research of Steffe and Cobb (1988).

Candy Shop/Candy Factory. This is a *sequence* of activities that uses a fantasy scenario of a Candy Shop/Candy Factory to support students' construction of conceptions of place value numeration and increasingly efficient multidigit addition and subtraction algorithms in Grade 2 and 3. The sequence begins with a scenario to situate the concepts. Next, the children make freehand drawings to aid in recording the process of packing and unpacking candies in rolls and boxes, then moves to the pupils' use of numerals to symbolize their methods and finally presents tasks on a factory form to enable students to numerically record their calculations in columnar format. This sequence of activities is intended to encourage the development of efficient algorithms for calculating multidigit numbers. These activities emphasize finding a limited number of efficient ways for solving problems. The work of Gravemeijer (1994) influenced the development of these activities.

Word Problems. Two types of word problem activities have been developed. In one case, the intention is to provide problems that can be solved using problem-solving heuristics (e.g., making a chart). In the other case, the word problem structures identified by Carpenter & Moser (1984) were used to create additive and multiplicative activities.

Note. From Wood and Sellers (1997). Reprinted with permission from the *Journal for Research in Mathematics Education.* Copyright © 1997 by the National Council of Teachers of Mathematics.

The ISTEP was given to students in the first (1990), second (1991), third (1992), and fourth grades (1993) by the classroom teachers during the first week of March. The results were used to compare the progress of three groups of students who progressed through different instructional sequences. All three groups received conventional textbook instruction in the first and fourth grades, but one group (Project-2) received problem-centered instruction during the second and third grades, another group (Project-1) received problem-centered instruction only during the second grade, and the third group (Textbook) did not receive any problem-centered instruction.

The results, shown in Table 12.2, support problem-centered instruction. At the end of the third grade there are significant differences between the three groups on the Computation subtest, but not on the Concepts and Applications subtest. At the end of the fourth grade, there are significant differences between the groups on both subtests.

Another test, the Arithmetic Test, was developed by project staff to provide a measure not only of computation skills but also of students' understanding of arithmetic. This test also consisted of two subtests. The Instrumental scale contained traditional arithmetic computation problems

TABLE 12.2
Effect of Problem-Centered Instruction on ISTEP Test Scores

	Group			
	Project-2 (2 years)	Project-1 (1 year)	Textbook (0 years)	F
Grade 3				
Computation	76.41	65.00	64.12	12.95*
Concepts & Applications	72.60	69.63	67.25	2.07
Total	77.54	69.31	67.72	7.84*
Grade 4				
Computation	74.10	62.12	64.29	10.27*
Concepts & Applications	77.37	64.77	66.53	11.22*
Total	78.23	64.96	67.13	13.27*

Note. An asterisk indicates that the group means are significantly different at the $p < .05$ level. From Wood and Sellers (1997). Reprinted with permission from the *Journal for Research in Mathematics Education.* Copyright © 1997 by the National Council of Teachers of Mathematics.

that were similar to the problems in the Computation subtest of ISTEP (see the top of Table 12.3). The Relational scale measured conceptual understanding by including a variety of items shown in the bottom of Table 12.3. Of particular interest for this book are the less challenging and the more challenging word problems that were derived from Carpenter and Moser's (1984) research on word-problem structures.

The results of this assessment showed that the three groups did not differ significantly on the Instrumental scale in either Grade 3 or Grade 4. However, the score on the Relational scale improved with more problem-centered learning and this difference was significant at both Grades 3 and 4. An analysis of the particular item types included in this scale revealed that the advantage of problem-centered instruction occurred for most item types, including both classes of word problems.

The Arithmetic Test produced results that are consistent with theory. We would hope that a curriculum based on the reform movement would lead to better performance on test questions in the Relational scale that measures understanding. We would not expect an increase for test questions in the Instrumental scale that measure computation skill, but it is gratifying that problem-centered instruction did not diminish computation skill.

The ISTEP test is also supportive of problem-centered instruction, but is more difficult to interpret from a theoretical perspective. Problem-based instruction lead to a significantly better performance on the Computation subtest and to a significantly better performance on the Concepts and Applications subtest only at Grade 4. The authors reported that these latter results are not surprising because despite the name, the Concepts and

TABLE 12.3
Sample Questions From the Arithmetic Test

Instrumental Scale
Total Number of Items (12)

| 12 | 49 | 658 | 37 | 71 | 502 |
| +47 | +32 | +284 | -24 | -37 | -365 |

Relational scale
Total number of items (41)

Sequence
　　Write the next number 52, 45, 38 ___

Everyday language
　　32 more than 59 is ___; 37 less than 71 is ___

Horizontal sentences
　　___ + 28 = 54; ___ -21 = 48

Multiplication picture
　　Each bag has 6 cookies in it. How many cookies are there? (Picture shows 9 bags in a
　　3 x 3 array.)

Multiplication/division
　　Mary, Sue, and Ann sold 12 boxes of candy each. How many boxes of candy did they
　　sell in all?

Money
　　Maria spends 87 cents. How much change does she get back from $1.00?

Numeration
　　Some cubes are hidden in the box. There are 57 cubes altogether. How many cubes
　　are hidden?

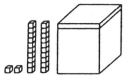

Less challenging word problems
　　Tom had 27 pennies. Then his grandmother gave him 12 more pennies. How many
　　pennies does Tom have now?

More challenging word problems
　　Jim has 43 baseball cards. Rod has 14 baseball cards fewer than Jim. How many cards
　　does Rod have?

Note. An asterisk indicates that the group means are significantly different at the $p < .05$ level.
From Wood and Sellers (1996). Reprinted with permission from the *Journal for Research in
Mathematics Education.* Copyright © 1996 by the National Council of Teachers of Mathematics.

Applications problems are computational in nature and test for knowledge of basic skills through traditional algorithms. Taken together, the findings indicate that problem-centered instruction was often helpful, and certainly did not diminish basic skills.

Cognitively Guided Instruction

The successful implementation of curriculum reform requires changing teachers' beliefs about instruction to make them consistent with the goals of the program. The University of Wisconsin team has been particularly interested in how teachers' beliefs about instruction influence the learning of their students. One of their more recent reports is a 4-year longitudinal study that tracked the beliefs of 21 teachers and related changes in their beliefs to learning in their classrooms (Fennema et al., 1996). Like the Purdue study, the teachers were in the lower elementary grades, but unlike the Purdue study, emphasis was on how teachers changed over 4 years rather than on how individual students changed over 4 years.

The goal of this program was to help teachers develop an understanding of their students' mathematical thinking and how their students' thinking can form the basis for learning more advanced mathematical ideas. This goal was implemented in workshops that showed videotapes of individual children solving word problems that were selected to illustrate critical aspects of children's thinking. Discussion focused on how distinctions among the problems were related to the ways that children thought about and solved the problems. The teachers were encouraged to carefully observe how students solved problems in their classrooms, but were not given a particular curriculum. They were told that an important criteria for making decisions about teaching was children's understandings and that children should not be asked to practice procedures that they did not understand.

The Wisconsin team collected both formal and informal data about the teachers based on audio tape transcriptions of classroom observations, interviews, belief scale scores, and field notes of informal activities. These observations were used to classify each teacher during each year of the study into one of the categories shown in Table 12.4. The categories in the table vary along a continuum from least to most cognitively guided. The levels are determined by the following dimensions: opportunities for children to solve problems, children sharing their thinking with peers and teachers, teachers' elicitation and understanding of children's thinking, and teachers' use of children's thinking as a basis for instructional decisions. Using these criteria, the investigators found that the instruction of 18 of the 21 teachers became more cognitively guided during the 4 years of the project.

TABLE 12.4
Levels of Cognitively Guided Instruction

Cognitively Guided Instruction
Description
Provides few, if any, opportunities for children to engage in problem solving or to share their thinking.
Provides limited opportunities for children to engage in problem solving or to share their thinking. Elicits or attends to children's thinking or uses what they share in a very limited way.
Provides opportunities for children to solve problems and share their thinking. Beginning to elicit and attend to what children share but doesn't use what is shared to make instructional decisions.
Provides opportunities for children to solve a variety of problems, elicits their thinking, and provides time for sharing their thinking. Instructional decisions are usually driven by general knowledge about his or her students' thinking, but not by individual children's thinking.
Provides opportunities for children to be involved in a variety of problem-solving activities. Elicits children's thinking, attends to children sharing their thinking, and adapts instruction according to what is shared. Instruction is driven by teacher's knowledge about individual children in the classroom.

Note. From Fennema et al. (1996). Reprinted with permission from the *Journal for Research in Mathematics Education.* Copyright © 1996 by the National Council of Teachers of Mathematics.

Children's performance on word problems and computational problems was also evaluated each year. Performance on the Concepts and Problem Solving tests showed consistent patterns of improvement for students at each grade level. The mean performance for first-grade students increased from 43% correct in Year 0 (baseline) to 65% correct in Year 3 of the study. The mean performance of second-grade students improved from 59% correct in Year 0 to 69% correct in Year 3. And the mean performance of third grade students improved from 75% correct in Year 0 to 86% correct in Year 3. Performance on a computational skills test showed very small and insignificant increases during the course of the study. Cognitively guided instruction, therefore, increased problem solving ability without diminishing computational skills.

Fennema and her colleagues reported that the gains in students' concepts and problem-solving performance appears to be directly related to changes in teachers' instruction. Gains in the classes of individual teachers tended to follow change in each teacher's instructional approach. Although it is not possible to directly connect the gains to specific changes, instruction changed along several dimensions that seemed to affect achievement:

- Teachers provided more opportunity for students to reflect on concepts and engage in problem solving;

- Children were provided opportunity to share their thinking and their thinking was valued;
- Teachers whose instruction was classified as more cognitively guided adapted instruction to the problem-solving abilities of children.

College Preparatory Mathematics

Curriculum changes are also occurring in high school as is evident from programs such as College Preparatory Mathematics (CPM). According to Kysh (1995), codirector of the CPM Project at the University of California, Davis, the goals of the program are to:

- Develop a rich, integrated mathematics curriculum that will enable more students to succeed in a college preparatory mathematics sequence;
- Base the curriculum on current knowledge of how people learn and the mathematics needed in an era of computers;
- Involve teachers in planning, developing, revising, and introducing the materials to their colleagues.

To find time to develop understanding through a problem-solving approach in the Math 1 (Algebra 1) course, the group decided to embed some of the initial material of Algebra 1 in larger problems and significantly reduce the amount of work on rational expressions and radicals. Although algebra was the main focus in the course, the problems used to develop the algebra were integrated with graphing, geometry, and sometimes probability and statistics. Table 12.5 shows an example in which the discussion of rate is related to algebraic ratios, graphing, and similar triangles.

Other design issues required compromises. The original plan was to pause periodically in the course so students could work on big connecting problems but teachers in a pilot version of the course did not have time to try the big problems. Teachers did notice, however, that students remembered certain problems that later helped them to solve similar problems. An example is the phone problem shown in Table 12.6. The course designers took advantage of this finding by naming instructional units after these memorable problems.

The Math 1 course is the first of three courses. Math 2 has a greater emphasis on geometry but builds on the Math 1 material by integrating the use of functions and algebra, while including trigonometry and geometric probability. Math 3 focuses on functions and graphing through the use of graphing calculators. The Math 1, 2, and 3 materials were used during 1994–1995 by over 1,700 teachers in over 700 schools throughout California.

TABLE 12.5
An Example From College Preparatory Math

| EF-67. | C. J.'s car gets 20 miles per gallon of gas |
| | a) Copy and complete the following table for C. J. |

# miles traveled	20	100	40	10	0	m
# gallons of gas used						

b) Use the table you made in part *(a)* to write an equation relating g, the number of gallons used, to m, the number of miles driven.

c) Does your equation in part (b) make sense for m = 20 miles?

d) Graph your equation with m, the number of miles, on the horizontal axis, and g, the number of gallons, on the vertical axis. Label both axes. Scale the horizontal axis so one unit represents 10 miles. Scale the vertical axis to one unit represents one gallon.

e) Use your graph to estimate the value for g when $m = 70$.

f) Draw the vertical lines $m = 20$ and $m = 70$.

g) Explain why the two triangles formed by your graphed line, the horizontal axis, and the two vertical lines are similar.

h) For these similar triangles, write an equation with two equivalent ratios.

i) Solve your equation from part *(h)* to find out how much gas C. J. used in driving 70 miles. Compare your solution with your estimate in part *(e)*.

Note. From Kysh (1995). Reprinted with permission from Mathematics Teacher. Copyright © 1995 by the National Council of Teachers of Mathematics.

During the 1996–1997 school year my youngest son took a CPM algebra course in eighth grade. As mentioned in chapter 1, the introduction of the CPM courses into the San Diego schools created a controversy between supporters of curriculum reform and supporters of traditional mathematics. Given the heated nature of the controversy, I was surprised that the CPM material (at least the homework problems) did not depart very far from traditional curriculum. There was plenty of practice on basic skills. For example, I estimate that my son worked on at least 60 homework problems on factoring equations during the course. He became very proficient at this so I stopped checking his solutions. There was also a lot of practice on plotting functions and using both the solution of algebraic equations and the intersection of two functions to find answers, such as the phone example in Table 12.6. There were some word problems that were challenging and I often had to help my son with these. To the best of my knowledge, I

TABLE 12.6
A Memorable Problem From College Preparatory Math

CP-88.   CHOOSING A PHONE PLAN

In a college dormitory, each student has a choice of two phone companies. Company A charges $7.46 per month plus 13 cents a call; Company B charges $6.17 per month plus 17 cents per call.

   a)   About how many phone calls do *you* make per month?

   b)   For each company, write an equation which represents the cost in a given month in terms of the number of phone calls.

   c)   Graph each equation you write in part *(b)*. Be sure to label each graph.

   d)   Discuss how your two graphs relate to the solution of the problem. When are the costs for both companies the same? When is company A a better choice? When is Company B a better choice?

   e)   How many calls do you think that the average student in your class makes?

   f)   How could you find out the answer to *(e)?*

   g)   Carry out your plan from part *(f)*.

   h)   Decide which students in your class should use which phone company and tell why.

Note. From Kysh (1995). Reprinted with permission from Mathematics Teacher. Copyright © 1995 by the National Council of Teachers of Mathematics.

answered them all correctly although I wondered if I would encounter a problem that I couldn't solve before the course ended.

The biggest difference between this course and the algebra courses I remember taking in high school is that I took them in high school. I was impressed by how challenging the material was for eighth grade. Because the course demanded a lot of practice on basic skills, I would urge all people who are involved in a debate over curriculum to take a close look at the content of the curriculum before dismissing it as either too new or too traditional. In my view, the concern of parents that their children would not learn basic skills was unfounded for this course.

Interactive Mathematics Program

Another California product is the Interactive Mathematics Program (IMP) developed at the San Francisco State University (Alper, Fendel, Fraser, & Resek, 1995). The 4-year program of problem-based mathematics integrates algebra, geometry, and trigonometry with the additional topics recommended in the NCTM standards such as probability and statistics. The curriculum challenges students to experiment with examples, look for patterns, and to make, test, and prove conjectures.

Unlike the College Preparatory Program that abandoned "big problems" for memorable ones, the IMP uses big problems to provide a focus for units that require from 5 to 8 weeks of class time. Motivated by the central focus, students solve a variety of smaller problems that develop the skills and concepts needed to solve the big problem.

Table 12.7 shows a big problem that was taken from a text on linear programming. The purpose of this unit, however, is not to teach linear programming but to help students learn how to manipulate equations and reason using graphs. Students need to work with many numbers in the problem, such as one dozen plain cookies requires a pound of cookie dough, one dozen iced cookies require .7 pounds of cookie dough, and there is 110 pounds of cookie dough available. Students use the constraints on the cookie mix, $x + .7y < 110$, to plot pairs of numbers that either satisfy or do not satisfy the inequality. They then plot other constraints to find a graph of the total set of constraints. The purpose of beginning with a very difficult problem is to help students see for themselves how procedures, such as solving two equations with two unknowns, would be useful to know. Once a useful procedure has been discovered, students practice using it in other situations, including situations that they propose.

A major premise of the IMP, as well as the other programs reviewed in this chapter, is that nearly all students are capable of thinking about mathematics and of understanding mathematical concepts. The purpose of a curriculum should be, therefore, to immerse students in thought-provoking situations. Teachers and other students should offer support, but all students are expected to be able to constructively work on problems. In a world that is becoming increasingly complex, people need to understand procedures well enough to apply them to new situations, and in some instances, even invent new procedures.

The program is being evaluated by Dr. Norman Webb at the Wisconsin Center for Education Research, as part of a 5-year grant from the National Science Foundation. One of their studies looked at transcripts of students graduating in 1993 from three high schools that began using the IMP curriculum in 1989. The results are reported in *Evaluation Update* (No. 2, Fall 1996), a publication of the IMP (Alper, Fendel, Fraser & Resek, 1996). The findings included:

- A higher percentage of IMP students took at least 3 years of college preparatory mathematics than students enrolled in the traditional Algebra-Geometry-Algebra II sequence (90% vs. 74%).
- For students completing 3 years of college preparatory mathematics, an IMP student was more likely to take a senior-level mathematics course (71% vs. 52%).

TABLE 12.7
A Big Problem From the Interactive Mathematics Program

How Many of Each Kind?*

Abby and Bing Woo have a small bakery shop that specializes in cookies.

They make only two kinds of cookies—plain cookies and cookies with icing. They need to decide how many dozens of each kind to make for tomorrow.

One dozen of their plain cookies requires a pound of cookie dough (and no icing), whereas one dozen of their iced cookies required .7 pounds of cookie dough and .4 pounds of icing.

The Woos know from experience that each dozen of the plain cookies requires about .1 hours of preparation time and each dozen of the iced cookies requires about .15 hours of preparation time. They also know that no matter how many of each kind the make, they will be able to sell them all.

Their decision is limited by the following things:

- The ingredients they have on hand—they have 110 pounds of cookie dough and 32 pounds of icing.
- The amount of oven space available—they have room to bake a total of 140 dozen cookies for tomorrow.
- The amount of preparation time available—together they have 15 hours for cookie preparation.

Why on earth should the Woos care how many cookies of each kind they make? Well, you guessed it! They want to make as much money as possible. They sell the plain cookies for $6.00 a dozen, and it costs them $4.50 a dozen to make these cookies. The iced cookies sell for $7.00 a dozen and cost $5.00 a dozen to make.

The Big Question:

How many dozens of each kind of cookie should Abby and Bing make so that their profit is as high as possible?

1. To begin answering the Big Question, find one combination of plain cookies and iced cookies that will satisfy all of the conditions in the problem, and find out how much profit the Woos will make on that combination of cookies.
2. Now find a different combination of cookies that fits the problem but that makes a greater profit for the Woos.

*This problem was adapted from Stockton (1963, 19-35).

Note. From Alper et al. (1995). Reprinted with permission from Mathematics Teacher. Copyright © 1995 by the National Council of Teachers of Mathematics.

- A separate study done at one of the three high schools targeted students who were classified as "high achievers" in mathematics, based on a 7th-grade mathematics skills test. Although the IMP and Algebra students had comparable pretest results, the IMP students taking the SAT test had a higher mean mathematics score (545 vs. 531) than Algebra students, even though a higher proportion of IMP students took the test (83% vs. 72%).

Another study that is currently being conducted is looking at the Class of 1998. This project is monitoring IMP students' growth from 9th through 12th grade in mathematical understanding, problem-solving ability, confidence, and communication. The study is following randomly selected target students in the IMP and in more traditional mathematics programs.

Some Impressions

Chapter 1 described a concern that the emphasis on a more problem-oriented curriculum in the reform movement would diminish basic skills. There is no evidence for that in the programs reviewed in this chapter. We saw that students in the Problem-centered Instruction program did significantly better on the Computation subtest of the Indiana Sequential Test of Educational Progress and did as well as control students in the computation section of the Arithmetic Test. These students also did better than the control students on tests that measured conceptual understanding. Students in the Cognitively Guided Instruction program maintained their level of performance on a computational skills test and showed consistent patterns of improvement on the concepts and problem solving tests. Curriculum reform efforts at the lower elementary grades, therefore, have been successful in improving students' conceptual understanding and problem-solving performance without diminishing their ability to perform basic computational skills. The evaluation of programs at the secondary level is more preliminary, although some of the "early returns" look promising.

Nonetheless, I believe there are two resources that have been underutilized thus far in the design of curriculum: computers and cognitive research. There were several instances in this book where I showed examples of how computer technology can facilitate instruction on word problems, although the curriculum reform efforts reviewed in this chapter have not relied on computers to implement the reform. We should expect to see an increasing role of technology in supporting mathematics education. For example, the affordability of graphing calculators has already made it possible to rapidly generate and explore the characteristics of functions and this has encouraged more emphasis on functional relations. However, the addition of computers to the classroom will have an even more dramatic impact, as pointed out by the designers of the CPM project:

> Teachers thought that schools could afford a graphing calculator for each pair of students for classwork but that to require a calculator for each student or to depend on the use of computers would put the new materials beyond the means of many schools and students at this time. The key words here are "at this time." We see this project as a transitional effort, an effort to design materials for immediate use, not as an ideal curriculum of the future. Every

decision was a balancing act between "Will I be able to use this next semester in my school?" and our aimed-for constructivist approach to an understanding-based, problem-solving oriented, situation-embedded, technology-using curriculum. (Kysh, 1995, p. 662)

There are several ways in which computers can improve mathematics education. First, parents are correct that their children should learn basic skills, and computers can speed up the process of learning these skills. As shown in chapter 2, the tutors developed by Anderson's group have been successful in teaching basic skills in much less time than required in traditional classroom instruction (Anderson, Corbett, Koedinger, & Pelletier, 1995). This should make available more time to focus on the mathematical thinking and problem solving activities emphasized in the curriculum reform movement.

A second important role of computers is that they can help students integrate different representations of problems in a way that will enhance their understanding (Kaput, 1992). For example, in chapter 10, I described my research in which I contrasted three different instructional approaches for improving students' conception of average speed—that the average speed for a round trip is not the arithmetic average of the speeds in each direction (Reed & Saavedra, 1986). I mentioned that the animation of the problem improved students' estimates of average speed but was not successful in developing a deep conceptual understanding of the situation. As an instructional designer, I would integrate all three instructional approaches to develop a deeper conceptual understanding by having students calculate answers to problems, view the consequences of their estimates in an animated simulation, and see the function (as shown in Fig. 10.1) that relates average speed to the traveled speeds. The integration of mathematical knowledge is one of the objectives of the NCTM standards and is a goal of many curriculum reform efforts.

If we want to integrate different representations we must be careful that we do not use computer technology to substitute one representation for another. I am concerned that this may be happening when I read descriptions of programs such as the Computer-Intensive Algebra program that focuses on solving problems by plotting functions, but de-emphasizes paper-and-pencil algebraic routines (Heid & Zbiek, 1995). One can solve algebra word problems by plotting and finding the intersection of functions, but integration is loss if one solution method is simply replaced by another. I hope that emphasizing the relation between the two methods of solution will enhance the understanding of each method.

A third use of computers is in designing interactive microworlds where students can explore ideas (White, 1984). The advantage of this approach is that it is consistent with the NCTM standards' emphasis on active learning in which acquiring knowledge is a constructive process. The need here is to provide a balance between exploration and computer-assisted guidance (Nickerson, 1995; Snir, Smith, & Grosslight, 1995).

Research Contributions

Computers need good software to be effective and research can contribute to designing effective instruction, with or without the use of technology. A goal of mine in writing this book was to make people more aware of research on mathematical problem solving (particularly word problems) in the hope that research would help guide curriculum reform. It is difficult to evaluate how much of the current curriculum movements are influenced by research, in part, because the description of curriculum changes focus more on global issues involving the delivery of instruction than on the details of problem solving. For example, project descriptions typically mention the basic constructivist approach (such as dividing students into small groups and using the teacher as a facilitator) rather than the details of how instruction helped students achieve a better understanding of specific problems.

We can, however, catch glimpses of curriculum reform being guided by research, such as the use of research on elementary word problems in the Problem-centered Mathematics Project and in Cognitively Guided Instruction. I must admit, however, that I was disappointed in my attempts to find documentation of more direct links between cognitively-oriented research and curriculum reform. In order to provide closer links, curriculum designers need to be aware of instructionally relevant research and researchers need to be aware of important trends in the curriculum reform movement. I hope this book will encourage a tighter link.

There is an opportunity for research to play a more explicit role in curriculum reform as the NCTM Standards are revised. In a guest editorial in the *Journal of Research in Mathematics Education*, Lindquist, Ferrini-Mundy, and Kilpatrick (1997) reported that during two sessions at the April meeting of the National Council of Teachers of Mathematics, their colleagues shared their thoughts regarding how theory, research, and practice ought to serve as a basis for revising the NCTM Standards. A draft of the revised standards is scheduled to be released in the fall of 1998 and the final document is scheduled to be released in 2000. According to Lindquist, Ferrini-Mundy, and Kilpatrick (1997):

> The current *Standards* documents contain relatively little explicit discussion of the theoretical perspectives they reflect and few citations of the research literature. Perhaps consequently, advocates and critics alike have sometimes misinterpreted the approaches taken in the Standards, with regard to content, teaching, learning, and assessment, seeing a unitary focus where more dispassionate observers might have seen a rather eclectic set of views. The writers

of what has been tentatively termed "Standards 2000" will need to address the twin questions (a) What perspectives on goals and content, on the learning process, and on the teaching and assessment process should be reflected in Standards 2000? and (b) How should these perspectives be expressed? (p. 394)

In looking at the current state of curriculum reform projects, I was impressed by how unevenly the instructional design and research efforts have been distributed across grade levels. Much of the effort has been devoted to the lower elementary grades and some effort has been devoted to secondary school. There has been less effort devoted to improving instruction in mathematics at the middle-school level (although this is beginning to change). It is perhaps not surprising that in the recently released results of the Third International Mathematics and Science Study, U.S. fourth graders made a stronger showing relative to other countries than U.S. eighth graders. A press release from the National Science Foundation attributed this difference to improvements in curriculum at the lower elementary grades and the lack of curriculum reform at the middle-school level (see Box 12.1).

However, even changes at the lower elementary levels are not widespread. As is evident from this chapter, many curriculum reform programs are still in the evaluation stage. As research on cognitive processes, evaluation of curriculum programs, and implementation of promising programs continues, we can expect to see further improvement in the capabilities of students.

Summary

This chapter briefly reviewed five programs that are representative of the curriculum reform movement. One of these programs, the Phases of Classroom Mathematical Problem-solving Activity, was designed by Karen Fuson and her colleagues based on the Conceptual Phase Model that was considered in chapter 1. The instruction involves six learning progressions along which children move during the academic year. The first progression is *types* of word problems such as Change, Compare, and Combine problems. A second progression monitors children's ability to create as well as to solve word problems. A third progression requires students to explain their solution. The fourth progression is math tools, beginning with objects, fingers, and drawings. The fifth progression is solution methods, which range from abbreviated counting to full modeling of the situation. This sixth progression is one of increasing the size of numbers in the problem. Research on cognitive processes guides the design of the instruction for each of these learning progressions.

Purdue's Problem-centered Instruction, like many other reform programs, is based on the constructivist belief that children learn better when they construct meanings for themselves, rather than simply listen to the teacher.

Solid Curriculum and Strong Teaching Outweigh Negatives in Math and Science Learning

U.S. fourth-graders' performance on the Third International Mathematics and Science Study (TIMSS) proves that students can overcome factors that traditionally are blamed for poor learning, if challenged by a solid curriculum based on national education standards coupled with competent teaching, according to officials of the National Science Foundation (NSF).

"The fourth-grade scores, released today in Boston and Washington, D.C. confirm NSF's policy to require standards-based curriculums and thorough teacher professional development in all of its educational programs," noted Joe Bordogna, NSF's acting deputy director, at a press conference in the nation's capital.

"The TIMSS results are proof of what is possible in a competent educational system," said Luther S. Williams, who heads NSF's education and human resources directorate. "As the TIMSS report notes, factors such as the amount of television watching, class size, and time spent in school cannot explain student performance. What really matters is the quality of the day-to-day interaction between teachers and students around a coherent curriculum."

The TIMSS fourth-grade results indicate that in science, U.S. students outperformed most participating nations in the study. In math, U.S. fourth-graders made a stronger international showing than U.S. eighth-graders, but were not yet among the best in the world.

Even so, Williams notes that the performance of fourth-graders has improved markedly on international comparisons between 1990 and 1995, a period which coincides with the application of standards-based curriculum and teaching methods in math supported by NSF. Even so, he added, too few school systems yet offer what NSF considers a competent math and science curriculum at any level.

Margaret Cozzens, who heads NSF's elementary, secondary, and informal education division, noted that U.S. students' showing in math can be traced directly to the influence of national standards for exemplary math teaching as well as NSF-developed instructional materials based on the standards.

Published in 1989 by the National Council of Teachers of Mathematics, the standards have slowly been incorporated into elementary school teaching, more so than at the middle-school level, and can be expected to have influenced student performance by the mid-1990's, when the latest TIMSS data were collected, she noted.

Williams also pointed out that the TIMSS also indicates that the sharp decline in U.S. student performance between the fourth and eighth grades is probably a result of an unfocused curriculum. He noted that a report released last October as part of TIMSS showed that the U.S. eight-grade math and science curriculum is vague and repetitive. The U.S. fourth-grade curriculum more closely resembles those in high-scoring TIMSS countries.

Box 12.1. Press release from the National Science Foundation (June 10, 1997).

The program emphasizes problem solving by pairs of students, followed by whole-class discussion that involves an extensive exchange of ideas among students and the teacher. A group that received problem-centered instruction during the second and third grades did significantly better on the computation subtest of the Indiana Sequential Test of Educational Progress. They also did significantly better on the concepts and applications subtest at the end of the fourth grade, and on a test designed to measure conceptual understanding during both the third and fourth grades.

The University of Wisconsin's Cognitively Guided Instruction program focuses on changing teachers' beliefs about how children learn. The investigators classified teachers during each year of a 4-year study based on opportunities for children to solve problems, children sharing their thinking with peers and the teacher, and the teacher's use of children's thinking as a basis for instructional decisions. Performance on a concepts and problem-solving test showed consistent improvement during the 4 years of the study at all three (first, second, and third) grade levels. Gains in conceptual understanding and problem solving appeared to be directly related to changes in the teacher's instruction, and the changes occurred without diminishing performance on tests of computational skills.

Two secondary-school programs being developed in California are College Preparatory Mathematics (CPM) and the Interactive Mathematics Program (IMP). The objective of CPM is to develop a rich, integrated mathematics curriculum based on knowledge of how people learn and the kind of mathematics needed in the age of computers. The Math 1 course, for example, focuses on algebra but integrates the content with graphing, geometry, and sometimes probability and statistics. The IMP also integrates algebra and geometry with additional topics recommended in the NCTM standards such as probability and statistics. This program uses big problems to provide a focus for units that require from 5 to 8 weeks of class time. Although these two programs have not been as rigorously evaluated as the programs at the lower elementary level, some preliminary results are encouraging.

The evaluation of these programs indicate that it is possible to enhance students' conceptual understanding without diminishing their ability to perform computations. The implementation of research on cognitive processes and the greater use of technology offer additional opportunities for further improvement in instruction. For practical reasons, computer technology has not yet played a major role in curriculum reform, although this should change as more schools acquire computers. Computers provide an opportunity to speed up the learning of basic skills, provide tighter links across different kinds of representations, and create "microworlds" where students can explore and try out their ideas. Research on cognitive processes is already having some influence on the design and evaluation of curriculum, and it is hoped that the information provided in this book will further encourage this trend.

References

Ahl, V. A., Moore, C. F., & Dixon, J. A. (1992). Development of intuitive and numerical proportional reasoning. *Cognitive Development, 7,* 81–108.

Alper, L., Fendel, D., Fraser, S., & Resek, D. (1995). Is this a mathematics class? *The Mathematics Teacher, 8,* 632–638.

Alper, L., Fendel, D., Fraser, S., & Resek, D. (1996). *Evaluation update* (No. 2). Emeryville, CA: Interactive Mathematics Program.

Anderson, J. R. (1983). *The architecture of cognition.* Cambridge, MA: Harvard University Press.

Anderson, J. R. (Ed.). (1993). *Rules of the mind.* Hillsdale, NJ: Lawrence Erlbaum Associates.

Anderson, J. R. (1995). *Cognitive psychology and its implications.* (4th ed.). New York: W. H. Freeman.

Anderson, J. R., Boyle, C. F., Farrell, R., & Reisser, B. J. (1987). Cognitive principles in the design of computer tutors. In P. Morris (Ed.), *Modeling cognition* (pp. 93–134). New York: Wiley.

Anderson, J. R., Corbett, A. T., Koedinger, K. R., & Pelletier, R. (1995). Cognitive tutors: Lessons learned. *The Journal of the Learning Sciences, 4,* 167–207.

Anderson, J. R., & Fincham, J. M. (1994). Acquisition of procedural skills from examples. *Journal of Experimental Psychology: Learning, Memory, and Cognition, 20,* 1322–1340.

Anderson, J. R., Reder, L. M., & Simon, H. A. (1996). Situated learning and education. *Educational Researcher, 25,* 5–11.

Anderson, N. H. (1983). Intuitive physics: Understanding and learning of physical relations. In T. J. Tighe & B. E. Shepp (Eds.), *Interactions: Perception, cognition and development* (pp. 231–265). Hillsdale, NJ: Lawrence Erlbaum Associates.

Anderson, N. H. (1987). Function knowledge: Comment on Reed and Evans. *Journal of Experimental Psychology: General, 116,* 297–299.

Baranes, R., Perry, M., & Stigler, J. W. (1989). Activation of real-world knowledge in the solution of word problems. *Cognition and Instruction, 6,* 287–318.

Bartlett, F. C. (1932). *Remembering: A study in experimental and social psychology.* New York: Macmillan.

Bassok, M., & Holyoak, K. J. (1993). Pragmatic knowledge and conceptual structure: Determinants of transfer between quantitative domains. In D. K. Detterman & R. J. Sternberg (Eds.), *Transfer on trial: Intelligence, cognition, and instruction* (pp. 68–98). Norwood, NJ: Ablex.

203

Bassok, M., & Olseth, K. L. (1995). Object-based representation: Transfer between cases of continuous and discrete models of change. *Journal of Experimental Psychology: Learning, Memory, and Cognition, 21*, 1522–1538.

Bassok, M., Wu, L., & Olseth, K. L. (1995). Judging a book by its cover: Interpretative effects of content on problem-solving transfer. *Memory & Cognition, 23*, 354–367.

Ben-Zeev, T. (1996). When erroneous mathematical thinking is just as "correct": The oxymoron of rational errors. In R. J. Sternberg & T. Ben-Zeev (Eds.), *The nature of mathematical thinking* (pp. 55–80). Mahwah, NJ: Lawrence Erlbaum Associates.

Blessing, S. B., & Ross, B. H. (1996). Content effects in problem categorization and problem solving. *Journal of Experimental Psychology: Learning, Memory, and Cognition, 22*, 792–810.

Bobrow, D. G., & Winograd, T. (1979). KRL: Another perspective. *Cognitive Science, 3*, 29–42.

Bransford, J. D., & Johnson, M. K. (1973). Considerations of some problems of comprehension. In W. G. Chase (Ed.), *Visual information processing* (pp. 383–438). Orlando, FL: Academic Press.

Brewer, M. A. (1988). *The role of diagrams in understanding the semantic relations in arithmetic story problems.* Unpublished master's thesis, San Diego State University, San Diego.

Brewer, W. F., & Nakamura, G. V. (1984). The nature and function of schemas. In R. S. Wyler & T. K. Srull (Eds.), *Handbook of social cognition.* Hillsdale, NJ: Lawrence Erlbaum Associates.

Brown, J. S., & Burton, R. R. (1978). Diagnostic models for procedural bugs in basic mathematical skills. *Cognitive Science, 2*, 155–192.

Brown, J., Collins, A., & Duguid, P. (1989). Situated cognition and the culture of learning. *Educational Researcher, 18*, 32–42.

Carpenter, T. P., Corbitt, M. K., Kepner, K. S., Lindquist, M. M., & Reys, R. (1980). Results of the second NAEP mathematics assessment: Secondary school. *Mathematics Teacher, 73*, 329–338.

Carpenter, T. P., & Fennema, E. (1992). Cognitively guided instruction: Building on the knowledge of students and teachers. *International Journal of Educational Research, 17*, 457–470.

Carpenter, T. P., & Moser, J. (1984). The acquisition of addition and subtraction concepts. In R. Lesh & M. Landau (Eds.), *Acquisition of mathematical concepts and processes* (pp. 7–44). New York: Academic Press.

Carraher, T. N., Carraher, D. W., & Schliemann, A. D. (1985). Mathematics in the streets and in schools. *British Journal of Developmental Psychology, 3*, 21–29.

Carraher, T. N., Carraher, D. W., & Schliemann, A. D. (1987). Written and oral mathematics. *Journal for Research in Mathematics Education, 18*, 83–97.

Case, R. (1992). *The mind's staircase: Exploring the conceptual underpinnings of children's thought and knowledge.* Hillsdale, NJ: Lawrence Erlbaum Associates.

Catrambone, R. (1995). Aiding subgoal learning: Effects on transfer. *Journal of Eductional Psychology, 87*, 5–17.

Catrambone, R. (1996). Transfer and modifying terms in equations. In G. W. Cottrell (Ed.), *Proceedings of the 18th Annual Conference of the Cognitive Science Society* (pp. 301–305). Mahwah, NJ: Lawrence Erlbaum Associates.

Catrambone, R., & Holyoak, K. J. (1989). Overcoming contextual limitations on problem-solving transfer. *Journal of Experimental Psychology: Learning, Memory, and Cognition, 15*, 1147–1156.

Cheng, P. W., Holyoak, K. J., Nisbett, R. E., & Oliver, L. M. (1986). Pragmatic versus syntactic approaches to training deductive reasoning. *Cognitive Psychology, 18*, 293–328.

Chi, M. T. H., Bassok, M., Lewis, M. W., Reimann, P., & Glaser, R. (1989). Self-explanations: How students study and use examples in learning to solve physics problems. *Cognitive Science, 13*, 145–182.

Chi, M. T. H., De Leuw, N., Chiu, M., & LaVancher, C. (1994). Eliciting self-explanations improves understanding. *Cognitive Science, 18*, 439–477.

Chi, M. T. H., Glaser, R., & Rees, E. (1982). Expertise in problem solving. In R. J. Sternberg (Ed.), *Advances in the psychology of human intelligence* (Vol. 1, pp. 7–75). Hillsdale, NJ: Lawrence Erlbaum Associates.

Chi, M. T. H., & VanLehn, K. A. (1991). The content of physics self-explanations. *The Journal of the Learning Sciences, 1*, 69–105.

Clement, J. (1982). Algebra word problem solutions: Thought processes underlying a common misconception. *Journal for Research in Mathematics Education, 13*, 16–30.

Cobb, P. (1996). Justification and reform. *Journal for Reseach in Mathematics Education, 27*, 516–520.

Cobb, P., Yackel, T., & Wood, T. (1992). Interaction and learning in mathematics classroom situations. *Educational Studies in Mathematics, 23*, 99–122.

Cognition and Technical Group at Vanderbilt. (1990). Anchored instruction and its relationship to situated cognition. *Educational Researcher, 19*, 2–10.

Corbett, A. T., & Anderson, J. R. (1991, May). *Feedback control and learning to program with the CMU LISP tutor.* Paper presented at the annual meeting of the American Educational Research Association, Chicago, IL.

Cummins, D. (1992). Role of analogical reasoning in the induction of problem categories. *Journal of Experimental Psychology: Learning, Memory, and Cognition, 18*, 1103–1124.

Cummins, D., Kintsch, W., Reusser, K., & Weimer, R. (1988). The role of understanding in solving word problems. *Cognitive Psychology, 20*, 439–462.

Davis, R. B. (1996). One very complete view (though only one) of how children learn mathematics. *Journal for Research in Mathematics Education, 27*, 100–106.

De Corte, E., & Somers, R. (1982). Estimating the outcome of a task as a heuristic strategy in arithmetic problem solving: A teaching experiment with sixth-graders. *Human Learning, 1*, 105–121.

De Corte, E., Verschaffel, L., & De Win, L. (1985). Influence of rewording verbal problems on children's problem representations and solutions. *Journal of Educational Psychology, 77*, 460–470.

Derry, S. J. (1989). Strategy and expertise in word problem solving. In C. McCormick, G. Miller, & M. Pressley (Eds.), *Cognitive strategy research: From basic research to educational applications* (pp. 269–302). New York: Springer-Verlag.

Derry, S. J. (1994). *Psychological foundations of the TiPS system: A handbook for system 1.0.* Madison, WI: Wisconsin Center for Education Research.

Dixon, J. A., & Moore, C. F. (1996). The developmental role of intuitive principles in choosing mathematical strategies. *Developmental Psychology, 32*, 241–253.

Dixon, J. A., & Moore, C. F. (1997). Characterizing the intuitive representation in problem solving: Evidence from evaluating mathematical strategies. *Memory & Cognition, 25*, 395–412.

Duncker, K. (1945). On problem solving. *Psychological Monographs, 58*(5, Whole No. 270).

English, L. D., & Halford, G. S. (1995). *Mathematics education: Models and processes.* Mahwah, NJ: Lawrence Erlbaum Associates.

Fennema, E., Carpenter, T. P., Franke, M. L., Levi, L., Jacobs, V. R., & Empson, S. B. (1996). A longitudinal study of learning to use children's thinking in mathematics instruction. *Journal for Research in Mathematics Education, 27*, 403–434.

Fisher, K. M. (1988). The students-and-professors problem revisited. *Journal for Research in Mathematics Education, 19*, 260–262.

Fuson, K. C., Carroll, W. M., & Landis, J. (1996). Levels of conceptualizing and solving addition and subtraction compare word problems. *Cognition and Instruction, 14*, 345–371.

Fuson, K. C., Hudson, K., & Pilar, R. (1997). Phases of classroom mathematical problem-solving activity: The PCMPA framework for supporting algebraic thinking in primary school classrooms. In J. Kaput (Ed.), *Employing children's natural powers to build algebraic reasoning in the context of elementary mathematics.* Mahwah, NJ: Lawrence Erlbaum Associates.

Gelman, R., & Meck, E. (1983). Preschoolers' counting: Principle before skill. *Cognition, 13*, 343–359.

Gentner, D. (1983). Structure-mapping: A theoretical framework for analogy. *Cognitive Science, 7*, 155–170.

Gentner, D., & Gentner, D. R. (1983). Flowing waters or teeming crowds: Mental models of electricity. In D. Gentner & A. L. Stevens (Eds.), *Mental models* (pp. 99–129). Hillsdale, NJ: Lawrence Erlbaum Associates.

Gick, M. (1986). Problem-solving strategies. *Educational Psychologist, 21*, 99–120.

Gick, M., & Holyoak, K. J. (1980). Analogical problem solving. *Cognitive Psychology, 12*, 306–355.

Gick, M., & Holyoak, K. J. (1983). Schema induction and analogical transfer. *Cognitive Psychology, 15*, 1–38.

Goldman, S. R., Pellegrino, J. W., & Bransford, J. (1994). Assessing programs that invite thinking. In E. L. Baker & H. F. O'Neal (Eds.), *Technology assessment in education and training* (pp. 199–230). Hillsdale, NJ: Lawrence Erlbaum Associates.

Greeno, J. G., Riley, M. S., & Gelman, R. (1984). Conceptual competence and children's counting. *Cognitive Psychology, 16*, 94–134.

Greeno, J. G., Smith, D. R., & Moore, J. L. (1993). Transfer of situated learning. In D. K. Detterman & R. J. Sternberg (Eds.), *Transfer on trial: Intelligence, cognition, and instruction* (pp. 99–167). Norwood, NJ: Ablex.

Greer, B. (1987). Understanding of arithmetic operations as models of situations. In J. A. Sloboda & D. Rogers (Eds.), *Cognitive processes in mathematics* (pp. 60–80). Oxford: Clarendon Press.

Greer, B. (1993). The mathematical modeling perspective on wor(l)d problems. *Journal of Mathematical Behavior, 12*, 239–250.

Greer, B. (1994). Extending the meaning of multiplication and division. In G. Harel & J. Confrey (Eds.), *The development of multiplicative reasoning in the learning of mathematics* (pp. 61–85). Albany, NY: State University of New York Press.

Greer, B., & Verschaffel, L. (1990). Mathematics education as a proving-ground for information-processing theories. *International Journal of Educational Research, 14*, 3–12.

Griggs, R. A., & Cox, J. R. (1982). The elusive thematic-materials effect in Wason's selection task. *British Journal of Psychology, 73*, 407–420.

Hall, R. (1989). Computational approaches to analogical reasoning. *Artificial Intelligence, 39*, 39–120.

Hall, R., Kibler, D., Wenger, E., & Truxaw, C. (1989). Exploring the episodic structure of algebra story problem solving. *Cognition and Instruction, 6*, 223–283.

Hatano, G. (1988). Social and motivational bases for mathematical understanding. In G. B. Saxe & M. Gearhart (Eds.), *Children's mathematics* (pp. 55–70). San Francisco: Jossey-Bass.

Hegarty, M. (1992). Mental animation: Inferring motion from static displays of mechanical systems. *Journal of Experimental Psychology: Learning, Memory, and Cognition, 18*, 1084–1102.

Heid, K. M., & Zbiek, R. M. (1995). A technology-intensive approach to algebra. *The Mathematics Teacher, 8*, 650–656.

Hiebert, J., & Carpenter, T. P. (1992). Learning and teaching with understanding. In D. A. Grouws (Ed.), *Handbook on research in mathematics and teaching and learning* (pp. 65–97). New York: Macmillan.

Hiebert, J., Carpenter, T. P., Fennema, E., Fuson, K., Human, P., Murray, H., Oliver, A., & Wearne, D. (1996). Problem solving as a basis for reform in curriculum and instruction: The case of mathematics. *Educational Researcher, 25*, 12–21.

Hiebert, J., & Lefevre, P. (1986). Conceptual and procedural knowledge in mathematics: An introductory analysis. In J. Hiebert (Ed.), *Conceptual and procedural knowledge: The case of mathematics* (pp. 1–27). Hillsdale, NJ: Lawrence Erlbaum Associates.

Hinsley, D. A., Hayes, J. R., & Simon, H. A. (1977). From words to equations: Meaning and representation in algebra word problems. In P. A. Carpenter & M. A. Just (Eds.), *Cognitive processes in comprehension* (pp. 89–106). Hillsdale, NJ: Lawrence Erlbaum Associates.

Hirsch, E. D. (1996). *The schools we need and why we don't have them.* New York: Doubleday.

Holyoak, K. J., Novick, L. R., & Melz, E. R. (1994). Component processes in analogical transfer: Mapping, pattern completion, and adaptation. In K. J. Holyoak & J. A. Barnden (Eds.), *Advances in connectionist and neural computation theory: Vol. 2. Analogical connections* (pp. 113–180). Norwood, NJ: Ablex.

Holyoak, K. J., & Thagard, P. (1989). Analogical mapping by constraint satisfaction. *Cognitive Science, 13*, 295–355.

Hudson, T. (1983). Correspondences and numerical differences between disjoint sets. *Child Development, 54*, 84–90.

Inhelder, B., & Piaget, J. (1958). *The growth of logical thinking from childhood to adolescence.* New York: Basic Books.

Johnson-Laird, P. N., Legrenzi, P., & Legrenzi, M. S. (1972). Reasoning and a sense of reality. *British Journal of Psychology, 63*, 395–400.

Kahneman, D. (1973). *Attention and effort.* Englewood Cliffs, NJ: Prentice-Hall.

Kaput, J. J. (1992). Technology and mathematics education. In D. A. Grouws (Ed.), *Handbook of research in mathematics teaching and learning* (pp. 515–556). New York: Macmillan.

Kaput, J. J. (1995). *A research base supporting long term algebra reform?* Paper presented at the 17th Annual Meeting of the North American Chapter of the International Group for the Psychology of Mathematics Education, Columbus, OH.

Kieran, C. (1992). The learning and teaching of school algebra. In D. Grouws (Ed.), *Handbook for research on mathematics teaching and learning* (pp. 390–419). New York: Macmillan.

Kieras, D. E., & Bovair, S. (1984). The role of a mental model in learning to operate a device. *Cognitive Science, 8*, 255–273.

Kieras, D. E., & Bovair, S. (1986). The acquisition of procedures from text: A production-system analysis of transfer of training. *Journal of Memory and Language, 25*, 507–524.

Kintsch, W. (1988). The use of knowledge in discourse processing: A construction-integration model. *Psychological Review, 92*, 163–182.

Kintsch, W. (1994). Text comprehension, memory, and learning. *American Psychologist, 49*, 294–303.

Kintsch, W., & Greeno, J. G. (1985). Understanding and solving word arithmetic problems. *Psychological Review, 92*, 109–129.

Koedinger, K. R., & Anderson, J. R. (1990). Abstract planning and perceptual chunks: Elements of expertise in geometry. *Cognitive Science, 14*, 511–550.

Koedinger, K. R., & Tabachneck, H. J. (1994, April). *Two strategies are better than one: Multiple strategy use in word problem solving.* Paper presented at the Annual Meeting of the American Educational Research Association, New Orleans, LA.

Kolodner, J. (1993). *Case-based reasoning.* San Mateo, CA: Morgan Kaufmann.

Kolodner, J. (1997). Educational implications of analogy: A view from case-based reasoning. *American Psychologist, 52*, 57–66.

Kysh, J. M. (1995). College preparatory mathematics: change from within. *The Mathematics Teacher, 8*, 660–666.

LaBerge, D. L., & Samuels, S. J. (1974). Toward a theory of automatic processing in reading. *Cognitive Psychology, 6*, 292–323.

LeBlanc, M. D., & Weber-Russell, S. (1996). Text integration and mathematical connections: A computer model of arithmetic word problem solving. *Cognitive Science, 20*, 357–407.

Lampert, M. (1986). Knowing, doing, and teaching multiplication. *Cognition and Instruction, 3*, 305–342.

Larkin, J. H., McDermott, J., Simon, D. P., & Simon, H. A. (1980). Expert and novice performance in solving physics problems. *Science, 208*, 1335–1342.

Larkin, J. H., Reif, F., Carbonell, J., & Gugliotta, A. (1988). A flexible expert reasoner with multi-domain inferencing. *Cognitive Science, 12*, 101–138.

Larkin, J. H., & Simon, H. A. (1987). Why a diagram is (sometimes) worth ten thousand words. *Cognitive Science, 11*, 65–99.

Lesgold, A. (1991). *An object-based situational approach to task analysis.* Paper presented at the NATO Advanced Study Workshop on Learning Electricity and Electronics with Advanced Technology, Marne-la-Valle, France.

Lesgold, A. (1994). Assessment of intelligent training technology. In E. L. Baker & H. F. O'Neil (Eds.), *Technology assessment in education and training* (pp. 97–116). Hillsdale, NJ: Lawrence Erlbaum Associates.

Lindquist, M., Ferrini-Mundy, J., & Kilpatrick, J. (1997). Guest editorial. *Journal for Research in Mathematics Education, 28*, 394–395.

Lobato, J. E. (1996). *Transfer reconceived: How "sameness" is produced in mathematical activity.* Unpublished doctoral dissertation, University of California, Berkeley.

MacGregor, M., & Stacey, K. (1993). Cognitive models underlying students' formulation of simple linear equations. *Journal for Research in Mathematics Education, 24*, 217–232.

MacGregor, M., & Stacey, K. (1996, July). *Learning to formulate equations for problems.* Paper presented at the Proceedings of the 20th Conference of the International Group for the Psychology of Mathematics Education, Valencia, Spain.

Marshall, S. P. (1995). *Schemas in problem solving.* Cambridge, England: Cambridge University Press.

Marshall, S. P., Pribe, C. A., & Smith, J. D. (1987). *Schematic knowledge structures for representing and understanding arithmetic story problems* (Contract No. N00014-85-K-0661). San Diego: Center for Research in Mathematics and Science Education.

Mayer, R. E. (1981). Frequency norms and structural analysis of algebra story problems into families, categories, and templates. *Instructional Science, 10*, 135–175.

Mayer, R. E. (1989). Models for understanding. *Review of Educational Research, 59*, 43–64.

Mayer, R. E., & Hegarty, M. (1996). The process of understanding mathematical problems. In R. J. Sternberg & T. Ben-Zeev (Eds.), *The nature of mathematical thinking* (pp. 29–54). Mahwah, NJ: Lawrence Erlbaum Associates.

Mayer, R. E., Larkin, J. H., & Kadane, J. B. (1984). A cognitive analysis of mathematical problem-solving ability. In R. J. Sternberg (Ed.), *Advances in the psychology of human intelligence* (pp. 231–273). Hillsdale, NJ: Lawrence Erlbaum Associates.

Mechmandarov, I. (1987). *The role of dimensional analysis in teaching multiplicative word problems.* Tel-Aviv: Center for Educational Technology.

Mekhmandarov, I., Meron, R., & Peled, I. (1996, July). *Performance and understanding: A closer look at comparison word problems.* Paper presented at the Proceedings of the 20th Conference of the International Group on the Psychology of Mathematics Education, Valencia, Spain.

Medin, D. L., & Ross, B. H. (1989). The specific character of abstract thought: Categorization, problem solving, and induction. In R. S. Sternberg (Ed.), *Advances in the psychology of human intelligence* (Vol. 5, pp. 189–223). Hillsdale, NJ: Lawrence Erlbaum Associates.

Minsky, M. (1975). A framework for the representation of knowledge. In P. Winston (Ed.), *The psychology of computer vision* (pp. 211–280). New York: McGraw-Hill.

Nathan, M. J., Kintsch, W., & Young, E. (1992). A theory of algebra-word-problem comprehension and its implications for the design of learning environments. *Cognition and Instruction, 9*, 329–389.

National Council of Teachers of Mathematics. (1989). *Curriculum and evaluation standards for school mathematics.* Reston, VA: Author.

Neches, R., Langley, P., & Klahr, D. (1987). Learning, development, and production systems. In D. Klahr, P. Langley, & R. Neches (Eds.), *Production system models of learning and development* (pp. 1–53). Cambridge, MA: MIT Press.

Nesher, P. (1992). Solving multiplication word problems. In G. Leinhardt, R. Putnam, & R. A. Hattrup (Eds.), *Analysis of arithmetic for mathematics teaching* (pp. 189–219). Hillsdale, NJ: Lawrence Erlbaum Associates.

Nesher, P., & Teubal, E. (1975). Verbal cues as an interfering factor in verbal problem solving. *Educational Studies in Mathematics, 6*, 41–51.

Newell, A., & Simon, H. A. (1972). *Human problem solving.* Englewood Cliffs, NJ: Prentice-Hall.

Nickerson, R. S. (1995). Can technology help teach for understanding? In D. N. Perkins, J. L. Schwartz, M. M. West, & M. S. Wiske (Eds.), *Software goes to school* (pp. 7–22). Oxford, England: Oxford University Press.

Novick, L. R. (1990). Representational transfer in problem solving. *Psychological Science, 1*, 128–132.

Novick, L. R., & Hmelo, C. E. (1994). Transferring symbolic representations across nonisomorphic problems. *Journal of Experimental Psychology: Learning, Memory, and Cognition, 20*, 1296–1321.

Novick, L. R., & Holyoak, K. J. (1991). Mathematical problem solving by analogy. *Journal of Experimental Psychology: Learning, Memory, and Cognition, 17*, 398–415.

Ohlsson, S. (1990). Cognitive science and instruction: Why the revolution is not here (yet). In H. Mandl, E. De Corte, N. Bennet, & H. Friedrich (Eds.), *European research in an international context* (Vol. 2.1, pp. 561–600). New York: Pergamon Press.

Ohlsson, S. (1996). Learning from performance errors. *Psychological Review, 103*, 241–262.

Okamoto, Y. (1996). Modeling children's understanding of quantitative relations in texts: A developmental perspective. *Cognition and Instruction, 14*, 409–440.

Pennington, N., Nicolich, R., & Rahm, J. (1995). Transfer of training between cognitive subskills: Is knowledge use specific? *Cognitive Psychology, 28*, 175–224.

Philipp, R. A. (1992). A study of algebraic variables: Beyond the student-professor problem. *Journal of Mathematical Behavior, 11*, 161–176.

Pirolli, P. (1991). Effects of examples and their explanations in a lesson on recursion: A production system analysis. *Cognition and Instruction, 8*, 207–259.

Putnam, R. T., Lampert, M., & Peterson, P. L. (1990). Alternative perspectives on knowing mathematics in the elementary school. In C. B. Cazden (Ed.), *Review of research in education* (Vol. 16, pp. 57–150). Washington, DC: American Educational Research Association.

Randhawa, B. S. (1994). Theory, research, and assessment of mathematical problem solving. *The Alberta Journal of Educational Research, 40*, 213–231.

Reed, S. K. (1984). Estimating answers to algebra word problems. *Journal of Experimental Psychology: Learning, Memory, and Cognition, 10*, 778–790.

Reed, S. K. (1985). Effect of computer graphics on improving estimates to algebra word problems. *Journal of Educational Psychology, 77*, 285–298.

Reed, S. K. (1987). A structure-mapping model for word problems. *Journal of Experimental Psychology: Learning, Memory, and Cognition, 13*, 124–139.

Reed, S. K. (1989). Constraints on the abstraction of solutions. *Journal of Educational Psychology, 81*, 532–540.

Reed, S. K., Ackinclose, C. C., & Voss, A. A. (1990). Selecting analogous solutions: Similarity versus inclusiveness. *Memory & Cognition, 18*, 93–98.

Reed, S. K., & Bolstad, C. A. (1991). Use of examples and procedures in problem solving. *Journal of Experimental Psychology: Learning, Memory, and Cognition, 17*, 753–766.

Reed, S. K., & de la Pena, K. (1996). *Predicting generalization gradients for adapting solutions.* Unpublished manuscript, San Diego State University.

Reed, S. K., Dempster, A., & Ettinger, M. (1985). Usefulness of analogous solutions for solving algebra word problems. *Journal of Experimental Psychology: Learning, Memory, and Cognition, 11*, 106–125.

Reed, S. K., & Evans, A. C. (1987). Learning functional relations: A theoretical and instructional analysis. *Journal of Experimental Psychology: General, 116*, 106–118.

Reed, S. K., Francis, F., & Actor, C. (1988). *Mixing solutions and mixing knowledge.* Unpublished manuscript, Florida Atlantic University at Boca Raton.

Reed, S. K., & Saavedra, N. C. (1986). A comparison of computation, discovery, and graph procedures for improving students' conception of average speed. *Cognition and Instruction, 3*, 31–62.

Reed, S. K., Willis, D., & Guarino, J. (1994). Selecting examples for solving algebra word problems. *Journal of Educational Psychology, 86*, 380–388.

Reeves, L. M., & Weisberg, R. W. (1994). The role of content and abstract information in analogical transfer. *Psychological Bulletin, 115*, 381–400.

Reimann, P., & Schult, T. J. (1996). Turning examples into cases: Acquiring knowledge structures for analogical problem solving. *Educational Psychologist, 31*, 123–132.

Reusser, K. (1988). *From text to situation to equation: Cognitive simulation of understanding and solving mathematical word problems* (Research Report No. 5). Bern, Switzerland: Universitat Bern.

Reusser, K. (1993). Tutoring systems and pedagogical theory: Representational tools for understanding, planning, and reflection in problem solving. In S. P. Lajoie & S. J. Derry (Eds.), *Computers as cognitive tools* (pp. 143–177). Hillsdale, NJ: Lawrence Erlbaum Associates.

Riesbeck, C. K., & Schank, R. C. (1989). *Inside case-based reasoning.* Hillsdale, NJ: Lawrence Erlbaum Associates.

Riley, M., Greeno, J. G., & Heller, J. I. (1983). Development of children's problem-solving ability in arithmetic. In H. P. Ginsberg (Ed.), *The development of mathematical thinking* (pp. 153–196). New York: Academic Press.

Ross, B. H. (1984). Remindings and their effects in learning a cognitive skill. *Cognitive Psychology, 16*, 371–416.

Ross, B. H. (1987). This is like that: The use of earlier problems and separation of similarity effects. *Journal of Experimental Psychology: Learning, Memory, and Cognition, 13*, 629–639.

Ross, B. H., & Kennedy, P. T. (1990). Generalizing from the earlier use of examples in problem solving. *Journal of Experimental Psychology: Learning, Memory, and Cognition, 16*, 42–55.

Rumelhart, D. E. (1980). Schemata: The building blocks of cognition. In R. Spiro, B. Bruce, & W. Brewer (Eds.), *Theoretical issues in reading comprehension.* Hillsdale, NJ: Lawrence Erlbaum Associates.

Schoenfeld, A. H. (1985). *Mathematical problem solving.* San Diego: Academic Press.

Schoenfeld, A. H. (1988). When good teaching leads to bad results: The disasters of "well taught" mathematics courses. *Educational Psychologist, 23*, 145–166.

Schoenfeld, A. (1992). Learning to think mathematically: problem solving, metacognition, and sense making in mathematics. In D. Grouws (Ed.), *Handbook for Research in Mathematics Teaching and Learning* (pp. 334–370). New York: Macmillian.

Schoenfeld, A. H., & Hermann, D. (1982). Problem perception and knowledge structure in expert and novice mathematical problem solvers. *Journal of Experimental Psychology: Learning, Memory, and Cognition, 8*, 484–494.

Schwartz, J. L. (1988). Intensive quantity and referent transforming arithmetic operations. In J. Hiebert & M. Behr (Eds.), *Number concepts and operations in the middle grades* (Vol. 2, pp. 41–52). Reston, VA: National Council of Teachers of Mathematics.

Sebrechts, M. M., Enright, M., Bennet, R. E., & Martin, K. (1996). Using algebra word problems to assess quantitative ability: Attributes, strategies, and errors. *Cognition and Instruction, 14*, 285–343.

Shepard, R. N. (1978). Externalization of mental images and the act of creation. In B. S. Randawa & W. E. Coffman (Eds.), *Visual learning, thinking, and communication* (pp. 133–189). New York: Academic Press.

Silver, E. A. (1981). Recall of mathematical problem information: Solving related problems. *Journal for Research in Mathematics Education, 12*, 54–64.

Sims-Knight, J. E., & Kaput, J. J. (1983). Exploring difficulties in transforming between natural language and image based representations and abstract symbol systems of mathematics. In D. Rogers & J. A. Sloboda (Eds.), *The acquisition of symbolic skills* (pp. 561–570). New York: Plenum.

Singley, M. K., & Anderson, J. R. (1989). *The transfer of cognitive skill.* Cambridge, MA: Harvard University Press.

Sizer, T. R. (1996). *Horace's hope: What works for the American high school.* Boston: Houghton Mifflin.

Smith, E. E., & Goodman, L. (1984). Understanding written instructions: The role of explanatory schema. *Cognition and Instruction, 1*, 359–396.

Snir, J., Smith, C., & Grosslight, L. (1995). Conceptually enhanced simulations: A computer tool for science teaching. In D. N. Perkins, J. L. Schwartz, M. M. West, & M. S. Wiske (Eds.), *Software goes to school* (pp. 106–129). Oxford, England: Oxford University Press.

Sowder, J. (1992). Estimation and number sense. In D. A. Grouws (Ed.), *Handbook on research in mathematics teaching and learning* (pp. 371–389). New York: Macmillan.

Sowder, L. (1985). Cognitive psychology and mathematical problem solving: A discussion of Mayer's paper. In E. Silver (Ed.), *Teaching and learning mathematical problem solving: Multiple research perspectives.* Hillsdale, NJ: Lawrence Erlbaum Associates.

Sowder, L. (1988). Children's solutions of story problems. *Journal of Mathematical Behavior, 7,* 227–238.

Staub, F. C., & Reusser, K. (1995). The role of presentational structure in understanding and solving mathematical word problems. In C. A. Weaver, S. Mannes, & C. R. Fletcher (Eds.), *Discourse comprehension: Essays in honor of Walter Kintsch* (pp. 285–305). Hillsdale, NJ: Lawrence Erlbaum Associates.

Sweller, J. (1988). Cognitive load during problem solving: Effects on learning. *Cognitive Science, 12,* 257–285.

Sweller, J., Mawer, R. F., & Ward, M. R. (1983). Development of expertise in mathematical problem solving. *Journal of Experimental Psychology: General, 112,* 639–661.

Tabachneck, H. J. M., Koedinger, K., & Nathan, M. J. (1994). *Toward a theoretical account of strategy use and sense-making in mathematics problem solving.* Paper presented at the Proceedings of the 16th Annual Conference of the Cognitive Science Society, Atlanta, GA.

Thompson, A. G., Philipp, R. A., Thompson, P. W., & Boyd, B. A. (1994). Calculational and conceptual orientations in teaching mathematics. In D. B. Aichele & A. F. Coxford (Eds.), *Professional development of teachers of mathematics* (pp. 79–92). Reston, VA: National Council of Teachers of Mathematics.

Thorndyke, P. W. (1984). Applications of schema theory in cognitive research. In J. R. Anderson & S. M. Kosslyn (Eds.), *Tutorials in learning and memory.* San Francisco: W. H. Freeman.

Toch, T., & Daniel, M. (1996, October 7). Schools that work. *U.S. News & World Report,* pp. 58–64.

Trismen, D. A. (1988). Hints: An aid to diagnosis in mathematical problem solving. *Journal for Research in Mathematics Education, 19,* 358–361.

VanLehn, K. (1989). Problem solving and cognitive skill acquisition. In M. I. Posner (Ed.), *Foundations of cognitive science* (pp. 527–580). Cambridge, MA: MIT Press.

VanLehn, K., Jones, R. M., & Chi, M. T. H. (1992). A model of the self-explanation effect. *Journal of the Learning Sciences, 2,* 1–59.

Vergnaud, G. (1984). Understanding mathematics at the secondary-school level. In A. Bell, B. Low, & J. Kilpatrick (Eds.), *Theory, research, and practice in mathematical education* (pp. 27–35). Nottingham, UK: Shell Centre for Mathematical Education.

Vergnaud, G. (1988). Multiplicative structures. In J. Hiebert & M. Behr (Eds.), *Number concepts and operations in the middle grades* (Vol. 2, pp. 141–161). Reston, VA: National Council of Teachers of Mathematics.

Vergnaud, G. (1994). Multiplicative conceptual field: What and why? In G. Harel & J. Confrey (Eds.), *The development of multiplicative reasoning in the learning of mathematics* (pp. 41–59). Albany, NY: State University of New York Press.

Verschaffel, L., & De Corte, E. (1993). A decade of research on word problem solving in Leuven: Theoretical, methodological, and practical outcomes. *Educational Psychological Review, 5,* 239–255.

Verschaffel, L., & De Corte, E. (1996). Word problems: A vehicle for promoting authentic mathematical understanding and problem solving in the primary school? In P. Bryant & T. Nunes (Eds.), *How do children learn mathematics.* Mahwah, NJ: Lawrence Erlbaum Associates.

Verschaffel, L., & De Corte, E. (1997). Teaching realistic mathematical modeling in the elementary school: A teaching experiment with fifth graders. *Journal for Research in Mathematics Education, 28,* 577–601.

Verschaffel, L., De Corte, E., & Borghart, I. (1996, July). *Pre-service teachers' conceptions and beliefs about the role of real-world knowledge in arithmetic word problem solving.* Paper presented at the Proceedings of the 20th Conference of the International Group for the Psychology of Mathematics Education, Valencia, Spain.

Verschaffel, L., De Corte, E., & Lasure, S. (1994). Realistic considerations in mathematical modeling of school arithmetic word problems. *Learning and Instruction, 4,* 273–294.

Wason, P. C., & Johnson-Laird, P. N. (1972). *Psychology of reasoning: Structure and content.* Cambridge, MA: Harvard University Press.

Wason, P. C., & Shapiro, D. (1971). Natural and contrived experience in a reasoning problem. *Quarterly Journal of Experimental Psychology, 23,* 63–71.

White, B. Y. (1984). Designing computer games to help physics students understand Newton's laws of motion. *Cognition and Instruction, 1,* 69–108.

White, B. Y. (1993a). Intermediate causal models: A missing link for successful science education. In R. Glaser (Ed.), *Advances in instructional psychology* (Vol. 4, pp. 177–252). Hillsdale, NJ: Lawrence Erlbaum Associates.

White, B. Y. (1993b). ThinkerTools: Causal models, conceptual change, and science education. *Cognition and Instruction, 10,* 1–100.

Winston, P. H. (1980). Learning and reasoning by analogy. *Communications of the Association of Computing Machinery, 23,* 689–703.

Wood, T., & Sellers, P. (1996). Assessment of a problem-centered mathematics program: Third grade. *Journal for Research in Mathematics Education, 27,* 337–353.

Wood, T., & Sellers, P. (1997). Deepening the analysis: Longitudinal assessment of a problem-centered mathematics program. *Journal for Research in Mathematics Education, 28,* 163–186.

Author Index

Subject Index